In Pursuit of Excellence

FOURTH EDITION

Terry Orlick

Human Kinetics

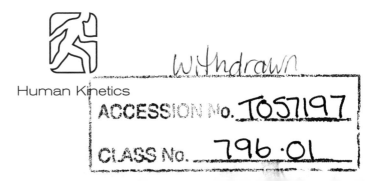

Library of Congress Cataloging-in-Publication Data

Orlick, Terry.
  In pursuit of excellence / Terry Orlick. -- 4th ed.
    p. cm.
  Includes bibliographical references and index.
  ISBN-13: 978-0-7360-6757-7 (soft cover)
  ISBN-10: 0-7360-6757-4 (soft cover)
  1. Sports--Psychological aspects. I. Title.
  GV706.4.O73 2008
  796'.01--dc22

                                        2007025190

ISBN-10: 0-7360-6757-4
ISBN-13: 978-0-7360-6757-7

Developmental Editor: Heather Healy; **Assistant Editor:** Carla Zych; **Copyeditor:** Robert Replinger; **Proofreader:** Pamela Johnson; **Indexer:** Nan N. Badgett; **Permission Manager:** Carly Breeding; **Graphic Designer:** Nancy Rasmus; **Graphic Artist:** Tara Welsch; **Cover Designer:** Keith Blomberg; **Cover photo:** courtesy of Topmost, Inc.; **Photo Asset Manager:** Laura Fitch; **Photo Office Assistant:** Jason Allen; **Art Manager:** Kelly Hendren; **Associate Art Manager and Illustrator:** Alan L. Wilborn; **Printer:** United Graphics

Human Kinetics books are available at special discounts for bulk purchase. Special editions or book excerpts can also be created to specification. For details, contact the Special Sales Manager at Human Kinetics.

Printed in the United States of America   10   9

The paper in this book is certified under a sustainable forestry program.

Human Kinetics
Web site: www.HumanKinetics.com

United States: Human Kinetics
P.O. Box 5076
Champaign, IL 61825-5076
800-747-4457
e-mail: humank@hkusa.com

Canada: Human Kinetics
475 Devonshire Road, Unit 100
Windsor, ON N8Y 2L5
800-465-7301 (in Canada only)
e-mail: info@hkcanada.com

Europe: Human Kinetics
107 Bradford Road
Stanningley
Leeds LS28 6AT, United Kingdom
+44 (0)113 255 5665
e-mail: hk@hkeurope.com

Australia: Human Kinetics
57A Price Avenue
Lower Mitcham, South Australia 5062
08 8372 0999
e-mail: info@hkaustralia.com

New Zealand: Human Kinetics
P.O. Box 80
Torrens Park, South Australia 5062
0800 222 062
e-mail: info@hknewzealand.com

This book is dedicated to YOU—for choosing to excel, for choosing to become what you are capable of becoming, for choosing to make a positive difference in your own life, for choosing to make a positive difference in the lives of others, for choosing to embrace a path with heart.

CONTENTS

ACKNOWLEDGMENTS

I would like to extend my heartfelt thanks to my daughters—Skye, Jewelia, and Anouk—for the wonderful gift of pure love and support that they have given me and continue to give me.

To the thousands of great athletes, coaches, students, and performers who have challenged me to give my best, find a better way, and continue to learn and grow as they have explored their own potential—

To the team at Human Kinetics who continue to help me share my experiences and visions of excellence in a clear and meaningful way with readers around the world: Rainer Martens and Ted Miller, as well as Heather Healy, Justin Klug, Nancy Rasmus, Robert Replinger, Tara Welsch, and Carla Zych—

To my colleagues and administrators at the University of Ottawa who have helped provide me with the freedom to pursue my personal and professional goals, and to my insightful and devoted graduate students who have been a continuous inspiration and joy to work with—

To all the inspiring athletes and performers who are quoted in this book and to those who agreed to share intimate details of their challenging journeys: Allison Forsyth, Kerrin Lee Gartner, Thomas Grandi, Chris Hadfield, Bruce Malmberg, Chris McCormack, Dan Nadeau, and Beckie Scott—

Thank you all for the ways in which you have inspired me and enriched my perspectives, my life, and the thoughts shared in this fourth edition of *In Pursuit of Excellence*.

PREFACE

This book tells you in simple and practical ways how you can excel in your life and live your dreams. You can turn challenges into opportunities in every part of your life so that you can succeed in your sport, school, profession, and relationships. You can make your focus work for you to raise the level and consistency of your performance. Perhaps most importantly, this book will help you see that you control your own destiny through your decisions and your focused actions. You are the only one who can take full control of you and your own focus—this alone puts you in a position to direct the course of your own life.

The strategies presented in this book work because they are derived from the hard-learned experiences of real people who have excelled in sport and many other high-performance domains. You can apply and adapt these lessons to surmount every conceivable challenge in your life. The recurring theme in their experiences is that focus is incredibly powerful. The focus you adopt in your life leads your performance and your reality in positive or negative ways. You decide.

As you read, keep in mind that different strategies work for different people, in different contexts, at different points in their lives. Clear your mind of clutter. Open your mind to possibilities and read with full focus and full intent to act on what is most relevant to you right now. I wish you the best in this quest.

Simple Joys,
Terry Orlick

FOCUS ➤

MENTAL READINESS ➤

POSITIVE IMAGES ➤

CONFIDENCE ➤

DISTRACTION CONTROL ➤

ONGOING LEARNING ➤

COMMITMENT ➤

PART I

Envisioning Excellence

CHAPTER 1

Choice of Excellence

Every journey to excellence is filled with challenges, victories, setbacks, lessons, and simple joys. I hope that the simple wisdom contained in these pages will make your personal journey richer and more joyful, and that you will apply what you learn to the various contexts of your life. I encourage you to act in ways that make your mission and my mission a reality.

My goal in writing this book is to help you become the person and performer you can be—to empower you to perform and live consistently closer to your potential. That is my mission.

If you picked up this book, you probably want to excel at something. In your heart, you know that you can be better and more consistent than you are right now. The great performers I have worked with have taught me how to live and perform closer to full potential—right now—and you can learn to do so as well.

Excellence in every part of your life is a decision—decide to excel.

Excellence is a choice—choose to excel.

Excellence is full focus—focus, focus, focus.

That's it! If you know exactly how to act on what you just read, you can close this book and simply act on it—every day, every opportunity, every interaction, every practice, every performance, every step along the way. If you are not quite sure how to act on what I have just told you to do, read the rest of this book to find out how other great performers do it and how you can do it.

The most important steps you can take to excel in any part of your life are the following:

Decide what it is that you really want to do.

Decide to do what you really want to do. Choose to do it!

Focus fully on doing what you want to do—every day.

Decisions and Choices

Virtually everything that you do or do not do in your life is ruled by the choices that you make. You can choose to excel or choose not to excel. You can choose to bring focus and quality to what you do or choose not to. You can choose to get stressed out about things beyond your control or choose not to. You can choose to let other people upset you or choose not to. You can choose to approach obstacles and react to challenging situations in positive ways or in negative ways. You can choose to dwell on the negatives or focus on the positives. You can choose to embrace your dreams and go after them or let them drift away without really trying. These are your choices, and your choices direct the quality of your performance and the joyfulness of your life. You decide.

I have never met an Olympic champion, world champion, or world leader in any field who did not decide that he or she was going to go after his or her goals with full focus. If you want to perform and live to your personal potential, at some point you have to decide to do it with full focus. After you decide to pursue your dream or follow a path with focus and commitment, the next challenge often becomes staying on that path when it becomes bumpy. The first big step is choosing to excel. The next big step, which is sometimes even more challenging, is deciding to persist through the obstacles. No one reaches his or her personal potential without facing obstacles, setbacks, and challenges along the way. Adversity is a normal part of the journey to excellence in every field.

People who are successful at persisting through obstacles, challenges, setbacks, bad patches, uncertainties, doubts, and sometimes fear find a way to keep a sense of purpose, passion, or perspective in their pursuit. They feel that they have meaningful reasons for doing what they are doing and are able to retain those reasons for doing it. What are your reasons for doing what you are doing, for pursuing what you are pursuing? Why are you doing it? What are you hoping your pursuit will give you in the short run and in the long run? What do you like or love about doing it? What do you hope it will give you and those who have supported you or those you care about?

If you can retain your passion for pursuing your dream and find sustainable reasons for doing it, pure excellence will become a realistic goal. If you lose your passion for pursuing your dream and are not able to find sustainable reasons for continuing to do it, pure excellence will become an elusive goal. Retention of passion, retention of purpose, retention of focus, retention of love or joy, and retention of choice are all essential for living your dream of personal excellence.

The Choice to Focus

In every pursuit, focus drives consistent high-level performance. The recipe for high-quality focusing is simple—stay positive and stay fully connected. Acting consistently on the recipe, however, is extremely challenging. You have to decide to focus, choose to focus, find good reasons for focusing, and commit yourself to work on improving your focus so that it works for you and not against you—every day, every assignment, every practice, every training day, every preparation session, every simulation, every meet, every game, every interaction, every presentation, every shift, and every part of every performance—from the first second to the last second.

You can choose to go through the motions, to slop through whatever you are doing, or choose to focus on performing with quality, to the best of your ability. You can choose to listen with full focus or choose to nod your head as if you are listening and not listen at all. You can choose to be wherever you are—fully focused with every fiber of your being—or choose to be only partially there or not be there at all mentally. You can choose to focus on the positives or the negatives. You make these choices every day.

When I am working with athletes, students, and other performers, I often ask, "If you are there physically (at practice, in class, at work, with another person, or performing), why not be fully there?" What is the point of being there physically but not mentally? Why not be there fully—fully focused, fully connected, and fully positive? I challenge you to see how long you can maintain a fully connected, positive focus in a class, conversation, practice, or performance. I challenge you to see how quickly you can regain a fully connected focus if your focus drifts away. I challenge you to find something positive in every situation you enter—to see it as an opportunity to test yourself, to learn, and to grow your focus.

When you get your thoughts and focus working for you and not against you, you immediately begin to take control of your destiny. You turn poor performances into good performances, good performances into great performances, and great performances into consistently great performances.

Perspective Is Everything

A powerful example of choosing to find a positive perspective in an extremely difficult circumstance came to me from Dan Nadeau, an officer and highly regarded instructor in the Royal Canadian Mounted Police (RCMP), a championship shooter, and father of three wonderful children. After reading a previous edition of this book, Dan wrote to me to share his story about how he got through what is every parent's worst nightmare.*

> I have read several of your books, and the one that has affected me the most was *In Pursuit of Excellence.* In your book you speak of athletes you have worked with and how they have enhanced their performance and reached their goals. I also have a success story that I will share with you, as your insight and knowledge has been a major contribution in my being able to live life and not simply exist in it.

*Excerpts from Dan Nadeau's letters courtesy of Dan Nadeau.

I have suffered the loss of my three children, Christan, Angela, and Kurtis. They were all born with cystic fibrosis. Angela passed away in 1979 while I was doing my RCMP training in Regina. Kurtis passed away in January 1995, and my oldest son, Chris, passed away 13 months later. As the children were growing up, it was a very painful and extremely stressful task to keep the boys positive toward life, despite their knowledge that if a cure was not found, their life expectancy was short.

In the early part of 1990, I was introduced to your work by my assistant coach. We were coaching a local high school volleyball team. Between the two of us we gathered as much material as we could find on the subject of focus, imagery, and visualization. It was at this time that my life as I knew it began to change. Through the acquired learning of the various life skills you detailed in your books and articles, I felt a surge of new-found inspiration. I brought this sense home with me. I would often find myself and my boys engaged in discussion on how powerful our minds are and how we can control our thoughts and feelings. This opened a door of communication between my children and me that completely changed how we perceived our situation. We were able to deal with the loss of Angela and finally able to discuss openly what each of us was feeling. The few years that followed provided us with many fun and exciting events. My boys have redefined the definition of courage. They were both visualizers and used it daily in keeping themselves positive. The last afternoon I spent with my son Christan, he said to me, "Dad, I can still see my dream. I'm just too tired to get there right now." He passed away that night.

Since then I have had some really trying times. When I lose sight of my focus, I bring myself back to those final few years I had with Chris and Kurtis. I can't begin to tell you how grateful I am for those years, how grateful I am to have been inspired by you and your knowledge.

I am presently instructing at the RCMP Academy in Regina and continuously pass on what I have learnt and continue to learn from you to the next generation of RCMP officers. I may not have a gold medal around my neck, but I have a comfort zone and thank you for that.

I wrote back to Dan, sincerely thanked him for sharing his story, and requested more details on how he used my material to get through the huge challenges that he was living. This was his response:

At the time I was introduced to your book my life was a living hell. On the outside I was a vibrant individual, police officer, volleyball coach—a community icon, as someone put it. Inside I was an angry, confused, and worn-out man. No one had any idea how afraid and depressed I was. I had never gotten over the guilt of not being there for my daughter when she passed away, and the outlook for my two sons was not good. They were getting older, and unless a cure was found, they would not be with me much longer. There was so much stress in my work and in my personal life that it just became a way of life—don't think, don't deal with it, just keep myself busy.

While reading your book the first time, in all honesty I got angry and frustrated. I was reading about athletes training mentally and physically to win, to stay focused, and to be positive. That's a great thing. As a coach that is what you want to see in all your players. But as a father with two young boys who were fully aware of their pending outcome, it was difficult to keep my perspective on life. My oldest son wanted to play slow-pitch ball, and the doctor advised that it would not be good for him. I decided it would and let him play. I was sitting in the bleachers watching my son play ball, and the tears were running down my face. He was having the time of his life. His first at bat, he got a hit right between first and second, all the way to the fence. He ran the bases and collapsed at third base, completely out of breath. That didn't matter to him—he hit a triple.

I continued reading your book, and upon finishing it, I found myself thinking more and more about the stress that I was feeling, all the hours I spent worrying, how I had no harmony in my life. The positive self-direction chapter was the catalyst, in a metaphoric sense, not in the perspective of an athlete, but rather a personal challenge for me in my life. The biggest revelation for me was the fact that I was coaching young athletes on how to play their sports well and how to make the connection to other productive aspects of their lives. My children needed coaching as well, and I wasn't coaching them.

As you put it, think of the process, not the outcome. All I thought about was the outcome. Quiet reflection—this is where the transformation took place. I started thinking a little more rationally. I felt I was slowly coming to terms with my situation. I was engaging in conversations with my sons more and more. We established a form of communication that allowed all of us to speak openly about our fears. What a gut-wrenching initiation. Many tears, many hugs, many "I love you guys."

I read your book a second time, and this time I shared with the boys my thoughts on how so many things in the book could be applied to life itself. Many good days followed that transformation. My sons have since passed on, but what fond memories I have to reflect on. The second reading was done in a totally different mind-set, which allowed me to heal, to learn, and to become aware of a man who wrote of simple joys. He showed me where to look. Because of your ability to express life in a pure, honest, and rational way, I have been able to celebrate my life every day and make a difference in many people's lives. When a loved one leaves you behind there is no filling the void, but you can make a conscious choice to continue living your life in honor of theirs.

A little over a year after I received Dan's first e-mail, he wrote to me to share how he had directed his focus (chapters 3 and 11) and imagery (chapter 8) toward a best-ever shooting performance and a major competition victory.

I simply wanted to share with you my experience in competing for the Connaught Cup. This cup is awarded to the best shooter in the RCMP. Each province is represented by their best shooter. I was representing our training academy. The event was held today, and I won the cup. As you know, you have been my mentor for many years. I can't begin to tell you how much you have contributed to the quality of life that I share every day with hundreds of cadets and coworkers.

In the days leading up to the competition, I prepared myself using your Focusing for Excellence audio CDs. Wow—what a tremendous help. Last night I listened to CD #4, *Performing in the Zone*, after which I sat down and did some focused imagery, seeing myself perform my best ever. Today I not only won the Connaught Cup but shot my all-time best. I'm still in a state of amazement in what one can achieve when inspired through the wisdom of a mentor such as you. On a final note, today my son Kurtis would have celebrated his 23rd birthday. He was a part of me today on the range, and I felt his spirit. Hard to explain. All I can say is that it felt good.

Over the three years since he first contacted me, Dan continued to update me about his success in applying the practical lessons from *In Pursuit of Excellence* to his work.

I am still instructing firearms for the RCMP and applying mental training with all the cadets. I continue to use the wheel of excellence as the basis of my instruction in the mental-training side of police work. As a result over 5,000 cadets have a better mind-set at the start of every shift. I personally make it a part of my cadets' training, and the senior officers are starting to take notice of the benefits. Since I have been instructing here I have not had one of my cadets fail firearms yet—knock on wood. I have been involved in coaching for 25 years. I know I have a natural ability to motivate and inspire people and over the years have gained a lot of experience. I have all this knowledge, I want to continue working in this area of expertise, and I know my potential—unlimited. I must say, Terry, you have been an unbelievable source of information and inspiration to many of us Mounties.

Learning from each experience and performance is a choice. You can choose to apply the lessons that you learn about your best and less-than-best focus in your next practice, experience, or performance. When you act on these choices, you become a better performer and better person. You separate yourself from those who never come close to living their true potential.

Choose to focus on the positives rather than the negatives.

Choose to focus on the opportunities rather than the obstacles.

Choose to bring a fully connected focus to your practices and performances.

Choose to focus fully on the step in front of you rather than on distractions.

Choose to live and perform closer to your potential.

The control that you have over your choices, your focus, and your destiny is real and powerful. It is the key to unlocking the door to your true potential.

CHAPTER 2

Wheel of Excellence

We are all performers living the drama of life in different ways, in different contexts. We are all capable of pursuing our dreams and reaching meaningful goals. We all pos-

> *Your focus leads your performance and your life.*

sess incredible strength when we draw on the full power of our focus. When we strengthen the quality and consistency of our focus, we add quality and consistency to our performances and joy to our lives.

Seven critical elements guide the pursuit of personal excellence: focus, commitment, mental readiness, positive images, confidence, distraction control, and ongoing learning. These elements combine to form the wheel of excellence (see figure 2.1), a puzzle of interconnected pieces that applies to every sport and performance pursuit.

Use the parts of the wheel that give you strength and focus. Choose to improve the parts that you believe can benefit from improvement. You can strengthen any part of the wheel of excellence at any stage of your development by deciding to do it and by focusing on making small improvements every day. After you have woven all the pieces of the wheel into their rightful place, the puzzle is complete, and the wheel runs smoothly, even in bumpy terrain.

Focus

Focus is the first and most important element of excellence. Focus is the core of excellence, the center of the circle, the hub of the wheel of excellence.

People who perform their best, or excel at the highest levels, have learned how to focus. To perform your best, you need to find a focus that frees you to be the way you want to be within your performance context and within your life. Excellence begins to blossom when you find ways to focus that connect you completely and absolutely with each step in the moment-by-moment process of your performance pursuit. A totally engaging focused connection frees you to raise the level and consistency of your performance.

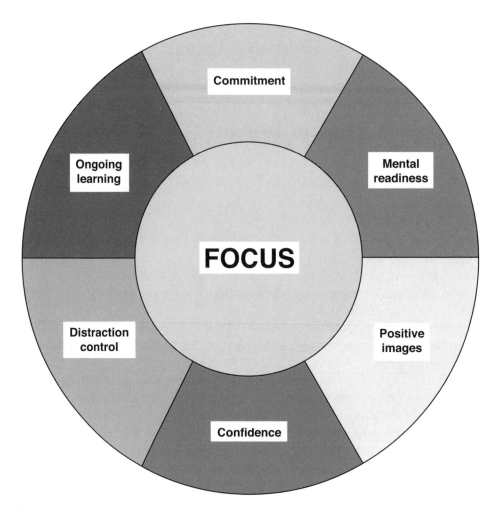

▶ **Figure 2.1** The wheel of excellence.

Improving your focus allows you to continue to learn, experiment, grow, create, enjoy, and perform closer to your capacity. Excellence flows naturally when you develop confidence in your focus and know that your focus will take you where you want to go. Consistent high-level performance depends on consistent high-quality focus. When you develop, direct, and connect your focus, you strengthen all elements of excellence that add quality and consistency to your performance and joy to your life.

The other elements of excellence (commitment, mental readiness, positive images, confidence, distraction control, and ongoing learning) grow out of your focus, take direction from your focus, connect you and reconnect you with your mission, and make excellence possible. The combination of the seven elements in the wheel of excellence empowers you to become the person and performer that you have the potential to be. And each of these elements is within your personal control.

Commitment

The heart of human excellence often begins to beat when you discover a pursuit that absorbs you, frees you, challenges you, or gives you a sense of meaning, joy, or passion. When you find something within a pursuit, or within yourself, that you are truly committed to developing, everything else can grow.

Do you have a vision of what you would like to pursue, where you want to go, or what you want to accomplish? If you do, make it clear in your mind. Think about it often. If you do not have a vision, think about where you might want to go, what you might like to accomplish, and how you might make it happen. Even if you don't start with a big commitment, simply getting fully focused on doing the good things that you want to do will cause good things to begin to happen. Your commitment, joy, and performance will grow.

Commitment is a key ingredient in guiding the pursuit of excellence. With focused commitment, you can achieve almost anything; without it, high-level goals that are within your grasp become virtually impossible to attain.

Your commitment requires a specific focus. Your commitment will grow when your focus is centered on

- ➤ continuing to learn and grow;
- ➤ pursuing your dreams or making a meaningful contribution;
- ➤ becoming the best that you can be;
- ➤ developing the mental, physical, and technical links to excellence;
- ➤ setting clear personal goals and relentlessly pursuing them;
- ➤ persisting through obstacles, even when they appear insurmountable or impossible;
- ➤ continuing to learn about how your focus affects your mood and your performance, and acting on the lessons learned about focus; and
- ➤ keeping the joy or passion in your pursuit.

The beginnings of excellence are kindled by engaging yourself in doing something that you want and like to do. Higher levels of excellence are inspired by having a positive vision of where you want to go—in your sport, performance, or life. To excel in any challenging pursuit, you must either have, or develop, a heartfelt reason or passion for doing it. You need a reason powerful enough to keep you pursuing your goals though the ups and downs. High levels of personal commitment grow naturally out of love for and joy in what you are doing, combined with positive visions of where you want to go. Commitment grows from embracing the special moments, absorbing yourself in your mission, and loving the experience of ongoing personal growth. Many personal reasons, or sources of commitment, can drive excellence:

- ➤ Pure enjoyment, passion, or love for the activity or pursuit
- ➤ The excitement of the pursuit and the feeling of being fully alive

➤ The feeling of being accepted, competent, needed, valued, important, successful, or special

➤ The feeling of pursuing a dream, living your potential, or becoming what you are capable of being

➤ The feeling of making a meaningful contribution or making a difference

➤ Pride in your performance, creation, or contribution

➤ The feeling of overcoming challenges, stretching limits, or proving something to yourself or others

➤ The feeling of giving something back to people who have supported you or giving something forward to people who will follow you

➤ The joy or love of ongoing learning

If you like what you are doing (at least parts of it) and are able to remain focused and committed to it, you will become competent at it—which is a worthy and beneficial goal. To become truly great at something, and to continue to perform at high levels over extended periods, you usually have to love it. Most performers who excel at the highest levels say that the pursuit itself becomes their passion and drives their lives for extended periods. They are passionate about their pursuits, love the joyful parts, and are willing to put up with or focus through the tough parts. They draw positive energy from the parts that they like and learn lessons from the parts that are not joyful. High-level performers are able to achieve most of their goals and gain from the journey by focusing on the positives and staying committed through the negatives or obstacles.

On the path to excellence, some obstacles may initially seem insurmountable. Every performer experiences this feeling, even the greatest performers in the world. If you believe that the obstacles are too great to overcome, you will prove yourself right even when you are wrong. Most seemingly impossible obstacles can be overcome by seeing possibilities, focusing on what is within your control, taking the first step, and then focusing on the next step and the next step after that. If your commitment wavers, remember your dream or mission and why it is important to you, find simple joys in your daily pursuits, rejoice in the little victories or small steps forward, and embrace the process of ongoing learning. With a positive perspective and persistence, you will get through, focus through, and find a way through all obstacles.

The commitment you make to yourself to go after your goals and persist through adversity is a huge part of reaching high-level goals. Equally important is your commitment to take time for mental, physical, and emotional recovery. Relaxation and regeneration are critical parts of consistent high-level performance, especially over the long term.

Sometimes the best way to enhance your performance and your life is to listen to your body, listen to your heart, and respect your basic needs for relaxation, rest, personal space, good nutrition, and joyful moments away from your performance domain. Failure to find some balance between quality exertion and quality rest, between stress and relaxation, will eventually affect your performance, your life, and your love for what you are doing. Commit to focus on doing what will be most beneficial for you and your ultimate goals.

Mental Readiness

There is a big difference between talking about what you want to do and being mentally ready to do it. Mental readiness has everything to do with being positive, focused, persistent, and fully committed to acting on your intentions. Excellence requires that you choose to get yourself mentally ready for focused, decisive action. Acting decisively every day is essential in training, work, and performance contexts because only action counts. Only focused action will take you to your goals. Excellence blossoms when you want to be somewhere rather than when you feel that you have to be there, when you choose to do something rather than when you feel forced to do it, and when you see opportunities rather than obligations.

Your mental readiness requires a specific focus. Your mental readiness will grow when your focus is centered on

➤ preparing, practicing, training, working, performing, and competing with full focus and the right level of intensity;

➤ bringing a positive focus into training, work, and performances;

➤ shifting back to a positive focus if you start to become negative;

➤ focusing in ways that bring out your best;

➤ creating positive learning opportunities;

➤ taking advantage of every training and performance opportunity;

➤ refining essential mental, physical, technical, and tactical skills necessary to excel in your pursuit;

➤ evaluating the effectiveness of your focus in practice, at work, and after every performance, and acting on the lessons learned at your next opportunity;

➤ continuing to find simple joys both within your performance pursuit and outside it; and

➤ relaxing, resting, recovering, and staying positive with yourself and others through the ups and downs.

To excel in any pursuit, you need to become mentally ready to think, focus, and act in positive ways. When you are mentally ready, you will find it much easier to learn essential performance skills, practice those skills to perfection, and perform those skills effectively under demanding conditions. The ultimate benefit of mental readiness is that you will be focused on getting the best out of what you have right now—at this point in your training, performance, season, career, or life.

You must also be mentally ready to draw lessons from each of your experiences and act on them. Great performers have effective action plans or focusing routines that prepare them mentally to accomplish whatever they want to accomplish each day and each performance, and to act on the lessons learned. To perform your best more consistently, challenge yourself to find effective ways to get yourself mentally ready and fully focused on achieving your goals. The following strategies can help you focus in positive ways:

➤ Think about some things that you have already accomplished.

➤ Think about some things that you still want to learn, improve, or accomplish.

➤ Think about specific goals that you want to achieve and write them down on paper.

➤ Think about what your goals are for today.

➤ Run through some of your goals in your mind and imagine yourself accomplishing them.

➤ Before going to practices or performances, think about what you are going to focus on to achieve your goals.

➤ Every day ask yourself, *What am I going to do today that will take me one step closer to my dreams? What am I going to focus on so that I can accomplish my goals today?*

➤ Continue to look for simple and effective ways to get yourself mentally ready to focus on achieving your goals.

➤ For specific exercises to improve mental readiness and focusing for excellence, refer to my Focusing for Excellence audio CDs, specifically *Practicing in the Zone* and *Performing in the Zone* (see page 303).

Positive Visions and Images

Many great accomplishments, new discoveries, and seemingly impossible feats begin with a single positive vision. Positive visions of what you want to accomplish and smaller visions of the steps that you are going to take to get there can drive the pursuit of excellence. Visions, big or small, often live in your mind before they become realities. Part of the ongoing challenge of pursuing excellence is sustaining positive visions and a positive perspective through the various stages of your journey.

Your visions or images depend on what you focus on. Your positive visions will grow when you focus on using the power of positive visions, thoughts, mental imagery, visualization, or *feelization* to

➤ create positive visions of where you want to go with your performance (or your life) and see what you have the potential to be;

- ➤ speed up the learning and integration of technical skills, tactical skills, mental skills, physical skills, race plans, game plans, focusing plans, and refocusing plans;
- ➤ create positive images of the steps that you need to take to get where you want to go;
- ➤ create positive visions, images, or thoughts that inspire you to continue to pursue your goals and go after your dreams;
- ➤ learn from your best performances and best parts of performances;
- ➤ identify clear and specific daily goals for ongoing improvement;
- ➤ mentally prepare yourself to follow your game plan or race plan and focus in ways that will free you to perform to your capacity;
- ➤ act and react in positive and decisive ways;
- ➤ strengthen your confidence; and
- ➤ improve the execution of your performance skills.

One of the main benefits of having a big positive vision and smaller step-by-step visions is to keep you focused on the positives and the possibilities (why you can do it, why you want to do it, and how you will do it) as opposed to focusing on the negatives (why you can't do it). Your chances of achieving high-level goals and living joyfully are greatly enhanced when you focus on positive thoughts, positive images, positive visions, and positive lessons.

Great performers do not begin their lives or pursuits as great performers. They work at getting into a habit of seeing things in positive ways and imagining themselves performing and executing technical skills in the way that they would like to perform them. In fact, most of the best performers in the world have highly developed imagery skills because they use these skills daily to create a positive focus for excellence. They draw on positive memories, recall the focus and feelings of previous best performances, and create positive visions of the future. They use their positive thoughts and positive imagery to prepare themselves mentally for quality practice, quality performances, and joyful life experiences.

To improve future performances, they carefully revisit positive parts of their current or past performances (so that they know what is working) and assess parts of their performances that can be improved so that they can make necessary adjustments. They often refine or improve their skills by running them through their minds. They think, see, feel, or imagine themselves making the improvement and being competent, confident, successful, and in control, which sets the stage for higher-quality performances. When learning new skills, procedures, routines, or tactics or when making refinements, they often run the desired actions through their minds many times, with quality and feel, to speed up the learning process. Some of them also use positive imagery to relax themselves or regain control when distracted.

©SportsChrome USA

▶ Great performers like Roger Federer learn to draw on previous best performances and to envision future successes.

You, too, can experience the benefits of positive visions. Performing at a high level in your mind (and feeling it in your body) allows you to create the conditions for success without having actually executed those performances in the real world. This focusing process can enhance your confidence, focus, and performance, leaving you with good feelings about yourself, your readiness, and your capacity to do the things that you want to do. With practice, you can preexperience and reexperience many desired actions, feelings, sensations, and skills that are important for the successful execution of your best possible performance.

Positive thoughts combined with positive images and positive feelings help create the mindset and focus required for high-quality performance. What do you want to accomplish in your performance domain or in your life? Can you imagine or envision yourself accomplishing those goals or living your dreams? What positive steps can you take today to move forward toward your ultimate performance goals? Think about how you want to perform in your next competition, challenge, or performance. Make it clear in your mind. Imagine it, see it, and feel yourself doing it. Let your positive visions lead your actions and your reality in positive ways.

Confidence

Confidence is an essential ingredient in guiding the pursuit of excellence. Confidence opens doors that an absence of confidence has previously slammed shut. Performance confidence rises or falls based on the quality of your preparation, the quality of your focus, and the extent to which you believe in your capacity. Confidence comes from committing yourself to do the preparation or quality work, talking to yourself in positive ways about what you have done and what you can do, drawing lessons from your experiences and acting on them, and remaining positive with yourself through the many challenges along the way. Confidence blossoms when you discover what focus works best for you, respect the power of that focus, and regularly call upon it.

Your confidence requires a specific focus. Your confidence will grow when your focus is centered on trusting or believing in

- ➤ your own potential,
- ➤ your capacity to overcome obstacles and achieve your goals,
- ➤ your preparation or mental readiness,
- ➤ your focus,
- ➤ your choices,
- ➤ the meaningfulness of your mission or pursuit, and
- ➤ those with whom you work or play.

We rarely begin performance pursuits with total confidence in our capacity to achieve our goals or execute certain tasks with quality and precision. We grow confidence by rejoicing in the things that we do well, acknowledging our improvements, learning from our successes and failures, absorbing the wisdom of others, and discovering that focus frees us to perform our best.

When you have unwavering belief in your capacity to carry out a mission and absolute focus on your performance, doors are open to the highest levels of excellence. When distractions or negative thoughts interfere with your confidence, your performance wavers—not because you are any less capable, but because you let those doubts interfere with your best focus. Pure confidence comes from feeling grounded in who you are and knowing in your heart and soul that you are capable of doing what you want to do. In the presence of pure confidence, you trust your focus and your performance soars. In the absence of confidence, you rarely touch your full potential.

The only way to increase your confidence is to strengthen your focus on the right things. Each element on the wheel of excellence can help you improve the quality of your focus, which in turn strengthens your confidence. Confidence in your focus is like a master key: It opens the door to higher levels of excellence, and higher levels of excellence open the door to greater confidence. The following strategies can help you strengthen your confidence:

- ➤ Remember that someone believes in you.
- ➤ Think in positive ways about your capacity.
- ➤ Think about why you can achieve your goals.
- ➤ Write down a list of reasons you can achieve your goals or reasons to believe that you can achieve your goals.
- ➤ Act as if you can do it.

➤ Focus on high-quality technical, physical, and mental preparation.

➤ Think about your successes in training, simulations, and previous performances.

➤ Find the positive parts of all your experiences and performances.

➤ Think about how you will achieve your goals. What will you focus on?

➤ Continually draw out the focus lessons to improve the quality and consistency of your performances.

Although you may occasionally perform well without feeling fully confident, you are much more likely to perform to your potential on a consistent basis if your confidence and your focus are working together for you. This gift comes from respecting yourself, respecting your best focus, and freeing your body and mind to perform without interference. Give yourself this gift. You are worthy of it.

Distraction Control

Distraction control refers to focusing through distractions or not letting distractions interfere with the quality of your performance or the success of your mission. Some distractions are external, arising from other people (competitors, fans, or media) and their expectations or from specific circumstances in your environment. Other distractions are internal, arising from your own thinking, doubts, worries, fears, or expectations. Regardless of what kind of distractions you face, maintaining a positive connected focus before, during, and after performances is important. Distraction control is especially important when you feel stressed, crowded, pressured, uncertain, or unappreciated, or when you are performing in demanding circumstances.

Your ability to control distractions requires a specific focus. Your ability to control distractions will grow when your focus is centered on

➤ reducing stress;

➤ maintaining a positive, effective focus in the face of distractions;

➤ regaining a positive, effective focus when distracted before, during, or after a practice, event, or performance;

➤ refocusing or reconnecting quickly with your best performance focus;

➤ performing consistently close to your potential;

➤ staying focused on executing your game plan;

➤ relaxing and getting adequate rest; and

➤ staying on your own best path for personal excellence.

Great performers activate positive shifts in focus by using simple reminders, images, or focus points that reconnect them with something positive that is within their immediate control. This process takes them back where they want to be—to a positive mind-set and a fully focused connection within the present performance moment. By strengthening your ability to refocus quickly, you will achieve greater consistency in your performance and experience more enjoyment in your life.

Effective refocusing grows most readily from developing a simple refocusing plan and acting on that plan. When you become distracted by negative thoughts, lapses in concentration, setbacks, or dips in confidence—before, during, or after a performance—the goal is to regain a positive perspective quickly and reconnect instantly to your best focus. You can learn to reconnect more quickly and effectively by reflecting on what works best for you to get you back on track quickly. Plan some reminders that you can use to regain control, to refocus on what you control, and to focus on what works best for you. Plan your best focus path and practice using your refocusing reminders whenever the opportunity arises.

Ongoing Learning

Consistent high-level performers follow their own best paths. They are superb self-directed learners. The pursuit of excellence is a process of self-discovery and stretching limits, in which you act on discoveries that lead you to your best focus and best performances. As you discover what works and feels best for you, remember to follow this path, even in the face of obstacles.

Ongoing learning requires a specific focus. Your skills for ongoing learning will grow when your focus is centered on

➤ finding joy in what you do well and in the small steps forward,

➤ drawing out relevant lessons from each experience or performance,

➤ reflecting on what you did well and what freed you to do it,

➤ reflecting on what you can improve and how you can make those refinements,

➤ reflecting on how your focus affected your performance and how to respect your best focus,

➤ targeting relevant focus areas for improvement, and

➤ acting on the lessons learned on an ongoing basis.

Personal excellence results from living the lessons that you gain from your experiences. Great performers attain high levels of excellence because they are committed to ongoing learning. They prepare well, focus well, deal well with distractions, do thorough postperformance evaluations, and act on the lessons that they draw from their experiences. They see their own good qualities, look for positive parts of their performances, and target relevant areas for improvement. They gain inspiration, confidence, and inner strength by finding simple joys within their pursuits, looking for personal highlights, and continuing to reflect on what frees them to live fully and perform their best. They also grow from setbacks by channeling their lessons and energy toward their improvement.

To live your true potential, continue to reflect on the focus that you carry into your most joyful experiences and best performances. Continue to extract the focus lessons from your best and less-than-best experiences and performances. Continue to refine your focus until it is consistently where you want it to be. Your rate of learning, the level and consistency of your performance, and the quality of your life are directly affected by the extent to which you engage in ongoing, constructive, personal evaluation, followed by positive action. Don't waste hard-learned lessons. Embrace them, remember them, and act on them.

Personal Excellence

Personal excellence is a lifelong journey that brings focus, challenge, meaning, joy, frustration, and perspective to life. As good or great as you are or become, you can always be a little bit better—a little more focused, confident, consistent, positive, or better equipped to deal with distractions. When Tiger Woods won his fifth consecutive PGA Tour event (7 wins in 14 starts that year and 53 PGA Tour event wins), he commented, "Everything can always be better. This game is fluid. It's always changing. It's always evolving. I could always hit the ball better, chip better, putt better, think better. You can get better tomorrow than you are today." Tiger's focus is on target, and his wheel of excellence is usually working on all cylinders—that's why he is a great golfer.

The wheel of excellence can serve as a personal guide for improving anything important in your life. Decide what is most important for you now. Then look at the wheel while keeping that goal in mind. Assess where you think your mental skills are strongest and where they need strengthening. Target a specific area for improvement that seems most relevant for you now. Write down a personal plan for making meaningful improvements in this area and focus on implementing it. Decide to do it and then do it! When you revisit the wheel later, select another target area that could help you improve. The following questions may help you clarify your personal direction for improvement.

Focus

➤ Do you know what kind of focus helps you perform best?

➤ Do you know what kind of focus helps you learn best?

➤ Do you have a plan that will consistently get you into your best, fully focused state?

➤ Are you working at improving the quality and consistency of your focus? Every day?

➤ Are you focusing on doing the little things that work best for you? Every day?

➤ Are you working at sustaining your best focus for the duration of each class, practice, work session, personal interaction, or performance? Can you do better? How?

Commitment

➤ Are your goals clear, challenging, and targeted at being your best?

➤ Are you doing something every day that takes you one step closer to your goals? What did you do today to take yourself one step closer to your goal?

➤ Are you working at improving something every day and in every performance?

➤ Is your commitment to quality focus in training, learning, practicing, and performing strong enough to take you to your goals? Could your commitment be better or could you act on it in a more consistent or focused way?

➤ Are you keeping an element of joyfulness in your pursuit and in your life?

➤ Is your commitment to respect your personal needs for rest and recovery strong enough to sustain you through this challenging journey?

Mental Readiness

➤ Are you carrying a positive mind-set into your work, school, interactions, practices, and performances? Can you do better? How?

➤ Are you looking for opportunities in everything?

➤ Are you carrying a perspective that centers on continued learning and growing?

➤ Are you mentally preparing yourself to focus fully on performing your best every day—in school, work, practices, relationships, and performances? Can you do better? How?

➤ Are you dwelling on the positives, not the negatives?

➤ Are you remaining open to new possibilities?

Positive Images

➤ Do you have a big vision of where you would like to go with your performance, your education, your profession, or your life?

➤ Do you keep that vision clearly in your mind? Do you visit it regularly?

➤ Can you imagine yourself performing exactly the way that you would like to perform, accomplishing the things that you want to accomplish, and being the way that you would prefer to be?

➤ Do you imagine yourself focusing the way that you would prefer to focus and achieving the goals that you would like to achieve? Often?

➤ Do you imagine yourself doing the little things, taking the small daily steps that will take you to your goals? Every day?

➤ Are you waking up your positive images or positive visions by acting on them in positive ways every day?

➤ Are your positive visions providing you with inspiration and direction to continue to pursue your goals and dreams?

Confidence

➤ Do you believe that you can reach your dreams or attain your goals?

➤ Are you looking for reasons to believe and focusing on why you can achieve your goals?

➤ Are you talking to yourself in ways that make you feel positive and confident?

➤ Are you choosing to be confident? Are you thinking about why you can achieve your goals and how you will achieve them?

➤ Are you putting yourself in situations that give you the best chance of believing in yourself and achieving your goals?

➤ Are you looking for the good things in every practice, in every performance, and in your life? Every day? Even if some parts didn't go well?

➤ Are you acknowledging your progress and rejoicing in it?

➤ Are you trusting yourself, your preparation, and your focus?

➤ Are you acting as if you can do it?

Distraction Control

➤ Are you carrying a perspective that allows you to avoid or minimize stress and distractions?

➤ Can you maintain your best focus even when you face setbacks or distractions?

➤ Can you refocus quickly and regain control when you encounter performance errors or setbacks? Can you do it consistently?

➤ Are you good at turning negatives into positives?

➤ Do you have an effective plan for dealing with distractions?

➤ Are you acting on that plan? At every opportunity?

➤ Are you working on improving your skills at focusing through distractions and adversity?

Ongoing Learning

➤ Are you committed to ongoing learning, to learning something from every performance and experience, and to using it to get better?

➤ Are you looking for the positives in yourself, others, and your performances? Every day?

➤ Are you drawing out relevant lessons from every performance and every important experience, both when things go well and when they do not go well?

➤ Are you acting on those lessons every day or at every opportunity, before your next performance, interaction, or event?

➤ Are you reflecting on the role that your focus plays in each performance and each important interaction?

➤ Do you act on those reflections? Consistently?

To make meaningful improvements in the quality and consistency of your performance, you do not have to reinvent the wheel. You just have to target a relevant area for improvement and act on it. In my consulting work with high-level performers (and those striving to be high-level performers), we almost always target two areas for improvement—focusing and distraction control. These two elements have an extremely powerful effect on the consistency of high-level performance.

When you look at the different success elements on the wheel of excellence and think about your performance and your life, you may immediately know where you are strongest and where you need the most work. Start there. And remember that these seven elements of excellence apply not only in sport but also in every other performance domain and every life pursuit. When implemented they add quality and joy to your performance, work, relationships, and life. These seven elements free you to attain what is important to you in life.

Whether your goals are expansive or modest, the success elements that make up the wheel of excellence will take you on an exciting journey toward your true potential in performance pursuits and life. Each of these mental links to excellence has the potential to strengthen your focus, take you closer to your capacity, and add joy to your life.

CHAPTER 3

Focus for Excellence

Focusing and refocusing are essential action components for learning, performing, and achieving excellence. Individuals and teams cannot perform consistently close to their potential without them. Effective focusing, which includes effective refocusing, is the key target in my work with high-performance athletes, coaches, business executives, students,

> *What you choose to focus on is totally within your control. You direct your focus, and your focus leads your performance. If you do not control your own focus, who does?*

and performers in all disciplines precisely because these skills are essential for consistent high-level performance.

Athletes, students, coaches, teachers, parents, children, and performers in all work settings and at all performance levels can gain from improving the quality and consistency of their focus. High-quality focusing enhances learning, joy, and performance in practices, training, preparation sessions, meetings, workshops, video sessions, classes, and all other learning contexts. High-quality focusing also enhances performance in all work and performance contexts and positively affects the quality of daily interactions at home, work, and play. Focus rules your performance, your day, your life, and your world. As shown in figure 3.1, focus is the sun that radiates energy, power, direction, and connection to all the elements of the wheel of excellence. Your focus affects everything you do in every area of life—just as the sun radiates energy for life and growth on our planet.

Using Focus-Centered Performance Enhancement

The single most important goal in any performance is to keep your focus centered on what connects you to your performance and frees you to perform your best. In the world of high-level performance, focus rules—for better or worse.

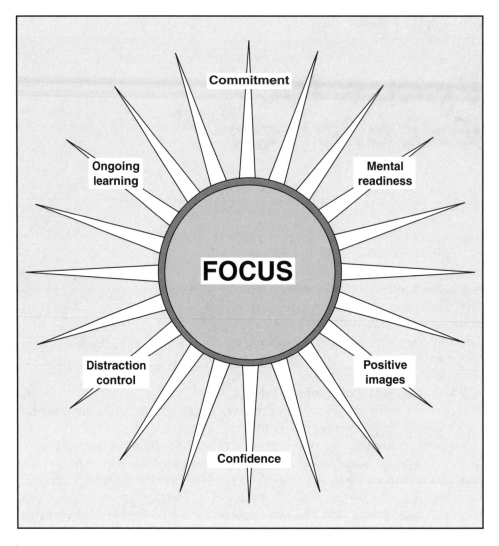

▶ **Figure 3.1**   Focus radiates outward, illuminating every aspect of life.

Performance, good or bad, is grounded in your focus. Is your focus fully connected during your performances and interactions, or is it not fully connected? Are you focusing in ways that are helping you or hurting you? Is your focus on target or off target? When your focus is fully connected and right where you want it to be, how do you get it there and keep it there? When it is not fully connected or not where you want it to be, how do you get it back on track?

To enhance the quality and consistency of your performance, you need to understand how your focus affects your performance. What focus frees you to perform, and what focus interferes with a free-flowing performance? When you begin to understand what works well and what interferes, you can more easily make a commitment to work on improving the quality and consistency of your focus. Focus-centered performance enhancement is grounded in taking what is presently your best focus in your best performances and working to make that kind of focus even better and more consistent.

Think about one (or two) of your best-ever performances, when you performed to your potential in a performance that was important to you. The goal of this exercise is to make your performance focus more consistent and reliable. The following questions will help you identify your best focus and your less-than-best focus:

➤ What were you focused on (or thinking about) going into that performance?

➤ What did you focus on seconds before you started to perform, compete, or play?

➤ How would you describe your focus or connected feelings during that performance?

➤ What were you focused on or connected to for most of that performance?

➤ How fully connected did you feel during that performance?

➤ Did you ever lose that focused connection?

➤ If you lost the connection, what did you do to get back on track?

➤ If you never lost the connection, what kept you connected?

Think about one (or two) of your most disappointing performances when you did not perform close to your potential in a performance that was important to you.

➤ What were you focused on (or thinking about) going into that performance?

➤ What were you focused on seconds before you started to perform, compete, or play?

➤ How would you describe your focus or feelings during that performance?

➤ What were you focused on or connected to for most of that performance?

➤ Did you ever feel a fully focused, high-quality connection?

➤ If you did feel fully connected, even for a short time, what did you do to get there?

➤ If you never gained or regained that focused connection, what kept you disconnected?

Think about your focus or focused connection when you have performed your best (in parts of performances or in complete performances) and compare it with your focus or focused connection when you have not performed your best. What kind of focus do you think will give you your best chance of performing to your potential on a more consistent basis? How can you make this happen?

Focus in Practice

A high-quality, fully connected focus in practice or training leads to better performance in both practice and competitions or performances. The goal in practice or training is to stay focused, stay positive, stay connected with the right things, improve in small ways every day, and not waste your time while you are there. Decide what focus you are going to carry into your practice or training session, commit to respect that focus, and focus fully on making good things happen. Remind yourself of the following facts to get the best out of each practice or training session:

➤ Quality practice and quality preparation create and enhance quality performance.

➤ Quality practice and quality preparation depend on quality focus.

➤ Quality practice depends on respecting a focus that brings out your best and works best for you.

➤ Quality practice depends on staying fully connected within the performance and quickly regaining a positive focus if it drifts away.

➤ Quality focus in practice includes listening attentively, focusing on quality execution, learning from feedback, focusing on making little improvements or corrections, and staying fully connected with what you are doing in the drill or simulation.

➤ Quality practice means focusing on doing what is required to perform well in competitions or performances and extracting the focus lessons from each practice to enhance ongoing learning and ongoing improvement.

Focus in Performance

The goal in performances, games, and competitions is to stay focused, stay positive, stay connected with the right things, perform to your capacity, and not waste an opportunity. Decide what focus you are going to carry into the performance, commit to respect that focus, and focus fully on making good things happen. Remind yourself of the following facts to bring out your best in each performance:

➤ Quality performance—in real performance situations, real games, competitions, and situations that count in your life—depends on your focus.

➤ Quality performance depends on respecting a focus that brings out your best and works best for you.

- ➤ Quality performance requires you to stay fully connected within the performance and to regain focus quickly if it drifts away.
- ➤ Quality focus in performances and competitions begins with deciding what you want to do in the performance, game, or competition and deciding what focus you are going to carry into the performance.
- ➤ Quality focus in performances and competitions requires that you respect your best focus, focus fully on connecting within the performance, and follow your game plan.
- ➤ Quality focus in performances and competitions requires that you commit yourself to maintaining your best focus in the face of distractions, focusing through distractions, and refocusing to get back on track quickly within the performance whenever necessary.

In critical situations and critical parts of your performance, performance is 100 percent mental. If you or your team members lose it mentally—if you lose focus, lose connection, or abandon hope—you will crash and burn. A loss of focus at critical moments negatively affects your performance and your team's performance. So, at least for those moments, performance is 100 percent mental, both in sport and in other high-performance pursuits such as negotiations, presentations, exams, and emergencies.

Nurturing Excellence

I have had the opportunity to learn from and work with many performers who have excelled in different disciplines. This group has included Olympic and world champions in sport, high-performance coaches, astronauts, exceptional surgeons, classical musicians, dancers, actors, leading business executives, and other people who excel at embracing their lives. The most striking revelation about these exceptional performers from all over the world is how similar they are with respect to their highly developed focusing skills, their positive performance perspectives, and their highly developed wheels of excellence.

In some ways people who excel at the highest levels are more like you than you might expect. They get nervous and sometimes fearful before they compete or perform in big events. They experience ups and downs in their confidence and sometimes have doubts about their ability to perform to their potential or repeat their best performances. They also like to have fun with what they are doing. Almost all great performers, from professional team-sport athletes to top classical musicians, speak of the important role of fun, joy, passion, or love for the pursuit (or parts of the pursuit) in freeing them to excel. The joy of the pursuit and their ongoing commitment to their mission helps them remain positive and focused through the ups and downs of their journey.

The reason that high-level performers are able to continue to perform well consistently is that they have developed effective ways to put away distractions,

© Jeff Topping/X 00284/Reuters/Corbis

▶ Steve Nash and other exceptional performers have learned to center their focus exclusively on the task at hand.

doubts, and fears and focus exclusively on doing their jobs when they get to the line and it is time to perform. What separates these people is their focus on fully developing themselves in one area of life and doing what is required to make their journey success-ful. In other parts of their lives these people often view themselves as normal or average.

All people have the capacity to excel, or become the best they can be, at something. To turn your capacity into a living reality, you have to make the decision to focus fully on doing it. You have to choose to pour your heart and soul into it. It is that simple. And it is totally within your control. When you make the decision to do something with commitment and quality, all the rest is focus. How far your journey takes you depends on the depth and direction of your focus.

Falling short of your potential in sport, performance, school, work, relation-ships, health, or life is usually a result of not focusing fully on being where you are or not focusing on the positive things that will help you achieve your goals. Make sure that the focus you take into your learning and performance contexts is helping you, not hurting you. The best path is to focus on remaining positive through the ups and downs and to focus fully on what you are engaged in while you are doing it. This approach will raise the level and consistency of your performance and the quality of your life. Decide to focus on acting on your good intentions—every day. After you decide to excel in your performance domain, or excel at living, and choose to pursue your goals with full focus, a thousand other little decisions fall naturally into place every day.

Attaining the goal of personal excellence is a choice. Choose to do everything in your power to fulfill your goals and dreams, to improve your focus, to raise the level and consistency of your performance, to experience a greater sense of enjoyment and personal satisfaction in your pursuits, and to enhance the overall quality of your life. Decide to do it! A performance goal (or relationship goal) does not have to become the only thing in your life in order for you to attain it, but it must be the only thing in your life while you are engaged in the process of doing it, experiencing it, or performing within it.

Everyone begins at a different departure point with respect to personal assets. When you develop and stretch those assets, even for short periods, you become better and more fully alive—you touch the essence of personal excellence. By improving your focus, you greatly increase your chances of journeying in positive directions and reaching your potential in different parts of your life. You can choose to go down this path of joy and excellence or choose not to. It's your decision.

Focusing With Beckie Scott

Beckie Scott was the first North American ever to win an Olympic gold medal in cross-country skiing. I started working with Beckie in the year leading into the Salt Lake City Olympics. In her previous Olympic experience, her best result was 45th. At the 2002 Salt Lake City Winter Olympics, she won Olympic gold. In 2005–2006, her final race season, she started the season by winning back-to-back World Cup races, was on the podium in 10 World Cup races, and won a silver medal at the 2006 Torino Olympic Games.

When we began working together Beckie was already highly committed to her training and competitions. To take the mental step up so that she could stand on the podium (and reach the top of the podium), Beckie had to fine-tune her race focus, decide to give everything she had in each race, race smart, and race to win.

She became a consistent winner by going into each race with a specific race focus plan, deciding to execute her race plan, being diligent in evaluating her race focus (in writing) after every race, drawing out the lessons (what went well and what could have been better), and planning to act on those focus lessons in the next race. By continually implementing and improving her race focus plans, she developed confidence in her focus and abilities, especially when she was challenged in a race or experienced severe discomfort (or lots of pain), which is part of endurance events.

Another important skill that helped Beckie become a better and more consistent high-level performer, and a better human being, was our work on dealing with distractions. Many distractions can affect high-performance athletes (and other high-performance people) over the course of their careers—poor results, setbacks, injuries, sickness, teammates, workmates, coaches, bosses, doubts, time away from home and family, and, in her case, the new expectations and time demands that came with becoming an Olympic champion.

Of course, distractions that you can never plan for will also occur. During Beckie's preparation phase for the 2006 Olympic year, I was at a training camp in Chile with the Canadian alpine ski team when I received an e-mail from Beckie. Her husband and training partner, Justin, had just broken his neck in a bad mountain bike crash. Fortunately, Justin's spinal cord was not severed. He recovered fully and was with Beckie at the Torino Olympics.

Distractions, large and small, are part of life. No one is immune to them. So the better your skills are for coping with them, dealing with them, focusing through them, and learning from them, the better you and everyone around you is likely to be. In the interview that follows, Beckie shares key components of her personal journey to excellence in the demanding sport of cross-country skiing.

Terry: What did we do together that helped you most in terms of pursuing and achieving your goals?

Beckie: I think initially it was the very thorough and detailed process of planning, executing, and evaluating that lay the groundwork for me and became the base for getting the best out of myself mentally in training, racing, and, ultimately, life. It was a step-by-step, day-by-day process that was in motion year-round. The process was always dedicated to improvement, the highest quality, and getting to where I wanted to go. It began with really detailed worksheets and a lot of careful thought and later evolved to a process that would become second nature.

I asked myself almost every day, *What am I going to do today to get closer to my goals? How am I going to do it?* And at the end of the day I asked myself, *What went well, and what could I have done better?* In the final year of my career, which I consider my most successful, I almost didn't have to ask the questions anymore. I knew exactly what I needed to do to reach my goals, how I was going to do it, and where to turn for a little help and support when I needed it. I was confident that when it was all over I could look back and say that I did everything I possibly could to get the best out of myself.

Developing and implementing a detailed race plan was another one of the crucial elements of my success. In the year before the Salt Lake City 2002 Olympics, we had the opportunity to race World Cup races on the same courses that we would be racing at the Olympics. I learned a tremendous amount during those World Cups about how the courses raced, and I felt very confident that given the opportunity, I could capitalize on this education.

During the year leading up to the 2002 Olympic Games, I also spent a great deal of time at the venue either by myself or with the team. I had decided to make a special effort to train on those courses as much as I could. When the Olympics rolled around, I had developed not only a tremendous level of comfort and familiarity with the environment and surroundings but also a specific race plan for the pursuit race. I was confident that if I could handle the physical aspect of the race, I had the best strategy going.

On race day, the pursuit race was two 5K races separated by about an hour and a half. I had followed my first 5K classic race plan to the letter and was sitting in a perfect position for the second 5K. A few seconds separated a group of about six women. I knew every uphill, corner, downhill, and flat on that course, and when the time came to make a move, I did. I didn't know how the other racers would react, of course, but I was even prepared for a sprint to the finish if it should happen—knowing I would swing wide out of the final corner and take the outermost lane if it came down to it. At the end of the day, I won that 10K Olympic race (the two 5K races combined) by one-tenth of a second. I know that all the homework I did beforehand and executing my race plan and strategy with full focus and precision had everything to do with it.

Terry: After you won the Olympic gold medal, there were lots of people wanting your time. How did you try to respect your own needs even though you had lots of people tugging at you?

Beckie: In the months that followed the Salt Lake City Games, there was an extreme level of attention and demand that came my way. Even though I felt completely ill—equipped to manage it initially, I resolved to enjoy as much of it as I could. Whenever it started to become stressful or unenjoyable, I just stepped away until I felt I could manage it again. I also really made an effort to strengthen and maintain my close friendships and relationships in this time because I recognized that these were the people who really cared and would always be there—Olympic champion or not.

Terry: Part of our plan for ongoing learning was ongoing evaluation and acting on the lessons learned—to pull out positive things from every performance, to assess your focus, and to learn from every experience. Can you comment on how you did that during the years we worked together?

Beckie: For five years (since we began working together), I sat down after nearly every single race, even time trials, and wrote out an evaluation that basically described what went well, what didn't go well, and what I needed to do to be better next time. This was an absolutely critical process for me in ensuring that no experience, good or bad, was ever wasted and that I continued to grow both as an athlete and as a person from each time I stepped to the starting line—whether it was a roller-ski time trial by myself with only my husband timing or an Olympic medal–winning race. On many occasions, through taking the time to go back and sift through what had happened, I picked up things that hadn't been obvious before. Every race was a learning opportunity.

Terry: What does being focused mean to you? Can you describe what it is, what it feels like, or how it unfolds for you?

Beckie: I think the best way I can describe being totally focused is through a description of a feeling. There aren't really any emotions attached to it, or specific thought patterns. It's almost like wearing special glasses where everything inside you is crystal clear. Your thoughts, feelings, physical sensations, and everything outside you that doesn't matter, or won't get in your way, is irrelevant and fuzzy and blurry. You are entirely present, in the absolute moment, and able to react, respond, and perform as you need to, in the way that you need to. You're just "there," and it is a good feeling.

Terry: Can you describe a specific race day when you had one of your best performances—from a focus perspective?

Beckie: On race days, your focus has to be able to move around a little as you change gears from task to task, such as warming up, testing skis, racing, and coping with the discomfort of racing. When you are in a good, clear frame of mind and the focus is right on, you are able to shift from each of these points easily and capably. For example, for me, parts of the race preparation morning have to be really relaxed and totally focused on conserving energy and making the right decision about skis. Then, 45 minutes later, I'm completely focused on squeezing the very last ounce of effort out of myself while sustaining the absolute physical limit of pain threshold and keeping my technique smooth and efficient.

One of my best performances this last season was a 15K mass start race in which I led from start to finish over an extremely demanding course in very cold conditions. I had decided beforehand that I liked cold weather (I actually don't), that I wasn't tired (I was), and that I could win if I skied a perfect race. I went into that race morning with my focus being positive, calm, and relaxed, but also absolutely 100 percent determined that I would have a great race, and I proceeded with the prerace morning routine in that frame of mind. Everything flowed out from there, and even if there were some snags, or inconsistencies, or things that didn't go quite right, I coped and dealt with them easily.

When we started to race, my focus shifted into competition mode, and I just became completely "in" the race. With mass start races, you begin a race surrounded by upward of 60 women, and you have to be able not only to ski your own race but also to react and respond to the race that is going on around you. We began racing, and even though I was aware of the competition behind and beside me, I stayed completely focused on the task in front of me, which was to get around the course as fast as humanly possible. This kind of complete focus (on the task and leaving the awareness door open) allows for self-talk during moments of pushing through extreme pain, allows for boosts and adrenaline rushes from the cheering crowds, allows for split-second decisions, and allows for adjustments and refinements when information comes in from coaches around the course.

The feeling when I crossed the finish line first, after 45 minutes of enduring some of the hardest, most physically demanding racing I had ever done, was not only sheer joy in the accomplishment but also tremendous pride in the fact that I had won this race more on pure mental determination and staying completely focused on doing what needed to be done to win than anything else.

Terry: Can you comment on the role of refocusing to get back on a positive track when a doubt or worry enters your mind and give a couple of specific examples that you have used?

Beckie: I think the most stressful moments of doubt and worry for me came in the form of illness and injury. When your body is your livelihood and you need to train as hard and as prolonged as we do to race successfully, being downed by illness or an injury has the potential to be tremendously upsetting.

I recognized this and was usually able to refocus, keep things in perspective, and keep myself on track with a couple of tactics. For illness, I would just tell myself that this was my body's turn, my body's way of saying, "Enough, I need to rest now." Often I would turn those days of hanging out on the couch or in bed into something constructive—trying to plan how I was going to come back after this bout with the flu or a cold better than ever. I used all that down time to my advantage and would be telling myself not only that was I going to come out of this super rested and super motivated but also that my training was going to benefit from the time off and that this little break was exactly what my body and my mind needed to get better.

With injury it was a little different. The summer before the 2006 Olympics I suffered an injury to my shoulder, my rotator cuff, so that for a month I couldn't use my left arm. I not only had to stay positive and believe that I would heal but also had to fight hard to overcome feelings of despair and frustration with being in that position in the year of the Olympics.

Finally, I realized that I had to make a choice, and I decided again to let this work to my advantage. Because I couldn't use my arms, I started training exclusively with legs-only technique. I decided that I was going to perfect my skiing technique from the waist down. When it came time to use my arms again, I just flew, because I had been doing legs-only intervals and legs-only strength work in addition to the regular distance workouts. In the end, I think that because I decided that the injury was going to work to my advantage and I was going to come out of it better than before, I did.

Terry: How did you get yourself to race smart and give everything through the really tough times, like the last two races of your career following the 2006 Olympics when you were sick and feeling exhausted?

Beckie: In the last season of my career, I was fighting for the overall World Cup title with a great Norwegian champion. We were separated by only a few points. The overall title was basically going to be determined in the last two races, and these races were coming on the heels of a killer race and travel schedule following the Olympics.

On the morning of the second-to-last World Cup race, I woke up with a raging sore throat, aching body, and headache. I also had terrible jet lag and was very depressed by the surroundings. We were in one of the worst, most industrial, polluted places I had ever seen in my life. The air was brown, you couldn't see the horizon or drink the water, and it was just such a downer.

I knew, though, that this was one of my last two chances left to claim the overall title and that somehow I had to overcome the physical aspect to compete. I had to convince myself that I could do this and decided to tell myself I was just having a severe allergic reaction to the pollution (even though I've never had an allergic reaction to anything in my life). I decided it wouldn't affect my capacity or performance.

I also went back to something you had said before, which was "the body is dumb, meaning your body will follow your focus . . . You can convince it of anything," so I set about convincing myself that I felt great and was going to race just fine. I had to race smarter than anyone, I had to race great, and I had to draw on everything I had to at least secure my position as second overall and close the gap on first. I had to ignore completely what my body was feeling and telling me and make it do what I needed it to do.

So, we began racing the heats, and I just self-talked myself through the entire day, racing very tactically, aggressively, decisively, and, thankfully, fast enough to keep advancing. I had really bad chills between rounds and had to wear every item of clothing I had brought, but I just told myself it was the humidity and kept moving around and trying to stay warm. I ended up second that night, and it blew me away. I look back on that now and think that of all my racing experiences, that day, for me, defines mental toughness.

After that race, we traveled from China on to Japan, and I basically spent the next three days in bed trying to recuperate and gather any strength I could for the final push to the World Cup overall title. In spite of being sick, I was completely relaxed during this time, knowing at that stage that I had nothing to lose, that everyone was getting tired, that the pursuit was my best event, and that regardless of what happened in the upcoming race, I had already had an amazing season.

I went to the start of that race having only seen the course in my warm-up that morning. When we were all lined up and ready to begin the race, the commentator announced, "This is Beckie Scott's last race today," and everyone in the starting area clapped and cheered. It was such a great feeling to know that I would be leaving this sport successfully and with so many good friends that I decided right there at the start line that if I could almost win in China feeling like I had, I could definitely win here in Japan with three good days of rest behind me. I focused with every fiber of my being, and I raced as smart, determined, and tactically as well as I possibly could. I took the opportunity when it arose to win, and gave everything I had to win the race. And I did. I won the last race of my career.

Terry: That was a great win! Over the course of your racing career you had a high commitment to ski racing, but you also seemed to maintain a commitment in your relationships with your family. How did you try to balance that?

Beckie: I have a very close extended family. To spend so much time apart from them and then stay focused on training and recovery in the brief periods that I was able to spend with them was really hard. But I just viewed it as part of my commitment to be the best racer I could be, and ultimately I saw the little time that I did have with them as critical to my overall happiness, balance, and enjoyment of life. Being with my family put things in perspective more often than not and probably kept me sane.

I also had an extremely supportive partner in Justin because he had been a cross-country ski racer and knew exactly everything I was going through. In the final years of my career, he became more and more of a training partner. Even when he wasn't able to take part in the actual training sessions, he would still be there. I'd be roller-skiing home as it was getting dark, hear the car pull up beside me, and look over to see our grinning golden retriever, Henna, sitting in the passenger seat. No matter how irritated I was from fatigue or the loneliness of training, I was uplifted and had to smile, because there they were, my unique little team, always ready to guide me home.

Terry: What do you think was the most important lesson that you learned from me?

Beckie: If I work backward from the present, more specifically this past season, I think the most important lesson I learned was the powerful nature of the deciding process and how things can be changed or affected just by deciding to do something. Even though that seemed to be one of the final chapters we worked on, I realize now it was present from the beginning, whether that was deciding to make every single day of training the highest quality possible with careful planning and evaluating, or deciding that adrenaline and nervous energy were a good thing and would help me ski faster instead of impeding me, or deciding that I was confident and fully prepared (even if preparations hadn't necessarily been ideal), or deciding to turn negative and potentially adverse situations into positive ones that could be beneficial or learned from. I think that virtually everything I was able to accomplish can be traced back to beholding the responsibility of decision making and the power that you have in just deciding something for yourself.

Terry: I am really interested in how your confidence in your capacity and your confidence in your focus changed over the years that we worked together. I know that this year you really knew that you could win or be on the podium consistently. How would you describe the strengthening of your belief or confidence in yourself and your focus?

Beckie: I remember asking a teammate at one of my first World Cup races in Europe when she thought Elena Valbe (a famous Russian skier who dominated women's skiing for years) would retire. I was 20 years old and had placed about 58th in that race, so there should have been a few more women I was thinking of other than just Valbe. But even way back then, and really with no signs of any great talent or ability on my part, I was determined I wasn't going to stay 58th my entire career and that someday I'd be good enough to challenge for World Cup wins. I was just unsure if I would be able to beat Valbe.

I think that every time I experienced success, or some measure of it, my confidence improved a little. With each new experience and training and all the little things, I was slowly piecing together a way to ensure success every time I stepped to the line. This evolved to the point where I had enough to start believing it was possible to win.

The final year of my career, I really felt that I knew exactly what I had to do to win or be on the podium consistently in all domains. Training, recovery, nutrition, psychology, everything—there wasn't one element from my overall approach to ski racing that I had overlooked or felt was lacking. Just having done this and trained and prepared for the season in this manner gave me a lot of confidence. I knew that when I went to the start line I was going in prepared as well as, if not better than, anyone there.

Terry: Any last comments, Beckie?

Beckie: I have to tell you that it is really a full-circle experience for me to think about being featured in your book. I remember getting my first copy of In Pursuit of Excellence when I was 18 years old from my coach Les Parsons in Vermilion, after having missed an entire season because of mononucleosis. He thought that reading your book would be a great way to start another training season, and from that point on, I basically carried the book with me everywhere. Later on, the year before the Salt Lake City Olympics, I received a revised copy, which is where I found your Web site in the back pages. I contacted you, and the rest is history! I could never have imagined at age 18 when reading your book that I would someday come to be one of the featured athletes in it. What an incredible journey it has been.

CHAPTER 4

Journey to Excellence

I reached one of my performance highs in sport when I mastered a quadruple twisting back somersault. I still remember how good that felt. At that time, there were only a couple of people in the world who had accomplished that feat in training, and I was executing it with precision in competitions. Some people might say, "So what? Who cares if you can spin your body in the air four times before landing? What difference does it make?"

We want not only to live but to have something to live for. For some of us, this means pursuing our potential through a sport or another challenging performance pursuit.

It might not have made a difference to anyone else, but it made a difference to me, and it taught me some important lessons about how to achieve other important goals in my life. It felt great to accomplish something that required a commitment and full focus to extend my personal limits. Perhaps even more important, although I didn't realize it at that time, was that my experiences as an athlete and performer taught me a great deal about the focus required to excel in other areas of my life.

The Quest

The quest to become your personal best—to excel, to attain the highest standards of performance, to be a leader in your chosen field—is a worthy human pursuit that can lead to ongoing personal growth, a higher level of contribution to others, and a more meaningful life. If none of us were concerned with the quality of our contributions, performance, work, creations, products, services, relationships, or interactions, our society would take a marked turn for the worse.

Yet achieving high levels of performance in any field does not come easily. We must overcome numerous obstacles and push aside many barriers along the way. Becoming a highly skilled person who contributes something of value in any field—sport, the arts, medicine, science, business, politics, technology, the trades, the service professions, writing, teaching, coaching, or parenting—is made possible by having a high level of commitment, envisioning positive possibilities, establishing an absorbing focus, and nurturing belief in your potential.

The greatest barriers in our pursuit of excellence are psychological barriers that we impose on ourselves, often without even realizing it. My failure even to attempt a quintuple twisting somersault is a good example. I never even entertained the possibility that it was possible. Perhaps it was like the four-minute mile. At one time breaking that barrier was viewed as impossible, until one man overcame it—and then almost immediately a host of others did the same. The physical or technical makeup of runners didn't change; what changed was their belief in what was possible. As our beliefs about limits change, limits themselves change.

While traveling through southeast Asia, I had the opportunity to see barefoot men walking across hot coals. Those glowing embers generated incredible heat, yet the walkers emerged unblistered and unscarred. Is this unbelievable feat

©Tami Chapell/Reuters/Corbis

► Players like Sydney Crosby inspire us to change our ideas about the limits of what's possible.

within the capacity of normal human beings? How many of us even believe that walking across extremely hot coals is possible? How many of us will ever call on this kind of capacity in pursuing goals that are important to us? Therein lie our limits. The firewalkers, and the world's best performers, are made of the same flesh and blood as you and I are, but their focus is different. Therein lies their strength. When you are successful at removing the barriers of "im" from impossible and focus on the possibilities, almost anything is possible. Focus and belief give birth to new realities in all human pursuits.

Have you ever done something that you initially thought was impossible to do? Have you ever thought, *I am never going to be able to do this*, *I am not going to be successful with this*, *There is no way this is going to work*, or *There is no way we can win this one*—and yet you were successful? You or your team accomplished a goal that initially seemed impossible to reach. Most of us have had experiences when we thought, at least momentarily, that we couldn't do something and then managed to do it. If you can recall a personal experience when this happened to you, think about how you (or your team) managed to reach your goal. What did you focus on to make it happen? There are some great focusing lessons in these experiences about how you and others can turn negatives into positives, impossible into possible.

Every year in team sports, even at the highest levels, teams who are not supposed to win beat teams who are highly favored to win. How do they do this? They win because their collective focus is centered on the right things. Everyone comes to play, everyone gives everything they have, and everyone is focused fully on achieving their mission, step by step, shift by shift, moment to moment, from start to finish. The players are so focused on doing what they believe is possible that they don't let any thoughts of impossible get in the way of achieving their mission.

The Pursuit

Many years have passed since I last competed in sport, yet I continue to have an abundance of joyful experiences engaged in physical activities, mostly in the outdoors, through trail running, kayaking, canoeing, cross-country skiing, alpine skiing, and biking. I never formally trained or competed in any of these activities, yet they offer ongoing challenge and joy. I love to run along an empty beach at sunrise or sunset with the surf rolling in, or wind my way along narrow trails in the woods or mountains, or paddle my kayak on a perfectly calm lake or into a strong headwind. These are often the highlights of my day, probably because they make me feel fully alive. They free me from everything else in my life and absorb me completely—physically, mentally, and emotionally.

One clear, crisp winter night, under a full moon, I set out with some neighbors to ski up a mountain trail to a small log chalet nestled among the trees. On this majestic evening, the snow sparkled like dancing crystals under the moonlight. At the chalet we made a fire, had a sip of wine and a bit of stew, and joked a little; then we headed back down the mountain. As I skied down, I became one with the mountain, not knowing where it ended and where I started. I embraced it and felt it as a part of me as I flowed along that narrow snow-packed trail. I moved into and out of shadows as the moonlight darted through the trees. I was totally absorbed in the experience. It was novel, challenging, sensual, fun, exciting, physically demanding, a meaningful encounter with nature—a highlight experience, the kind that makes it great to be alive. In few other contexts do we have such close contact with other people, and ourselves, as we do in nature and sport.

Sport, physical activity, nature, and other engaging pursuits provide abundant opportunities to free ourselves for short periods to enjoy special moments not readily available elsewhere in our lives. We can live out our quest for excitement, connection, joy, personal control, or risk by deliberately accepting challenges that we then pursue with passion. Experiences like this make us feel more fully alive and more capable of directing at least part of our own destiny. Great satisfaction comes from embracing the experience, becoming competent, and feeling connected and in control. The continual process of seeking out and meeting challenges that are meaningful to us and within our stretched capacity ensures that we continue to learn and grow.

As a white-water canoeist I discovered that the challenge of running a river is not a conflict between human and nature, but rather a melding of the two. You do not conquer a river—you experience it, you work together to find the right path. The calculated risk, the momentary sense of meaning, and the intensity of the experience let you emerge feeling exhilarated and somehow better. This experience is a quest for connection and self-fulfillment rather than a quest for victory over others or over the river. Embracing each experience becomes the goal, and each experience may lead to personal growth, improved performance, self-discovery, or greater awareness, or the experience may simply be interesting, joyful, or meaningful in its own right.

Finding a sense of meaning or purpose in what you are going through, doing, or pursuing can make the difference between excellence and mediocrity, between life and death. Although meaning for each of us is unique and changes over our lifetime, it flows most readily when we are fully connected to something or striving toward some goal that we find worthy or think is worthy of us. We can experience joy and meaning by committing ourselves to certain goals, ideals, or values; by embracing simple joys; by experiencing someone or something of value to us; by being creative; by honoring others or choosing to do something for others; or by doing something with others or by ourselves that we deem worthwhile. Sport and other meaningful high-performance pursuits are wonderful mediums for providing a sense of purpose and continuous challenge, as well as a range of intensity and emotion that is difficult to experience elsewhere. These pursuits can be rich and rewarding if we approach them on our own terms, with a sense of perspective. They offer numerous opportunities for personal growth and for stretching the limits of human potential—physically, mentally, and emotionally.

Personal excellence is a contest with yourself to bring out the positives and the potential that lives within you. Excellence is a pursuit in which you must cooperate with yourself, drawing on the natural reserves within your mind and body to develop and stretch your capabilities to the fullest. Each of us begins this journey at a different point—mentally, physically, emotionally—and with respect to the support that we are given. Look for the opportunities within each situation that you enter. Develop your strengths. Make the most of what you have, whatever that may be. The true joy and challenge lies in pursuing ongoing personal growth, loving the pursuit, and living the various textures of your life.

Kerrin Lee Gartner's Journey

I began working with Kerrin Lee Gartner when she was a 16-year-old on the Canadian women's alpine ski team, and I continued to work with her throughout her racing career. After eight years on the national team, Kerrin won the gold medal at the 1992 Winter Olympics in Mirabel, France, in women's downhill on what at that time was considered to be the fastest, most difficult women's race course ever. I conducted the following interview with Kerrin shortly after her Olympic victory. Our discussion focused on her path to personal excellence. I did a short follow-up interview with her in 2006. Her experiences show how you can act on the wheel of excellence in the real world of high-level performance in sport and life after sport. Perhaps her experiences can serve as an inspiration or guide in your continued pursuit of personal excellence.

Commitment

Terry: You have achieved the highest goal in downhill skiing, and you were able to do it in a very stressful situation. How would you describe your commitment to go after that goal?

Kerrin: The commitment is more than 100 percent. It's committed through the ups and downs. Committed through the good results and the bad results. Committed when you're coming in 50th, and it looks like there's never an end to the bad results. You still have to be committed and still focused and still trying to win every race. I think the day that you let your commitment go is the day you don't have a chance to win.

Terry: How long did it take you to get ready for this one little run (the 1992 Olympic downhill)?

Kerrin: A lot of people assume it's an overnight success story. It's taken me nine years of hard work in international competition and many years before that. I think that all of your work with me during this time shows how long it has taken me.

Terry: Over the last eight or nine years you've had lots of setbacks, lots of challenges to overcome, lots of injuries, and maybe some people not believing in you as much as you believed in yourself. How did you get yourself to keep going after your goals through some of those struggles?

Kerrin: The obvious struggles were my knee injuries, and each one took six months to about a year and a half to really recover from. It wasn't just the physical recovery. The mental recovery was the hardest part. There are always waves in life, and when you're down in ski racing, with a physical disability like my knees were, it was always important to keep my goals set, to always believe in myself, and to look at the reasons why I was going through these struggles, to look at the end result really. I made little tiny goals for myself—little tiny steps, focused on little things. I stayed focused through every single bad thing, stayed focused, stayed focused, stayed focused. I think that's the only way through it, to go gradually and continue believing in yourself the whole way. That's the key to everything when you're down.

Focus

Terry: When you talk about being focused in training, focused in races, can you describe what that is?

Kerrin: My very best focus is when everything happens naturally. I don't even think about it. A lot of people want to know exactly what I am thinking in certain parts of the course, or what I'm thinking in the start gate, or when I go through the finish. It's almost a feeling. The focus is so clear that you shut your thoughts off and you trust yourself and believe in yourself. You've already prepared for years. All you do is go; it's very natural. The focus is so crisp. You're so connected. That happened to me at the Olympics. There are so many words to describe it—there's autopilot, connection, tunnel vision, or just being 100 percent focused. It's all more of a feeling. It turns from thoughts into feelings and natural motions on skis. You don't really have any distinct thoughts when you're going down. You don't see the people on the side of the hill. You don't see anything. You're just naturally doing what you do.

Mental Readiness

Terry: When you talk about mental readiness, what does that mean to you?

Kerrin: It means years of mental preparation. My first meeting with you was when I was 16 years old. I remember it clearly. I was not very good at imagining myself skiing. I didn't understand why I even had to do it. Now it's come to a point where it's a part of my everyday life. If I'm hanging a picture in the living room, first I imagine where I want it. Then I imagine how high I want it, and how far away from the wall. I can see it all clearly. Then I hang the picture, and it's in the right spot. That's a simple example of what I can do when I ski, but when I ski I'm doing something dangerous. I'm doing something that I want to do very well. It's not worth making a mistake, so I have to use my imagination and my imagery constantly throughout the whole year.

Terry: How did you approach your training runs for the Olympic downhill?

Kerrin: I just tried to stay very relaxed, work on certain parts of the course all week long, and keep my goals small. I worked on a 30-second section instead of the whole thing. That way I kept the pressure off myself as well. I didn't feel the need to win every single training run. I just felt the need to ski certain parts of the course well, and I think that was the key to a lot of it. It allowed me to stay relaxed. It kept the press away a little bit. The press didn't think I was a key person, even though I thought I was.

Terry: You skied each section well, but you picked different sections to go after on different training runs.

Kerrin: Yes. We only got to ski the top 30 seconds of the course twice, and that was where I had trouble at the beginning of the week. The last training run, I concentrated solely on the first 30 or 40 seconds, and then relaxed and basically just skied the rest. I still had a very good run, so I knew I was ready to do well.

Terry: What were your reminders going into the race?

Kerrin: Actually, I kept it pretty simple. I just had the reminder to just go for it, take the advantage, and I knew I had the chance to make it my day. I was very relaxed, which was obviously a key to it all.

Positive Images

Terry: Did you do much imagery in preparing for your Olympic race?

Kerrin: I've been doing imagery of the Olympics for about four years, but I started this course last February and have run it hundreds of times in my mind. So by the time I actually had the race-day run, I had done it many times before. I just hadn't won it in reality yet!

Terry: What do you experience in your imagery of the race run?

Kerrin: I think a lot of people assume that imagery is pictures in your mind, and actually when I was 16, when we first started working together, it was very much like watching a videotape. I could watch anybody with my eyes closed and picture anybody skiing in a certain part of the course. It's advanced itself to the special state where now it's more of a feeling. I can feel the feelings of skiing, and feel the motions. My thoughts almost turn into feeling. I think that is important for athletes to do that in any sport.

Terry: What about imagery for getting through your injuries and back on track? Did you do anything there?

Kerrin: The first injury I had, I remember talking to you, and you said, "Remember to ski in your mind." I thought, *The last thing I want to do now is ski, because I'm injured.* But I remember it didn't take me very long to get back on my skis in my mind. I skied [in my mind] basically every single day through my injury and through the recovery. It helped me keep my focus on what I was going through it for, and it made the pain and struggle a lot easier to take because I was still doing something enjoyable in my head. Even if I was on crutches, in a cast, it made it a lot easier.

Terry: How did your first run go after those injuries?

Kerrin: I think by keeping my imagery there, it made it much simpler to get out on the downhill skis. In a real course, it made the speed adjustment much quicker. With the second injury, it just happened naturally. I had already succeeded in being able to imagine myself skiing perfectly, and I did it throughout the six months of recuperation. When I put my skis on, it was like I wasn't even off them.

Confidence

Terry: I am interested in how your confidence in your capacity has changed over the years. I know this year you really knew you could do it. How would you describe the strengthening of your belief?

Kerrin: Actually, it's amazing because people naturally assume you always believe in yourself from day 1. When your results aren't there, the first thing that shatters is your belief and confidence. That's a key to success, and over the years I've developed belief in myself. I knew I could be on the podium, and I knew I would be a winner, but as much as I know and as much as I can believe, until it happens, 100 percent belief isn't there. I really talked myself into it this year. I knew I was skiing as well as anybody on the World Cup circuit. I've had top five results consistently in the last two years, and I really, really believed, with 110 percent of myself, that if there was a course that I had a chance to win on, it was the Olympic course. Just by believing in myself, and always talking to myself positively, and putting positive thoughts in my mind, it only encouraged the belief I already had.

Terry: So how would you talk to yourself positively?

Kerrin: I would turn anything negative into a positive. If I had a bad run, I would take a positive out of it anyway. If I had a run where I was only good on half of it, I would take a positive and build on it. That made me believe in myself more each time I ran the course. Each time I did anything, I could build positive emotions on it. On race day at the Olympics, it was very flat light, very foggy, which is not pleasant in downhill. The first positive thing I did was say to myself, *You're good in flat light; you're one of the best skiers in flat light. This is your opportunity right now; go for it!* I really am one of the better skiers in flat light. Although I don't like it any more than anyone else, I can still be aggressive and I can still ski like I want to ski.

Distraction Control

Terry: The Olympic Games are a huge distraction for most athletes. How were you able to come through with a great run under the most distracting circumstances?

Kerrin: I've taken lessons from a lot of different races. One of the races I took a valuable lesson from was the 1988 Olympics. I was very distracted in 1988. I wanted to win badly. In preparing for 1992, what I did was take everything I learned, which included putting myself first, putting what I need first, and concentrating on what I needed to concentrate on in everyday races. I was relaxed. I knew what my job was. All I had to do was go out and do it. Once I was on the chair lift in the morning, everything was fine. I took an hour or two to deal with all the distractions in a one-block period. I left the rest of the time to myself. I think it's important to make sure that you're relaxed and ready to go. If you get too distracted, then you can't focus anyway, and you don't have a chance to win.

Terry: So you dealt with some of the people and media things and then had a time that you just clicked off to get away from it all?

Kerrin: Yes. Once I left the hill and the race site, which is where most of the stress and distractions are, I was on my own. It was like my normal everyday life—playing card games, reading books, and just staying relaxed. I remember in Calgary, all I did was think about the race all day long. In Mirabel I couldn't have been more relaxed.

Terry: What about on-site? What perspective allowed you to focus on your performance instead of the outcome?

Kerrin: I had a good teacher, Terry! I think I've learned, definitely, not to focus on the outcome of any event. Although you dream about it, and I dreamed about the gold medal for many years, I think the best thing for me is that I've learned to concentrate on what I need to concentrate on. I needed to concentrate on having a good warm-up in the morning, concentrate on being very smooth, very quick, looking for speed in the course. It carried right through to my race. I went to the start, and I wasn't concentrating on the final result; I was concentrating on what I needed to do to ski my best. It just became natural for me. I went through the same motions as I go through every race. It just happened naturally.

Terry: Were there any points where you had to refocus to get back on track within the race?

Kerrin: There was one, actually. It didn't show up too well on TV, but there was one spot where I caught my ski and it went out from underneath me. It really caught me off balance, and I remember my mind slipping away a bit there. It didn't take long to get it back. I just said, *Come on*, to myself. I got it right back together, and the bottom half of the course was exceptionally good.

Terry: A lot of athletes who win gold medals really struggle in their next races because of the expectations placed on them and the expectations they place on themselves. You had great races in your subsequent World Cups. How was your focus in those races?

Kerrin: Actually, I was tired going into the first World Cup race after my Olympic win. I wasn't expecting much of myself. I went out in the morning, and my warm-up didn't go as planned. I didn't ski as well as I had hoped. I had been thinking a lot about the outcome. I realized it right away, and I changed my thought pattern by admitting it and by getting the focus into my mind that I really needed to focus on. I changed into the mode that works for me. I thought of going for it, being aggressive, and of all my key thoughts. When I was standing in the start gate I knew that I had an opportunity to win the race. I pushed out of the gate and went into my automatic pilot without thinking about anything other than my key thoughts. I just kept my focus. I was second by three one-hundredths, and that's pretty close to winning. I was happy with that result after everything that had happened.

Terry: If a negative thought slips into your mind, what do you find is best for getting back on track?

Kerrin: When I notice myself thinking thoughts that I don't want to be thinking and don't work for me, or when I start thinking about the outcome or final result, I try to notice it first, and rectify it by thinking of things that work for me.

Terry: Has it taken a while to be able to get your thoughts working for you like that?

Kerrin: It's taken a long time. I remember races in the past where I wouldn't even realize why I had blown it in that race until a year later. Last year at a downhill in Lake Louise I had been doing very well, winning training runs. On race day, I came in fifth, and I realized after the race that my approach was wrong. I was thinking the wrong things. Now I've started to realize when I'm thinking the wrong things before I even race. This gives me a chance to have a good race before racing.

Terry: So you change your thinking, or your focus, before the race begins, to have a better chance at performing well?

Kerrin: Exactly. If I wake up and I realize my head is there, in the right place, I let my thought patterns work naturally and I have a good race. If it's not there or something distracts me in the start or warm-up in the morning, then I know my refocusing thoughts. I know what brings me back to my good results and good focus.

Ongoing Learning

Terry: Part of your ongoing evaluation plan is to pull out positive things from every performance to enhance your confidence or feel good, as well as to learn from the experience. Can you comment on that?

Kerrin: It's taken me many years to pull something out of each run. If I'm last in a race I've learned to still pull something out of it. Most times I give 110 percent effort, and that's enough for me. If you try as hard as you can try and you give the effort you can give, you have to be satisfied with the result because you really couldn't have done more anyway. The lessons that I pulled out of the Olympics and applied to other World Cups afterward were to stay relaxed and to concentrate on what I know works.

There are certain key thoughts that work for me on race day, and most of it is just relaxing and going for it, counting on my natural instincts to take over. When that happens, I have my best races.

Terry: I've noticed over the past couple of years that you are more willing to follow your own path, to do things that you know help you, even when some people may not agree. How has that unfolded?

Kerrin: I'm in an individual sport that is run in a team manner, so sometimes it's hard to do things like an individual and to follow my own path. I've come to realize that I must trust myself 100 percent and believe in myself. When I need something a little bit different from what the rest of the girls need, I am willing to take a risk and go for that to get the win.

Terry: So now that you know what you need to perform your best, you are able to respect those patterns and gain from them.

Kerrin: Exactly. You learn about yourself throughout your career. I've been out there for eight years, and I've learned a lot. I've taken lessons from many different things. Now I can apply those lessons. At the Olympics, I knew I had to be away from the team and had to be on my own and away from the distractions of the village. I did that, and it paid off.

Terry: Now that you have won the gold medal, lots of people are wanting your time. How are you planning to respect your needs even though you have people tugging at you?

Kerrin: At first it was difficult because it was hard for me to say no. I wasn't used to being an Olympic champion or having that much attention. I've realized I really have to listen to my insides. I have to listen to what I feel, and when I'm run down and tired, I have to say no. I have to say, "I'm sorry, I can't do it tonight, or next week, or the week after; I need a couple of weeks off." I've realized it's OK to say no and to look after myself first, because my career is not finished. I know I can still win out there.

Terry: It's better to listen to yourself and to your body and do something positive about it before you are totally exhausted, rather than after.

Kerrin: Exactly. I think you have to learn to do that as an athlete. You really have to learn to respect your body. Often you realize a week before it happens that you are getting close to being too tired, and you have to take a week off. It's important to be able to listen to yourself and follow your feelings as well. If I think I need time off, I take it off instead of listening to other people. Because if I don't believe I'm on the right program, then I won't win a race. I really have to believe in what I'm doing 100 percent. The program has to be right for me.

Terry: You had a high commitment to ski racing, but you also seemed to maintain a commitment in your relationships with your family. How did you try to balance that?

Kerrin: I am from a large family of five children, and we were very close throughout my childhood. I think with the support that they gave me, it was natural for me to put them number one. Although my career was ski racing, and that was important to me, I think it's also important to keep my private life alive and separate. A lot of people were worried that when I got married my focus would be gone and I wouldn't be able to concentrate on winning a race. Surprisingly, it's done wonders for my skiing. It's made me relax, try hard, but know that it's not the end of the world if I don't win the race.

Terry: What are the most important lessons that you learned from me?

Kerrin: Hmm! The most important lesson is probably always to learn something from everything that happens and apply it to the next event. To stay relaxed. I've taken a lot of lessons from every race I've had. I've learned a lot about myself, and now I can be a lot more relaxed. My imagery is as clear as I could ever want it. I know exactly how to focus, and I just know how to apply everything that I know how to do. I know how to apply it on race day.

Terry: What advice might you have for other people who are in pursuit of excellence?

Kerrin: From everything I've learned through ski racing, the first and foremost thing is you have to believe in yourself and what you've chosen to do. No matter what profession you're in, I think if you try 100 percent to be as good as you can be, it doesn't matter how good you are as long as you believe within yourself that you've tried as hard as you can.

Terry: Are you applying the mental skills that you've been developing through your skiing to other areas of your life?

Kerrin: The mental skills I learned through ski racing come into play every single day, all the time. Learning to deal with distractions comes into play now with the press, or if you have an argument or a setback, it's learning to get through that. I have to deal with that and still get on with my life . . . staying relaxed, taking the good points out, always taking something positive and still feeling good about yourself and about the situation. I think everything that I do in sport relates to real life. It relates to everybody's career. It really relates to everything. I think that's the key to it all. Once you're relaxed and confident upstairs in your mind, then everything else will follow. Being completely focused is the only way you can achieve your goal.

A Look Back at the Journey

I conducted this short follow-up interview with Kerrin in the latter part of 2006, almost 15 years after our initial interview. At the time of this interview Kerrin was married and had two lovely daughters, ages 10 and 11. She had been working as a TV commentator for alpine skiing for the previous three Winter Olympic Games and many World Cup seasons. She had also been active in raising money for children in orphanages as well as other meaningful projects. I included her responses here to illustrate how you can continue to act on the wheel of excellence in your life after sport.

Terry:	What did you learn from ski racing and the work we did together on strengthening your focusing skills that you are still using in your work and daily life? What are the sustainable mental skills or perspectives that you learned in sport that you are carrying with you now?

Kerrin:	All my mental training for ski racing has helped me in all avenues of my life. I think the reason that the transfer of skills was so easy and works so well is that you need many of those same skills to be successful in anything.

Since retiring from ski racing, I have worked at three Winter Olympics for CBC as an analyst for alpine skiing. We call the races live, as they happen. Every now and then, I will make the mistake of mixing up my stats or saying something completely different than what I intended to say. Once this verbal mistake pops out on live television I don't really have time to dwell on it. So I just focus on the next step that is within my control. This is a simple example of how my training at focusing and refocusing has come in handy many times on occasions as simple as this. As a former Olympic champion, I have also been asked to speak at all kinds of functions. The simple message woven through each presentation remains the same:

➤	Decide what it is you want to do. Dream!

➤	Make the plan, do some goal setting, and adjust the goals as needed along the way.

➤	Prepare, work hard, analyze, learn, and work some more.

> ➤ Believe in your dream, your goals, your plan, and your preparation. Believe in yourself.

> ➤ Be determined, be focused, and be persistent.

> ➤ And always remember to try to enjoy the challenges and have fun!

Terry: Nice reminders! What has been the most important mental skill or perspective that you learned in your sport that you have carried into your life after high-performance sport?

Kerrin: The toughest lesson for me to start believing in as a racer happens to be the one thing that has changed me most as a person. As a racer, it was difficult for me ever to believe that I was good enough. I always saw my mistakes, dwelled on them, and compared myself to others, which only made me doubt myself and my abilities. The end result was often one of me trying too hard in all the wrong ways and ultimately not being at my best. As an athlete, it took a couple of years for me to believe in the benefit of learning from my mistakes and acting on them. It took a while to really understand that more can be learned from an oops that you act on than from a random success.

The process of trying, analyzing, learning, and trying again—with the benefit of that lesson—became one that I continue to use today in work, play, and parenting. This process creates belief, confidence, and ongoing improvement in whatever I am attempting.

Are there times when I still have doubts? Of course, but I have come to believe, as I did in skiing, that my best is good enough. And yes, some days my best just isn't quite what it was the day before. That is fine, too, because I will learn a lesson from it.

PART II

Preparing the Mind for Excellence

CHAPTER 5

Self-Examination

The pursuit of excellence begins to flourish when you take the time to get to know and understand your focusing patterns. This process is simply one of becoming more aware of your focusing capabilities, strengths, and areas that need improvement. You must also become more aware of what you really want to do with your performance and your life, as opposed to what others want of you. With this awareness, you can establish priorities and thereby pursue the things that are really important to you and avoid the things that are not.

Change and growth take place when a person has risked himself and dares to become involved with experimenting with his own life.

Herbert Otto

You know yourself better than anyone else in this world knows you. You just have to begin tuning in to how you usually think, feel, and focus when you perform your best and when you perform less than your best; how you interact and react in different contexts when you are at your best and when you are less than your best; and how you cope with different kinds of challenges and demands when you are at your best.

Performance settings provide wonderful opportunities for knowing yourself better. You can listen to your body and feelings. You can talk to your body and adjust your focus so that your mind and body do what you want them to do. You can discover what focus works best for you, what focus works against you, and what focus empowers you to turn things around from negative to positive. You can nurture your best focus and make it more consistent to meet ongoing and exciting new challenges. Take time to know yourself. Discover your best focus. Knowing what it is will serve you well, now and in the future.

Getting to know your focusing patterns also involves becoming aware of the direction of your focusing errors. Do you usually err by overreacting or by underreacting, by giving too little or by giving too much? Do you decide too early or too late? Are you too emotional or not emotional enough, too relaxed or not relaxed enough, too intense or not intense enough? Do you think too much or too little? Do you free your body and mind to perform? What focus patterns are related to your best performances and your performance flaws?

Finding out what your patterns are is a critical first step that can lead you to consistent improvement and consistent high-level performance.

Focus Control and Commitment

Even the best performers can continue to improve their focus so that it is consistently where they want it to be. How can you improve the quality and consistency of your focus? Begin by reflecting closely on where your focus is in your best and less-than-best performances and learning experiences. Then identify any focusing strategies or reminders in this book that will help you to improve your practice and performance focus. Develop a focus plan to improve the quality and consistency of your focus. Practice focusing fully every day, at every opportunity, both inside and outside your performance domain.

Besides improving your focus control, you should work to improve your focus commitment. What can you do to improve your commitment? Take an honest look at your level of commitment to act on things that will take you where you want to go. Given your current performance level, is your commitment strong enough to take you to your goals? If not, you can choose to raise your level of commitment to bring it in line with your goals. The other option is to adjust or lower your performance goals so that they are more realistic in terms of your current level of commitment. If your commitment and goals are not aligned, you may experience continued frustration.

The self-assessment scales in figures 5.1 and 5.2 are based on qualities that leading performers and coaches around the world use to describe the kind of commitment and focus required to become a great performer in a variety of performance domains. A rating of 10 means that the statement is completely true for you, a rating of 1 means that it is completely false for you, and a rating of 5 means that it is midway between being true and false for you.

Performers who excel at the highest levels rate themselves higher on both commitment and focus control than less-accomplished performers do. Top performers tend to have total scores in the 100s on both the commitment scale and the focus control scale, or average scores of 9 or above for most individual items on both scales. The better your focus and higher your commitment, the more likely you are to achieve your highest level of excellence.

Mission to Excellence Process

When I coach people on how to enhance their performance in any field, I usually begin by asking a series of performance-related questions to which they respond. Together we discuss options for self-growth, some of which they implement. With some basic guidelines to follow, most students, athletes, and performers who really want to improve are fully capable of asking themselves these same questions and can successfully implement their own performance-enhancement strategies.

Figure 5.1 Focus Control Rating Scale

Rate yourself on each item. Then go back and identify your strengths and the areas that might require improvement if excellence or being your absolute best is to become a realistic goal.

1. I am so focused during my performances (or in my work, school, or personal interactions) that everything else disappears. I get so absorbed in what I am doing or pursuing that nothing else in the world exists for me during that time.

   never   2   3   4   5   6   7   8   9   10   always

2. I focus on keeping my performance focus totally in the present, in the here and now (for example, one shot, one step, one move, one moment at a time).

   never   2   3   4   5   6   7   8   9   10   always

3. I refocus quickly, back into my completely absorbing, best focus, even if I become momentarily distracted or nervous or make a mistake in performance situations.

   never   2   3   4   5   6   7   8   9   10   always

4. I maintain a high-quality, fully connected focus in practice or preparation sessions.

   never   2   3   4   5   6   7   8   9   10   always

5. I quickly regain a high-quality, fully connected focus when distracted in practice or preparation sessions.

   never   2   3   4   5   6   7   8   9   10   always

6. Before I perform, I focus on things that make me feel confident and ready.

   never   2   3   4   5   6   7   8   9   10   always

7. Before I perform, I decide to bring my best focus into this performance.

   never   2   3   4   5   6   7   8   9   10   always

8. I have a strong inner confidence that I can do anything I set my mind to do, if I focus fully on doing it.

   never   2   3   4   5   6   7   8   9   10   always

9. I focus through errors, bad calls, or situations that go against me within a performance; I focus right back on the step in front of me.

   never   2   3   4   5   6   7   8   9   10   always

10. I stay motivated and completely focused even when behind, when facing obstacles or setbacks, or when down in points.

    never   2   3   4   5   6   7   8   9   10   always

11. I focus on learning from setbacks, criticism, or errors and turn them into positive opportunities to improve.

    never   2   3   4   5   6   7   8   9   10   always

12. After a performance I focus on what I did well and how I can be better in my next performance, and I act on those lessons.

    never   2   3   4   5   6   7   8   9   10   always

From T. Orlick, 2008, *In Pursuit of Excellence, Fourth Edition* (Champaign, IL: Human Kinetics).

Figure 5.2   Commitment Rating Scale

Rate yourself on each item. Then go back and identify your strengths, as well as those areas that may require reassessment or realignment if excellence is to become a realistic goal.

1. I am willing to put aside other things to excel in my sport or other chosen pursuit.

   never   1   2   3   4   5   6   7   8   9   10   always

2. I really want to become an excellent performer in my sport or other chosen pursuit.

   never   1   2   3   4   5   6   7   8   9   10   always

3. I prepare myself mentally for each practice or learning opportunity so that I can continue to improve and get the best out of myself.

   never   1   2   3   4   5   6   7   8   9   10   always

4. I prepare myself mentally for each performance so that I can continue to improve and get the best out of myself.

   never   1   2   3   4   5   6   7   8   9   10   always

5. I am determined never to let up or give up (for example, I remain committed to achieving my goals, making the move, or completing the mission), even in the face of difficult challenges or obstacles.

   never   1   2   3   4   5   6   7   8   9   10   always

6. I take personal responsibility for my mistakes and work hard to correct them.

   never   1   2   3   4   5   6   7   8   9   10   always

7. I give 100 percent focus and effort in practices or preparation sessions, whether it's going well or not.

   never   1   2   3   4   5   6   7   8   9   10   always

8. I give 100 percent focus and effort in performances or competitions, whether it's going well or not.

   never   1   2   3   4   5   6   7   8   9   10   always

9. I give everything I can, even when the challenge seems insurmountable or beyond reach.

   never   1   2   3   4   5   6   7   8   9   10   always

10. I feel more committed to improvement in my performance domain (or other chosen pursuit) than to anything else.

    never   1   2   3   4   5   6   7   8   9   10   always

11. I am totally committed to making my focus as good as it can possibly be.

    never   1   2   3   4   5   6   7   8   9   10   always

12. I find great joy and personal satisfaction in my performance domain (or other chosen pursuit).

    never   1   2   3   4   5   6   7   8   9   10   always

From T. Orlick, 2008, *In Pursuit of Excellence, Fourth Edition* (Champaign, IL: Human Kinetics).

The following six-step process is designed to help you explore and act in positive ways to achieve your personal goals:

1. Select a target area for improvement within your sport, performance domain, or life. Select a situation in which you would like to have greater personal control. Choose an essential mental skill from the wheel of excellence that you would like to strengthen. Your specific target may be anything that can increase the level or consistency of your performance or bring you closer to reaching your potential or living your dreams. Make sure that you choose a meaningful target area on which to set your sights for positive change.

2. Complete the mission to excellence self-assessment (page 67), keeping your target area in mind. This self-assessment will help you pinpoint the circumstances within your situation or chosen target area that are related to your best performances or greatest control and your less-than-best performances or least control. Reflect closely on what may have already worked well for you or what focus has worked best for you in some situations.

3. Review some of the strategies for excellence provided in this book. Choose the ones that you believe will be most relevant for you to make the improvements that you are seeking. Draw on anything that you think might be useful in helping you accomplish your mission to excellence. If you want additional practical examples of how students, developing athletes, top athletes, and many other great performers in a variety of domains have strengthened their focus and mental game, see the additional resources listed on page 303.

4. After you have selected a target area for improvement, completed your mission to excellence self-assessment, and chosen some relevant strategies to guide your improvement, write down your plan of action for enhancing your performance or personal growth. More specifically, write down what you are going to do to initiate the change that you are seeking, when you are going to do it, how often you are going to do it, and in what circumstances you are going to do it or practice doing it.

5. Experiment with your plan by practicing and applying the various strategies that you selected in different situations so that you can move closer to your goals. After implementing a strategy in a practice or a performance situation, take a few minutes to think about what worked well, what didn't work, and what you need to refine or change to improve your plan and your performance. To continue to move closer to your goals, assess and refine your plan by drawing out and acting on the lessons from your ongoing experiences. Make a personal commitment to ongoing learning and ongoing improvement. Decide to make it happen.

6. Where feasible, get together with other people who are pursuing personal growth or excellence (classmates, teammates, colleagues, partners, friends, or family members). Share your experiences on the challenges that you are facing and what is helping you get through those challenges successfully. Share views

on effective ways to pursue your goals, enter and maintain a fully connected focus, and deal better with distractions.

This mission to excellence project is a great opportunity for you to apply relevant focusing skills to something that you believe is extremely important in your life. If you approach this six-step process with focus and commitment to make a positive change, it will be an extremely valuable learning experience, and the chances of accomplishing your mission, or actually making the positive changes that you are seeking, are very high. You can use this process to bring about positive improvements in any part of your life.

Mission to Excellence
Self-Assessment

The purpose of this self-assessment is to clarify your desired areas of improvement and target specific ways to make those improvements. Your mission to excellence can focus on something that you would like to do or something that you would like to stop doing. Or you can focus on living, interacting, working, or performing better, more consistently, or more joyfully. Analyze in detail the precise circumstances and focus that surround your best and less-than-best experiences or performances in your targeted area. You need to know what you already do that allows you to perform well at some times or in some situations and what you do that interferes with your good performances or good parts of performances. Use a performance notebook or diary to record your reflections on how your focus has affected and is now affecting your performance or experiences positively or negatively. This approach can help you understand more fully the kind of focus that works best for you and against you.

Specific events within your environment and within your thinking or focus lead to good or bad experiences and consistent or inconsistent performances. Only at certain moments does focusing become a problem. For one Olympic figure skater, this loss of focus happened only at important competitions, "when I see the judges peering over me as I begin and I start to think about being judged instead of focusing on the movement." For a world champion water skier, it was "when I approach the first buoy on my slalom run and I think, *Uh-oh, I'm probably going to blow this.*" For a national team basketball player, it was "when the coach yells at me during the game and I start to worry about him instead of concentrating on playing ball."

You should assess precisely when a focusing problem arises and become aware of what you are thinking or, more important, what you are focused on at that moment. You should also become aware of what you focus on when the situation or your performance improves.

The following self-directed questions are designed to help you assess your focus and find your best focus for positive change. These questions have been used effectively as a guide to strengthen focus and enhance performance in sport, the performing arts, school, health, business leadership, and other areas of life. Ask yourself the following questions and record your responses.

1. What is it that you want to improve most at this time (for this mission to excellence)?

2. What are you doing that you don't want to do, or failing to do that you would like to do more often? Specifically, what would you like to change, make better, do, or act on more consistently?

3. When, where, and under what circumstances is the greatest need for change or improvement? In what situations does a problem usually come up? What kinds of demands or expectations are being placed on you at that time? What are you usually thinking, feeling, or focusing on at that time?

4. How important is it for you to improve your focus, connection, reaction, or performance in this target area? Why is it important to you to improve in this area?

5. Think about the times when you have been in a given situation and your focus, connection, response, or performance has been at its best. What was going on then? What were you doing or saying to yourself? What were you focused on?

6. Think about the times when you have been in this situation and your focus, connection, response, or performance seemed to be at its worst. What was going on then? What were you doing or saying to yourself? What were you focused on?

7. What seems to be the major difference in your focus when you compare your best and less-than-best performances, actions, responses, or experiences in this situation?

8. What do you think you can do to improve this situation, your response to it, or your performance within it? What would be your ideal or best focus within this situation?

9. Do you think that you can improve your focus in this situation if you

   ➤ focus on bringing a more positive perspective or more connected focus into this situation or performance?

   ➤ focus more fully on what you control within this situation or performance?

   ➤ focus less on what is going on around you, or what others around you are doing or not doing, and more on yourself and your performance?

   ➤ focus on taking better care of your needs for rest, nutrition, personal space, or simple joys outside this situation or performance context?

10. How strong is your commitment to make a positive change in this target area? Are you committed enough to practice and work regularly at improving your focus, connection, response, and performance in this area? If yes, great! If no, can you decide to make a full commitment to do what is required to make this positive change right now?

From T. Orlick, 2008, *In Pursuit of Excellence, Fourth Edition* (Champaign, IL: Human Kinetics).

Selecting Improvement Strategies

After you have completed your mission to excellence self-assessment, you face the delightful challenge of selecting effective strategies for making the positive changes that you are seeking. "How do I choose the best one to start with?" you're asking, right?

After completing the mission to excellence self-assessment, you might already know what will work best for you or what you need to focus on to make the positive changes that you are seeking. If not, before choosing a strategy for improvement, read through the various focus and performance enhancement options in the remainder of this book, along with the examples that show how different performers have used them. Some approaches will be immediately more attractive to you than others, and some may seem particularly suitable for your situation. Try any strategy that makes intuitive sense to you. If just reading about it feels right, try it.

Through my ongoing consultation and interactions with tens of thousands of athletes and other performers, one thing has come through loud and clear—the uniqueness of individual mental preparation, best focus plans, motivation, and effective ways of coping. An approach that may work beautifully for you may have the opposite effect on someone else. For example, in the same precompetition situation, one athlete may prepare best by thinking about something relaxing, another athlete may prefer to focus on reviewing the task at hand, and a third performer may embrace the excitement and channel it into executing his or her performance.

Your belief about the potential effectiveness of a particular strategy influences your commitment to work on it and, consequently, how well it will work for you. You are unlikely to have gone through life without knowing something about how you function. So your beliefs about what will or will not work for you often rest on a sound foundation. They are based on the number of years that you have lived and the extent to which you have experimented with what focus works best for you in your performances and life. Read through the various options for excellence with an open mind and then follow your gut feelings on strategy selection.

Select several approaches or a few focusing strategies that seem most appropriate for your particular situation. Then experiment with them until you can isolate the one or two that work best for you. You may choose a single approach, a combination of several interrelated approaches, or a personal strategy that you come up with yourself. Keep in mind that something that has not yet worked for you may at some point work beautifully for you. Often all that you need is more persistence in practicing, refining, and focusing on the strategies that have already been somewhat successful in your past. When you find something that really works for you, use it; that's the main goal.

CHAPTER 6

Intensity and Relaxation

Intensity and relaxation are not necessarily opposites; they can work together in complementary ways to bring out the best in you and your performance. You need an optimal amount of intensity to perform your best—not too much and not too little. More intensity is not necessarily better, even in high-intensity pursuits. There is a point with intensity where less is more. Trying too hard or pushing too much can work against you. The goal is to free yourself to perform rather than force yourself to perform.

You need a certain amount of tension to be able to go. On the other hand, if you are too far gone, you just go off the deep end, you lose control. So it is just being able to find that little narrow comfort zone.

Steve Podborski, overall World Cup downhill ski champion

What usually works best to free yourself to perform is relaxed intensity, relaxed attack, or relaxed power. You go after your goal with full focus, you push your limits, and at the same time you relax enough to free your body to perform in a powerful yet flowing way. Have you ever listened to high-intensity music blasting in your car, on your stereo, or on your portable music player? When you crank up the volume to the highest level, the device starts to vibrate or shake a bit, and the sound is no longer clear and crisp. If you turn down the volume a notch, the vibration stops and everything becomes clearer, crisper, more focused—right where you want it be for high-quality performance.

In sport and other high-performance domains, tuning your intensity level to that sweet spot can make a big difference in your performance. You can enter your ideal intensity zone by trusting yourself to do what you are capable of doing, by relaxing your breathing and your body, and by connecting fully with the doing part of your performance.

Turning down the intensity a little when it is too high frees you to be powerful and fluid, but not forced. You become less rigid, less tense, more supple, more flowing, and more focused on the step in front of you. You are free to engage yourself fully in the process of performing, reading and reacting intuitively so that you can successfully greet whatever challenge lies before you. On the other hand, turning up the intensity a little when it is too low can also free you to be more powerful and fluid and take you to your goals. You can often raise the level of your intensity by thinking about your goals and why you have been pouring all these hours into your pursuit. The goal of relaxed intensity is to help you find that sweet spot where you are most powerful, fluid, and focused on the right things, and to be able to reach that state consistently.

Maintaining Intensity

A leading Chinese coach once said to me, "You can jump over a very high fence when a big bull is chasing you." I haven't tried doing that yet, but I think that a bull charging at me would give me a little lift. Being pumped up or energized can help you achieve greater heights, as long as you channel that energy in the right direction. But in your haste to avoid the horns of the big bull, you don't want to trip and fall before you reach the fence or run into the fence rather than go up and over it. The point is that that increased intensity can either help you reach greater heights or make you fall flat on your face. The result depends on the intensity level, whether you are guiding that intensity in the right direction, and the extent to which you are focusing on the right things at the right time.

Most performers are naturally more intense, or up, before important games, competitions, or performances, and they do not require additional motivation to heighten their preperformance or precompetition intensity. If you do need a lift, you will most likely need it when fatigue sets in toward the latter part of the game, race, or performance—when every stroke, every stride, every rush, every movement, every inch counts. At that point the image of a charging bull, or your deciding to give it everything you have, may be most helpful.

Maintaining optimal intensity and full focus for the duration of the game or performance is the goal of many great performers. Achieving this goal separates great performances from lesser performances and differentiates teams that win when it really counts from teams that don't.

Your challenge is to discover how you can attain and maintain your best focus and ideal level of intensity, not only for the duration of one race, shift, period, game, work session, or performance but also over the course of your season and career. Maintaining an ideal level of intensity and focus comprises two important parts—what you do with your focus on-site and what you do to recharge your batteries when you are away from your performance arena.

Do you know what works best for you to enter and maintain an ideal level of focused intensity? You will have to discover and continue to work on this to consistently perform closer to your potential. Many different approaches can work to bring a delicious level of focused intensity to your pursuits, and what works best for you may change over time. The heart of focused intensity among the great athletes and performers I have worked with is quite basic. They simply decide to go out there and play or perform with full focus—with fully focused and relaxed intensity—every second. Before every performance, race, game, period, or shift, they make a commitment to themselves to go out there and do that.

Finding the right level of focused intensity is a decision that we make, because we are all capable of bringing a certain level of focused intensity to our pursuits and we are all capable of relaxing inside and outside our performance arena. Consistently great performers make a commitment to themselves to relax through the intensity and to get adequate rest away from the performance site so that when they return to it, they have the energy required to play, perform, and focus with high intensity from the first second to the last.

Fear of failure, injury, or embarrassment can sometimes increase focus and intensity. Fear can also paralyze performers, usually because they lose their best performance focus or become too tense or tentative. Performing well or winning can sometimes result in increased intensity, but it can also result in complacency. The same is true with losing. How you respond depends on how you perceive the particular situation and how you direct and connect your focus.

To relax in situations that may have previously created feelings of fear or stress, clear your mind of any thoughts about outcomes, slow your preevent pace, breathe easily and slowly, and let your body move freely. Focus fully on your preevent preparation and your warm-up, and then connect fully only with what you are doing once you begin performing.

One way to maintain ideal levels of focus and intensity over time, through the ups and downs, is to draw on your positive emotions and the passion that you have for your pursuit. Think about positive possibilities, personal bests, highlights, positive opportunities, and the possibility of taking a step up and making a positive difference every day, every performance. Find ways to keep the positive passion, pride, joy, excitement, possibilities, and absolute focus in your daily pursuits.

Athletes who consistently bring a high level of focused intensity to everyday practices are often the ones who consistently maintain high-intensity focus for the duration of their performances or games. Practicing with fully focused intensity establishes a positive pattern that performers often carry into games and performances. For that reason, among others, high-quality, fully focused practice is important. A team made up of players who are able to generate and maintain an ideal level of focused intensity throughout practice will perform well in games or performances.

Perhaps most important is deciding for yourself that you are going to bring your ideal level of intensity and focus to practice and committing yourself to doing it—every day. Commit to performing in practice with focus and intensity. This approach will make a huge difference in your performance. If you don't train with focus and intensity, somebody else will—and that will give your competitor an advantage. By setting specific focus goals for practice and thinking about how you will achieve those goals on the way to practice, you can generate focus and intensity in situations in which you might otherwise feel bored or unchallenged. Creating personal challenges or competitive challenges in practice can also raise the level of focus and intensity. For example, you can hold scrimmages; compete against teammates or the clock; train with good or great athletes from other teams or other countries; or bring in officials, judges, or spectators. Some of our best athletes use a personal challenge or a competition against opponents of greater or lesser skill as a challenge to meet personal performance goals and as an opportunity to practice their best focus in preparation for more important events.

Practices and performances provide many opportunities for you to discover the level of intensity and kind of focus that help you perform your best in your sport or performance domain. Practice getting into this zone and maintaining it, so that it becomes your natural way of performing. After you discover how to focus for your best performance, your goal becomes maintaining that focus whenever and wherever you need it. You do this by deciding to do it, planning to do it, practicing doing it, and focusing on doing it.

On some occasions, relaxing is more productive than being physically intense, such as when you are recovering from an injury, are sick, or are extremely fatigued (when, for example, you are in the middle of a long, hard season that has included extensive travel). In these cases, the best approach is often to take time off to rest or to do light, low-intensity training. You will benefit more from rest than from hard exertion.

Continue to reflect on how you can improve your focus and how you can relax through intensity to perform your best more often. Decide to do what works best for you right now—this day, this race, this game, this performance, this run, this opportunity, this season, this life. The better you become at focusing and relaxing, the better your performance and your life will become. Make this your mission over the next few days, weeks, months, years, and decades.

Understanding Relaxation

People have different bodily responses to the onset of stress. Some feel tension in their neck, back, or shoulders. Others experience shaky legs, queasiness in the stomach, a rapid increase in heart rate, sweaty palms, hot flashes, pounding in the head, dizziness, a feeling of being out of control, or a loss of focus. What do you feel when the stress in your life, or the stress before a performance, begins to rise? Stop and think about it. This is a first step in gaining an effective strategy for relaxing under pressure. As you become more aware of your early signals of stress, you can use them as reminders to relax and shift focus back to what you control. The goal is to understand your patterns and begin to identify and manage your responses, usually by refocusing, before you become uptight or lose control.

To relax, some people focus on relaxing different muscle groups (for example, in the legs, shoulders, arms, or neck) or focus on breathing slowly and easily while thinking about relaxing fully with each exhalation. Others imagine themselves in a familiar, relaxed setting with family or friends, or on the beach relaxing as waves wash gently onto the shore.

You may find it relaxing to spend time alone in a quiet place with no distractions, talk with someone who places no demands on you, go for a walk, listen to music, have a massage, go to a beautiful natural outdoor setting, or do something else that you love to do. There is no right way to relax. Whatever makes you feel more relaxed, less stressed, more joyful, more peaceful, or more in control of you and your life is right for you.

Try to become familiar with various possibilities for relaxing in different contexts. Simple reminders such *relax, breathe, calm,* or *be here* can help you relax or shift focus instantly if you practice the techniques and call on them before, or as soon as, you start to feel tense. Self-initiated relaxation, as well as relaxation assisted by activities within your environment—a long run, a warm bath, a facial, a massage, or time with a loved one—can be helpful in reducing stress or easing tension.

Two things happen to initiate effective relaxation. The first is psychological. Your focus shifts away from what caused the increased tension—such as thoughts about how you are scared, or are going to blow it, or feel like a failure—to a full focus on executing your task, connecting fully to the step in front of you, and taking the next step forward. In short, your focus shifts from outcomes, fear of failure, or fears of rejection to a positive, constructive, and absorbing focus. The shift away from self-evaluation and worry alone renders you less anxious and puts you more in control. The second part of

▶ Effective use of relaxation allows players like Ken Griffey Jr. to maintain focused and controlled movements.

effective relaxation is physiological. Your heart rate slows, your breathing slows and becomes more regular, your oxygen consumption decreases, your muscles become less tense, and you begin to feel a sense of calmness or control within your body and mind.

I remember one athlete saying to me while going through a relaxation exercise, "I don't need to relax in here; it's out there that I need it." It is out there, when the stress begins to rise, that we all need it. But if relaxation or a refocusing strategy is to be effective in high-stress contexts, you must be able to activate that response in the space of one deep breath. To do this successfully, you usually have to practice—first under low-stress conditions, then under medium stress, and finally under high-stress conditions (out there in the real world). To ready yourself for the performance arena, take advantage of all the stressful situations that you face so that you'll be practiced at responding effectively. Then you will be ready—out there—when you need to be.

If you take time to learn and practice effective relaxation, you will become more aware of your body's internal environment and better able to adapt to your external environment. You will become more in control in potentially stressful situations that count.

Practicing Relaxation

Most people, especially those involved in demanding challenges or high-performance pursuits, enjoy and benefit greatly from practicing some kind of relaxation every day—between practices or work sessions, at the end of the day, or before going to sleep at night. If one of your goals is to develop your ability to call on a relaxation response quickly in a stressful setting, then conclude some of your relaxation sessions by repeating to yourself a reminder, such as *relax, breathe, calm,* or *focus,* every time you exhale. You can also imagine being in a stressful context and remind yourself to relax and focus. This way of practicing will strengthen the association between your reminder and total relaxation or total focus. Begin to use your reminders to relax and focus in a variety of settings.

The process for practicing relaxation goes something like this. Think to yourself *breathe, relax, calm, let go, loose, focus, connect.* Let that calm, relaxed sensation spread throughout your mind and body. Then scan your body for any areas of tension. You may find it helpful to imagine a beam of light scanning through your body. The light beam is charged with relaxation, so if any area of tension exists, you can simply zap it with a light beam of relaxation.

Experiment with this process first in a quiet setting and then start to do it in less quiet settings. In the beginning, you may need a few minutes to get yourself feeling completely relaxed. Your goal is to be able to bring on a relaxation response with one long, slow, deep breath, or in a few seconds. Try using your relaxation and focus reminders to relax yourself while sitting, reading, listening to music, standing, walking, running, talking, listening to another person, driving, in class, at school, at work, at meetings, at workouts, on the beach, in bed, and so on. Simply relax and focus.

You can try these techniques right now. Breathe in, breathe out, and then say to yourself, *Re-lax . . . re-lax . . . re-lax*. Now scan your body for any areas of tension. Are your shoulders relaxed? Relax your shoulders. Are your hands relaxed? Relax your hands and arms. Are your legs, ankles, and feet relaxed? Relax your legs, ankles, and feet. Is your jaw relaxed? Relax your jaw. These are good checkpoints. Zap any area of tension that you find in your body with a warm beam of relaxation. Set a goal to relax on the spot two times today. You've already done it once—one more to go.

Next, practice plugging your relaxation response into potentially stress-provoking situations. If performance or competition settings have resulted in unwanted stress or tension, begin to simulate performance conditions in practice and practice using your reminders to relax and focus. Move from simulated conditions in practice to performance or competition conditions, from less important competitions to more important ones, while continuing to use your relaxation and focus reminders. This approach will allow your preferred on-site relaxation and focus responses to become well learned and practiced for those times when you need them most.

Taking an exam, participating in a tryout, speaking in front of a class or group, going to the dentist, having an argument, responding to a customs official, or getting a parking ticket—all provide valuable practice opportunities. When you detect any personal signals of tension, take a deep breath, exhale slowly, and think to yourself, *Re-lax, calm, focus*. With practice, this process itself can bring on a relaxation response. Relaxation alone is not likely to eliminate all stress in a highly stressful situation, but it will help you reduce the stress to a manageable level and get you focused on what will allow you to achieve your goal.

In my consulting work, many athletes and performers in other fields have expressed a desire to be able to clear their minds and relax more completely, primarily for the following purposes:

➤ To experience a deep and restful sleep, especially before and sometimes after an important performance, game, or competition

➤ To remain calm and conserve energy during the final hours leading up to an important performance, game, or competition

➤ To relax and revitalize the mind and body between demands, shifts, runs, races, periods, quarters, or events

➤ To rest and recover physically and mentally while traveling from one game, performance, competition, presentation, or meeting to the next

➤ To hasten recovery from illness, injury, or personal setbacks

➤ To focus more completely on what they are engaged in

➤ To experience more simple joys in life

In response to requests by many athletes, and with their guidance and feedback, I developed a number of relaxation and focusing CDs (see "Additional Resources," page 303.) One of my scripts for a relaxation exercise is reproduced in figure 6.1. You can read the script yourself, have someone read it to you, listen to my voice on CD with relaxing music playing in the background, or create your own system. Whatever your method, try to get totally absorbed in the feeling of relaxation and focusing so that you can fully benefit from it and recall that feeling in the future.

If you want to use the exercise to relax and go to sleep, just lie down, play the CD, and listen. Chances are good that you will relax completely and drift off into a deep, restful sleep. The three-part relaxation exercise is designed to free you to enter a state of complete relaxation through muscle relaxation, relaxed breathing, and imagery related to a relaxing place.

To use the exercise as a lead-in to performance imagery, remind yourself before you begin listening that at the conclusion of the exercise, while you are still in a deeply relaxed state, you will imagine and feel preselected performance skills flowing perfectly in your mind and body. If you want to use the exercise to calm yourself before an important competition, select an appropriate time to listen—a time when you want to be more relaxed and when you do not yet need to be highly activated for competing.

To use the exercise as a lead-in to strengthening your confidence, remind yourself before you listen that at the conclusion of the exercise you will repeat to yourself your many assets, your strengths, and your many reasons to be positive and confident in yourself, your focus, and your capacity. In this case, you might want to write down some positive statements to think about before you begin the relaxation exercise. If your objective is to heal your body from an injury or speed your recovery from a strenuous or stressful day, then prepare yourself to send healing thoughts and revitalizing images to various parts of your body, both during and after the relaxation exercise.

Relaxing Through Exertion

When Florence Griffith-Joyner broke the women's 100-meter world record in 10.48 seconds, she commented, "The 10.60 [run in the first round of the competition] made me realize if I continued to focus on what I'm doing and stayed relaxed, my times would continue to drop." And they did!

Sue Holloway, following her Olympic silver medal performance in kayaking in pairs, spoke of the importance of relaxing through the exertion within her performance:

> Almost every three seconds or so toward the end of my race, I'd say, *Relax*, and I'd let my shoulders and my head relax, and I'd think about putting on the power, and then I'd feel the tension creeping up again, so I'd think about relaxing again, then power, relax. . . . I knew that

Figure 6.1   Relaxation Script

Get yourself into a comfortable position. Let yourself relax. Feel the relaxation spread through your body. Breathe easily and slowly. Become aware of your feet. Move your toes slightly. Let them relax. Now think into your lower legs. Let your calf muscles totally relax. Think into your upper legs. Let them totally relax. Feel your legs sink into a completely relaxed state. Relax your behind.

[Pause.]

Focus on the muscles in your lower back. Think relaxation into those muscles. Feel that relaxation spread into your upper back. Feel your whole body sink into a deep state of relaxation. Now focus on your fingers. Feel them tingle slightly. Think warmth into your fingers. Let them totally relax. Relax your forearms, your upper arms, and your shoulders. Totally relax. Relax your neck [pause] and your jaw. Feel your head sink into a totally relaxed and comfortable position.

Scan your body for possible areas of tightness and relax those areas. Feel your entire body encircled with soothing warmth and relaxation. Enjoy this wonderful state of complete relaxation.

[Pause for one minute.]

Now focus on your breathing. Breathe easily and slowly.

[Pause.]

As you breathe in, allow your stomach to rise and extend. As you breathe out, let your whole body relax. Breathe in—feel your stomach rise. Breathe out—relax. Breathe in—feel your stomach rise. Breathe out—relax. [Do this three times.] For the next 10 breaths, each time you breathe in, feel your stomach rise. Each time you breathe out, think to yourself, *Relax . . . relax . . . relax.*

[Pause for 10 breaths.]

Feel yourself sink deeper and deeper into a calm and wonderful state of complete relaxation.

Now in your mind you are going to a very special place. You can go here whenever you want to find peace and tranquility. In your special place the sun is shining. The sky is blue. You are totally relaxed, enjoying the warmth and tranquility.

[Pause.]

Feel the warmth. Enjoy the beauty.

[Pause.]

You can be here alone or you can share this place with a special friend. It is your place. You decide.

In your special place, it is so relaxing. You are calm, relaxed, confident, and happy to be alive. You are in control. You feel great.

Feel the calmness spread through your entire body and mind as you rest gently, enjoying the peace and tranquility of your special place. You are feeling so good and so relaxed. You are comfortable; you are warm; you are safe. You are in control of your body and mind. Enjoy this wonderful, restful state.

Available on the CD *Relaxation and Stress Control Activities* (see "Additional Resources" on page 303).

From T. Orlick, 2008, *In Pursuit of Excellence, Fourth Edition* (Champaign, IL: Human Kinetics).

in order to have that power I had to be relaxed. You can be powerful but tense, and the boat won't go. You windmill, and you stay on the spot and dig yourself into a hole. I wanted to feel the power, the boat coming up, lifting and going. Crossing the line, the thing I remember was just letting the emotion go and being able to say, *That's it, it's over!* I just knew that we'd gone our very hardest.

At first glance, exertion and relaxation may seem to be a contradiction in terms. But most of the best performances in sport occur when athletes feel loose and relaxed in the process of extending themselves. When Larry Cain paddled at a blistering pace to win Olympic gold, a definite sequence of reach–power–relax occurred with each stroke. He pushed his limits, but he also paddled relaxed. With top runners you see a similar sequence of stretch–power–relax accompanying each stride. Champion runners often speak of running relaxed after shattering world records.

To develop the skills that allow you to relax during exertion, set a goal to focus on doing this during training sessions and then remind yourself to relax while you are going hard in training. Think of on-site reminders that might help you enter a relaxed but highly focused channel (for example, *loose–powerful, power–relax, reach–pull–relax, stretch–grab–relax, relax shoulders, relax ankles*). Experiment with using reminders at appropriate times before and during practices, simulated competitions, and progressively more important performances or competitions. In activities that involve repetitive sequences, reminders can be timed to go with the rhythmical flow of the activity.

Marathon runners would not be breaking personal barriers, running 26 miles in a little over two hours in some cases, unless they were stretching, pushing, reaching, and relaxing through their limits. The best distance runners run relaxed, breathe steadily and consistently, relax muscles with periodic exhalation, scan muscles for tension, and focus on localized relaxation of tense areas. They use only those muscles required, relax nonessential muscles (including jaw and shoulder muscles), and relax working muscles in the recovery stage to conserve energy and run more efficiently. You can learn to relax your nonworking muscles while other muscles are working hard and to relax your working muscles in the recovery phase of sequential movements—if you focus on doing it in training. You know where all those muscles are; you simply have to practice tuning in to them and telling them what to do at critical moments.

By relaxing and focusing on specific things that you want to happen within your body, you can effect physiological changes in your muscle tension, heart rate, blood pressure, respiratory rate, blood flow, and body temperature. You can even influence your rate of recovery from injury. When attempting to direct such changes, clearly visualize or think into the part of the body that you want to influence. Then imagine and feel the desired change taking place (see chapter 9 and "Additional Resources" on page 303 for more about this technique).

Applying Intensity and Relaxation

Think of your own performances. Did you ever fall short of your goals because you were too tight, rigid, anxious, tense, or stressed? Did you ever fail to achieve your best performance because you were too complacent or not really going after your goals? If the answer to these questions is yes, the way to resolve the problem is to "flip your switch" so that you bring your best focus into your performance and remain fully connected throughout your performance. Personal best performances occur when mind and muscle combine through focus and execution in a free-flowing way.

Thomas Grandi's Story

The story of Thomas Grandi, a world-class skier and person, demonstrates the critical role of focus and combining intensity and relaxation to reach high-level goals. I met Thomas Grandi at a dryland training camp in 2004 and worked collaboratively with him for the remainder of his athletic career. When we met he had been racing against the best skiers in the world on the World Cup circuit for over 12 years. He was 32 years old and still dreamed of winning a World Cup race.

Thomas' skiing events (giant slalom and slalom) require putting together two great runs on the same day because the times for two separate runs are combined for the final result. On some occasions Thomas had a great first run but a disappointing second run, and on other occasions he had a disappointing first run and a great second run. He had never been able to put together great back-to-back runs to win a World Cup race.

Thomas had the potential to win. He had been right up there with the best in the world on one run. Athletes do not lose their technical or physical skills from one run to the next, so it was clear to me that his success was related to his race focus and taking the right level of relaxed intensity into each race run.

In our first meeting we talked a lot about focus and intensity, consistency of best performances, his dream goals, and his reasons for wanting to achieve those goals. His reasons for still competing on the World Cup circuit were to live his dream of winning a World Cup race, to be the first male skier from his country ever to win a World Cup race in his disciplines, to give something back to the people who had supported him over the years, and to inspire younger ski racers who looked up to him and who would follow in his footsteps or ski tracks.

I asked Thomas what he focused on in his best-ever race run. He said that he mentally prepared himself for that run and that at the top of the hill about a minute before the start, he decided to really go for it—to attack from top to bottom. When he had a poor second run following a great first run, it was usually because he didn't want to blow it, or ski out of the course, because then he would have no result at all. When he had a great second run after a poor or mediocre first run, he really attacked the second run to make up for the poor showing on the first run and thought that he had nothing to lose.

So I said to Thomas, "Why don't you just decide to do it, to really go after it, before every race. Prepare well for the specific race, and a minute or two before that race run, just decide to do it—first run and second run! Attack from top to bottom and everywhere in between. What are you waiting for?"

He laughed and I laughed, but the question was a serious one that had serious consequences for his goals and his career in ski racing. At 32 or 33 years old, time starts to create some urgency about doing what you really want to do while you are still fully capable of doing it. Thomas was already starting to have recurring back problems and later some knee issues. We spoke about the urgency of deciding to do something now—this year, this season—while he was still capable and motivated to do it.

Within the first few races of the new season he put together great back-to-back race runs and won his first-ever World Cup race. The following week at the next World Cup race, he did the same thing and won again. Back-to-back World Cup wins against the best ski racers in the world—finally, he was living his dream. He had the best season of his life and followed that up the next year with an even better overall season.

Shortly before the beginning of the 2006–2007 World Cup race season, I asked Thomas if we could do a short interview together so that I could share some of his journey with the readers of the fourth edition of *In Pursuit of Excellence*. He said that he would be honored to do it. Here is a portion of that interview.*

> Terry: What did we do together that you feel helped you most in terms of pursuing and achieving your goals?
>
> Thomas: I think that by talking about certain aspects of ski racing, I learned more about myself and the areas that I needed to improve. I can remember sitting down with you and talking about what I thought I needed to break through the last mental barrier. We talked about creating a sense of urgency that would make me ski the way I wanted to ski, taking risks, skiing every run like it was my last, and really taking advantage of every race. I created my sense of urgency by telling myself I was getting older, that each race was an opportunity I could never have back, and that I needed to seize every opportunity like it was my last. We also talked about creating a greater purpose, which would help me on those days when I didn't feel like pushing the limits and taking risks. My greater purpose was to put ski racing and specifically my events, GS and SL, on the front page. These two elements enabled me and pushed me to get out of my comfort zone and discover what was possible.
>
> Terry: What are the most important lessons that you learned from me?
>
> Thomas: One of the best lessons I learned from you was to analyze my race right after it, look at the good and bad, make notes of both

*Excerpts from Thomas Grandi's e-mail interview courtesy of Thomas Grandi.

and how I could be better in the next race, and move on. I used to have trouble dealing with both good and bad races. When I had a good race I would relive it too often and forget to prepare for the upcoming race. When I had a bad race I would also relive it and punish myself for my poor performance, beating myself up mentally. By writing race debriefs I learned to take the good and the bad, figure out how I could be better, and move on. I think this process really freed me to perform well consistently.

Terry: What does being focused in training and focused in races mean to you? Can you describe what it is, what it feels like, or how it unfolds for you?

Thomas: I would say that my focusing ability has evolved since I started working with you. I think a lot of athletes, including me, are constantly looking to get into the elusive "zone." You taught me that it doesn't have to be elusive, that I can actually control and enter the zone when I want to, by focusing to my fullest. In my two victories I can remember being fully focused. In Flachau, for example, after my first win, I was so relaxed that I knew exactly when to flip the switch. Ten minutes before my run I put my music on, cut out all the distractions in the start area, and enter my own world. I have done my warm-up by this point, so now I am actually calming myself down. My breathing becomes very steady, and I am not concerned about what anyone else is doing. It's all about me.

If I look at someone I look right through them. If I see people talking or laughing, their words don't register. I become fully grounded and present in the moment. When I enter the start, I tell myself, *This race is now, and I can never have it back. I need to ski with aggression and no regrets.* Occasionally I'll have one technical cue that I focus on. But in Flachau I was confident that everything was in me, so I didn't need to think at all. As long as I was present, I could react to anything and everything. I skied as though time were standing still. Although I was skiing the fastest I had ever skied and skiing a very aggressive direct line, I felt as if I had all the time in the world. I was truly enjoying my performance. I was in complete control. I could change the radius of the turn if I chose to.

On the second run the course started in complete sunshine, but halfway down it plunged into dark shadows that made it extremely difficult to see. I can remember saying to myself, *Holy shit, I can't see a thing.* For a split second I hesitated until I told myself my refocusing cue, which at the time was *Go now!* Those words clicked, and I charged through the flat light carving the last turns to the finish. In the finish when I saw my time I started to laugh, because I had taken the lead by over a second. I was living my dream and enjoying it to the fullest. I just let it come pouring out of me, and it was one of the best moments of my life.

Terry: That was a great example of refocusing instantly within the heat of the race when you moved into shadows and couldn't see. Can you comment on the value of refocusing to get back on a positive track in your sport?

Thomas: An alpine skier rarely has a mistake-free run. It happens occasionally, but typically you make one or two mistakes coming down the course. The ability to refocus quickly is critical. When a mistake happens there is no time to think about why it happened—it is a time to start racing again as quickly as possible. I have some key words to refocus, and it's as simple as *Come on!* I have learned to refocus and recover quickly and get back up to speed as quickly as possible.

Terry: How did you get yourself to continue to go after your dreams when things weren't going well?

Thomas: It sometimes surprises me that I did make it through the rough times. I guess I had this deep belief that I could do what I had set out to do, even though the results I was having showed the contrary. I learned to surround myself with positive people who believe anything is possible.

Terry: Part of our plan for ongoing improvement was to pull out positive things from every performance, to assess your focus, and to act on the lessons learned. How did you do that during the years we worked together?

Thomas: The biggest part of evaluating my performances was my race debriefs. Because I was committed to doing one after every race, good or bad, I learned the hard lessons that usually I would have rather swept under the rug and forgotten. It also showed me that even in a bad race there are positives, and in a good race there are lessons to be remembered and improved on. We refocused on a simple game plan based on what I knew worked best for me. If I had followed my instinct to forget all about my bad performances without analyzing what had gone wrong, I can guarantee that I would have never won those two races.

Terry: What kind of a commitment did it take to achieve your goals in your sport?

Thomas: Every decision I make is weighed on whether or not it will help me in my quest. If something is not going to help me in this quest, it probably won't happen. To reach the top of any sport requires a huge time commitment and huge desire.

Terry: I am interested in how your confidence changed since we began working together. Can you comment on that?

Thomas: The biggest change in how I approach ski racing is definitely in my confidence to focus when I need to. When I started working with you, the fact that you had such a successful track record, and that you believed in me and what I was doing gave me a big boost. Then when we designed my race plan I knew I was doing all the right things leading up to my races. The race plan routine set me at ease and allowed me to relax in the start gate. As I realized the race focus plan worked, I gained more and more confidence in it. This freed me. It allowed me to really relax so that I could attack from the first gate all the way to the finish. The more I race, and the more I put myself in situations that require me to focus, the more I am learning that I can fully focus whenever I choose to.

Part of what allowed Thomas to live his dream was all the work that he did on developing the physical and technical skills required to compete and win at his level. He had already developed those skills before I met him. The other part, the part that was missing, was deciding to take full control over his destiny by focusing in ways that would allow him to live his dream. The final step up, the one that took him to the top of the podium, came from focusing on the right things at the right time and understanding that the control switch was always within his own focus—first run, second run, and every run.

During the time that we worked together, Thomas and I had regular e-mail contact to prepare for the season and stay on track during the season. Some key points from our interaction that he believed helped him achieve the best results of his life appear here. I hope that they help you on your mission to personal excellence.

Race Perspective

The perspective and focus that you take into your races or performances sets the stage for how you perform. In a very real way, your performance outcomes are dictated by what you do, think about, and focus on before your game, race, or event even begins. You can set yourself up for success or failure based on the perspective you carry into your performance and the extent to which you respect your best focus for the duration of your performance. A positive race perspective allowed Thomas to perform his best.

Every race presents a unique opportunity to win, to learn, to grow, to live my dream. My goal for every race, every run, is to seize each opportunity. I race every race with the intention of winning. I race to win! I focus fully on doing what will free me to win. Today's race, this moment, this opportunity will never exist again. Today can never be lived again, so I embrace it with my absolute focus and my heart and soul.

Training Goals

The focus that you take into your training sets the stage for how you perform. The purpose of training is to prepare you to do the great things you would like to do in your races, games, performances, or competitions. Ensure that your training prepares you to do the things you have to do to perform to your true potential in your races or performances. This focus in training allowed Thomas to train his best.

> I push myself harder in training, not every run, but at least a couple per day. I go past my comfort zone so that I know I can go there and still pull it off. I pick the runs that I want to push hard in, in advance, and then commit to doing it. Going past my comfort zone in training will help me race to my potential more often.

Performance Reminders

In high-performance pursuits, reminders are important. Reminders of what you want to do and how you intend to do it are important because they allow you to achieve the consistency that you are seeking, in both training and competitions. Your personal reminders will be specific to you and your performance discipline. Some athletes benefit from technical reminders during their warm-up before competitions. The following technical reminders worked best for Thomas:

➤ Push the line longer and straighter down the hill. Open the stance and be super relaxed in the ankles and knees.

➤ Stand taller and stay ahead of the course, anticipate, and react well to rhythm changes. Push the line down the hill longer and smoother into the new turn.

To make sure that your technical reminders are fresh in your mind and body shortly before you perform, imagine the feeling of performing that way. Recalling that feeling will free you to perform your best more automatically, without having to think.

Final Prerace Reminders

Thomas took the following final focus reminders into his best races. The purpose of these reminders was to help him focus in ways that consistently brought out his best possible performance. As you read over his race-day reminders, notice that three interrelated themes are present: (1) attack and really go for it, (2) stay relaxed, and (3) trust yourself and your focus. See what you can find in the following focus reminders that might help you in your pursuit of excellence:

➤ Trust myself. No matter what happened in training leading up to this day, I can do it on race day when it counts. In the morning, I know that I am going to attack the hill, relax, and do it.

➤ Ski relaxed, smooth, and aggressive. Charge down the pitch and keep the skis going down the hill, as clean as possible.

➤ Remember how I felt last year. I had a chance to podium, but I watched as others came down and knocked me off the podium. I could have skied faster, but instead I hoped that others would make a mistake. That isn't the way to win. I control my own destiny. Go out there and get it!

➤ Out of the start, attack right away. Relax from the first gate right to the bottom. Do a great inspection—know exactly where to go. Get the direction, trust it, and go. Free myself to take the chances I need to be fast.

➤ There are no sections on this course that I can't rip. Rip it from top to bottom, with no backing off. Stay grounded, stay focused top to bottom for two runs, and be relaxed and aggressive. Trust myself.

➤ Charge out of the start, look for speed, and push the line.

➤ Focus forward, keep my body forward, and use a relaxed attack. Don't save anything. Spend everything I have.

➤ Go full out from top to bottom. Have super-relaxed ankles and knees (grounded in my boots) and supple legs. Look for speed.

Race Debriefs

The major purpose of performance debriefs is to help you understand what focus works best for you and what interferes with your best performance focus. When something goes well you must embrace and remember the lessons related to what made it go so well. When something does not go well, it is equally important to draw out the lessons about why it did not go well.

In two of his best-ever races, Thomas included the following comments in his race debrief:

> The morning of the race I went through my reasons for urgency and really cued in on this: Every race is a new opportunity, and my opportunities are numbered. Had a great warm-up before the race, one free run beside the race hill, and one run in the gates. Ten minutes before my run I flipped the switch.

> Before my runs I was so focused I was almost meditative. I had a clear mind and was extremely grounded in the present. I remember thinking when I got in the gate that I'd rather be nowhere else in the world but here. It was my turn for a minute and a half, and I was *on!*

Even when you reach the top of your field, you have to continue to respect and fine-tune your best focus if you want to perform consistently at that level.

The following exchanges with Thomas and the lessons drawn from these exchanges provide specific examples of how you can turn disappointment into positive focused action.

Thomas: I was not feeling 100 percent going into today's race. My GS skiing has not been feeling like it should. In training I have been making small mistakes far too often. I am attacking as hard as I can, and I am not very fast.

Terry: You are attacking as hard as you can, but are you also relaxing enough? Are you using your relaxed attack—relaxed ankles, supple legs? Sometimes relaxing a little more gives more fluidity and more speed.

Lesson: Sometimes when you are feeling pressure to perform, you let your focus slip away from what will free you to perform your best. In this situation, the attack was in full force but the relaxing was missing.

Thomas: I was feeling the pressure of being the defending champion and having a lot of supporters out to watch the race. I also drew number 1, which always creates a little more tension. But I skied aggressively. I attacked the hill as hard as I could, but I didn't ski as cleanly as I can. I know that I could have run the last part of the course straighter.

Terry: When you are feeling pressure, shift focus to the doing. The way to the results that you are seeking is to let go of thoughts of results and focus fully on how you are going to race this course. It always comes back to full focus on the doing, on being in the moment, on getting your focus in the right place—body forward, focus forward, relaxed ankles, relaxed attack, straighter line. Free yourself, trust yourself, and trust your focus. When you race, most things happen too fast to think your way down the course, so let your focus lead you, focus ahead, ski by intuition, and go for it—top to bottom.

Lesson: When expectations are high, you must focus fully on the doing and nothing else. Go back to the focus that freed you to perform your best. Remind yourself of that focus. Respect that focus. Keep things simple. Use one or two reminders and go.

Thomas: I skied aggressively. I attacked the hill as hard as I could and relaxed my ankles. I am happy with my approach to stay focused in light of the pressure and distractions. I know that I could have run the last part of the course straighter, but I am skiing really well.

Terry: Great—build on this! Keep working on your relaxed attack. Then everything will be where we want it to be.

Lesson: You can refocus and get back on track even when your focus has temporarily shifted to outcomes. When you bring your focus back to doing what frees you to perform well, the outcomes take care of themselves.

Ups and downs are always present in high-performance pursuits. As long as you keep returning to a focus that is positive and constructive for you, you will arrive at your desired destination. Remind yourself of the focus that has brought out your best in the past. Focus on what is most relevant for you right now and act on that focus.

Simple Reminders to Guide You

- ➤ Decide to do what you really want to do.
- ➤ Once you have decided, connect fully with your performance.
- ➤ Let nothing get between you and your performance. Pure focus, pure connection, is the only place to be.
- ➤ Remember that you are fully capable of performing your best.
- ➤ Free your body to do what it is capable of doing.
- ➤ Free yourself to perform with relaxed intensity.

Essentially, performance excellence is all about flipping the focus switch to absorb yourself completely in what works best for you, and doing it consistently, not just for one run, one race, one shift, one class, one interaction, one performance, one period, one at bat, one inning, one quarter, one round, one shot, or one game, but for every experience—top to bottom, start to finish, first second to last second.

Remember, you can choose the perspective and focus that you take into your performance. You can decide to perform with relaxed intensity. You have many reasons to believe in your capacity. You are fortunate to be out there doing what you love. Embrace the simple joys.

CHAPTER 7

Distraction Control

If I were asked to identify one mental skill that distinguishes great athletes, great teams, and other great performers who remain at the top of their game from all others, I would name their ability to adapt, refocus, and stay positive and focused in the face of distractions. If you want to perform near your best consistently and be your best in your most important events, you must master the critical skill of distraction control through positive focus planning and regular practice. You must learn to sustain your best focus in the face of potential distractions and be able to refocus quickly to regain a positive and absolute connection if your focused connection is broken. Athletes and teams who remain positive and fully focused in the face of distractions will win the big events.

Heart in champions has to do with the depth of your motivation and how well your mind and body react to pressure—that is, being able to do what you do best under maximum pain and stress.

Bill Russell, winner of 11 NBA Championships

Distractions come from a variety of sources, such as winning; losing; your own expectations and those of others; teammates; coaches; competitors; officials; media; management; sport organizations; sponsors; financial and educational concerns; changes in your performance level; and changes in familiar patterns and in your thinking before, during, and after performances. Distractions are an ever-present, ongoing part of sport and life.

Empowering Yourself to Change

When you enter competitive situations, demanding work or performance environments, or highly charged emotional contexts, the number of potential distractions increases substantially. But you decide whether you let those things distract you, upset you, lower your confidence, put you in a negative frame of mind, take you out of your best focus, or interfere with your best performance. How you respond to challenges is your choice. Something becomes a distraction only if you let it distract you. Otherwise, a potential distraction is simply something that happens as you go through your day, your preparation, your competition, or your performance. You can choose to be distracted by it or not, to dwell on it or let it go. You decide, and you live with the consequences of your decisions. Your focus is always within your control.

The point is that you don't have to let what you have normally seen as a distraction have a negative effect on your mood, focus, or performance. You don't lose your performance skills because of distractions; you let yourself lose the focus that allows you to execute your skills effectively.

You may face a situation or decision that you feel is unfair or you may experience a performance that does not go as planned. You may find these situations frustrating, but you are not obliged to react by putting yourself or others down, giving up, or questioning your own value or capacity. Unexpected disruptions may occur, such as schedule changes, delays, incompetent people, lack of personal space, or differences in food or facilities. You don't have to let these events overcome you or let your positive focus slip away. You may want a good result more than anything else, but you don't have to focus on worrying about the outcome. You can simply remind yourself to focus in a way that will allow you to perform your best, given the conditions that you are facing. Even when you are competing in a context that is different from anything you have ever experienced before, you can respect the preparation routines and focus that have worked best for you in the past.

You can find a way over, around, or through almost all obstacles by committing yourself to remain positive, by turning negatives into positives, by drawing out lessons, and by maintaining or quickly regaining a fully connected, positive focus. By reacting emotionally to distractions or potential obstacles, you defeat yourself—your emotions take you away from your best

▶ Sheryl Swoopes doesn't let distractions shake her confidence. You, too, can choose to overcome distractions.

© Rocky Widner/Getty Images

performance focus and leave you mentally and physically drained. Constantly reacting to potentially stressful situations in a negative or emotional way wastes a lot of energy and puts you at risk of becoming exhausted or getting sick, which obviously can hurt your performance and add still another stress factor. Don't waste your emotion on things that are not within your control, that will not help your performance, or that don't really matter in the bigger picture of your life.

When you are facing stress, additional rest is a blessing. If you are well rested, you will cope and focus better. Take time to relax, rest, and do some simple things that lift you after stressful experiences. Setting simple daily goals and planning each day to ensure that you get some rest, have some quiet time to relax, do something that you enjoy, and gain some sense of control over your life is helpful in managing stressful environments.

At major competitions or in other demanding situations, if you step back and look at distractions from a distance, you realize that most of them are little things that are quickly resolved. They aren't worth the expenditure of a lot of emotional energy. The following pointers will help you stay on a positive track or get back on track quickly:

➤ Commit yourself to remaining positive.

➤ Focus on doing what will help you stay positive and in control. A strong positive focus protects you from distractions.

➤ Get yourself into a positive state of mind before the event and stay focused on your job within the event; then things will flow.

➤ Look for advantages in every situation, even if the conditions are less than ideal. Look for reasons you can still be positive, focused, confident, and optimistic.

➤ Find the positives in the situations that you are experiencing or currently living. Find the good things in yourself, in others, and in each day.

➤ Remind yourself that distractions do not have to consume you. At a tournament, competition, or performance site, things may happen to you that are unfair or unexpected. You cannot control those circumstances, but you can control how you react to them. Why compound the problem by focusing your energy on things that are beyond your immediate control?

➤ Expect conditions to be different at important events or major competitions. Expect a faster pace, a busier place, and more waiting around. Prepare yourself to face these potential distractions in a relaxed, positive way. If something begins to irritate you, let those feelings go with as little wasted energy as possible. They are not worth your reaction. Let them bounce off you easily.

➤ Expect people to behave differently at stressful events, even those who normally would be calm, supportive, and understanding. Observe them with interest, but don't take responsibility for their behavior. Look for your own strength. Remind yourself of what you came here to do and where your focus should be.

➤ Know that you can enjoy this experience and perform well, regardless of the circumstances. Embrace the simplest joys.

Distraction control can be a valuable asset in all facets of your life. In preparing yourself to make positive focusing and distraction control a way of being, you have to move beyond thinking to acting. Consider the following actions:

➤ Make a commitment to yourself to remain positive and focused every day and act on that commitment. Challenge yourself to think and act in positive, self-enhancing ways. If things are not going well, refocus by finding your own space, doing some relaxed breathing, focusing on the positives, or connecting fully with something joyful, meaningful, or within your control.

➤ Practice getting back on track quickly. For example, when things don't go well in training, while performing, or in your personal life, take advantage of the opportunity to practice changing mental channels and refocusing into a more positive state of mind.

➤ Remind yourself repeatedly that you can change your focus and perspective. Then focus fully on doing it.

➤ Remain open to possibilities for staying focused or dealing better with stress or distractions. Some athletes with whom I worked found it helpful to imagine themselves surrounded by an invisible bubble or force field that protected them from unwanted stress or distractions at the performance site. Negative comments, distractions, or hassles simply bounced off a protective shield as they focused on moving toward their goals.

➤ Do the best that you can do with your focus today—draw out the lesson, learn from it, act on what you learned, and then move on. Continue to focus on what is within your control.

➤ After a good day or a mediocre day, be proud of your effort and of what you have done well. Draw out the positive lessons. Then start tomorrow as a fresh new day.

➤ If you want additional exercises to become better at focusing through distractions and finding the positives in each day, listen to my audio CDs *Focusing Through Distractions, Relaxation and Joyful Living,* and *Performing in the Zone* (see "Additional Resources" on page 303).

Your best on-site focus is usually limited to preparation for your own performance—something over which you have complete control. Focus on following your best preparation patterns. Think only of what focus works best for you.

Bring yourself into this frame of mind—it is the only place to be. You are not asking yourself to do anything unreasonable, only to focus as well as you can and perform as well as you can. Execute your task the way it can be done, the way you can do it. Focus on the doing—that is your goal. Your body follows your focus. Send a clear, positive message and then just let it happen. Trust your preparation. Trust your body. Focus ahead and go.

Creating a Refocusing Plan

Think of a recent situation at work, practice, competition, or in your daily life when you lost it—blew your cool, lost your temper, abandoned your positive focus, or lost your connection with your performance. Think about how you could have responded more positively or more effectively. Then imagine that you are confronting the same situation, but you don't let it bother you. You stay positive, focused, and in control. You rise above the distraction. Everything that you might have previously seen as negative bounces off you with minimal disturbance. You stay cool, calm, focused, and effective, and you get back on track quickly. That is what I want you to be able to do in your real world. How can you get yourself to do it?

Your focus dictates whether something becomes a distraction or problem for you in the first place. Your focus also has the power to eliminate the distraction or potential problem. Essentially, your focus can create the problem or distraction and can also allow you to eliminate it, which is why developing an effective focus is so critical to your performance and your life.

Every self-initiated positive change begins with three simple steps:

1. Create a vision. In this case, create a vision of a better way of viewing and responding to potential distractions.

2. Form a plan. In this case, develop a plan for how you can respond to distractions or potential distractions in a positive, effective way.

3. Make a decision to act on the plan, again and again and again.

Developing a personal refocusing plan and acting on it will help you make the changes that you are seeking, so that you are more in control and more focused on the right things when you face potential distractions in your performances and your life. You can begin designing your personal plan for distraction control right now by responding to the following questions:

1. What do you want to change about how you see and respond to distractions or potential distractions in your practices, performances, work, or life?

2. Why do you want to change how you see or respond to distractions or potential distractions in these parts of your performance or life? Why is it important for you to make these changes?

3. If you come up with a personal distraction control plan right now, can you decide to act on this plan repeatedly until you gain control over your focus and your distractions? If your answer to this deciding question is yes, then you will make the changes that you are seeking. If your answer is no, then rethink why it is important for you to act on your plan, because to control distractions or to focus through distractions in the real world, only action counts.

After you have answered the three distraction control questions, you are ready to complete the distraction control plan (see figure 7.1). Many of the athletes I have worked with have successfully used this tool to help them pinpoint their distractions and their reminders for dealing effectively with those distractions. Some of them carry that one-page plan with them to competitions and major events until their reminders are automated and inside their heads.

Figure 7.1 Distraction Control Plan

Distractions	Usual response	Preferred response	Refocus reminders

From T. Orlick, 2008, *In Pursuit of Excellence, Fourth Edition* (Champaign, IL: Human Kinetics).

In the first column on the distraction control plan, list the major distractions or refocusing situations that you have faced in the past or are likely to face in the future, those that have interfered with your best focus or best performance. Think about the key events that happen in your world or in your mind that prevent you from being your best, feeling your best, or performing your best. The distractions that you list and target for improvement can be in any area relevant to you. For example, you might identify something that happens to you before, during, or after a practice, competition, or performance, or what happens at home, at school, at work, or within your daily interactions or relationships.

In the second column, indicate your typical response to these distractions in the past. Consider what you were thinking, saying to yourself, or focusing on when you faced these distractions. In the third column, indicate how you would prefer to respond in each of these situations now and in the future. What would you prefer to think, say to yourself, or focus on the next time that you face this potentially distracting situation?

In the fourth column, write down a strong refocusing reminder that you can use in that situation to get your focus back to where you want it to be, back to where it is most beneficial to you and your performance. List key reminders that you can say or think to yourself the next time you face each of the distractions that you have listed in the first column. Write down reminders that you can use in the heat of the moment to refocus and quickly get back on a positive track.

Effective real-world refocusing reminders in potentially stressful situations often begin with a reminder to breathe. You are probably breathing anyway, so you can just focus on your breathing—take one long, slow deep breath in followed by one long, slow, deep breath out. Then you can shift to a focus reminder that has personal meaning for you. Here are some examples:

- ➤ Breathe, relax.
- ➤ Focus, focus, focus.
- ➤ Decide, decide, decide.
- ➤ Change channels.
- ➤ Focus only on my preparation—my game plan.
- ➤ Focus only on what is within my immediate control—nothing else matters
- ➤ This does not have to bother me—*park it* or *tree it*.
- ➤ Let it go and focus on the next step.
- ➤ I can perform well regardless of what happened before this moment.
- ➤ Be totally here. Be in this moment.
- ➤ I control my focus—it's my choice.
- ➤ Shift focus back to what will do me the most good—now!

You only need one or two simple but powerful reminders that you decide to act on to stay in control or to regain control. Remember that the control switch always lies within you. Decide to flip the switch. Decide to change channels whenever you feel that it is in your best interest to do so.

Acting on Your Plan

Once you have a refocusing plan that specifies how you would prefer to focus in specific important situations, your goal is to act on your plan. Use every available opportunity to practice responding more effectively to situations that have distracted you in the past as well as other situations that arise when you are distracted or begin to lose your best focus. Practicing will help you fine-tune your skills for focusing and refocusing through distractions and improve your overall performance.

The next time that something distracts you—a negative comment, a missed move, too much thinking, a loss of focus—challenge yourself to turn it around within that setting. Set a goal to regain your positive focus or total connection with your performance as quickly as possible. The next time that you are about to become upset because of someone or something, shift to a focus that will allow you to respond in a more positive way. Refocusing in a constructive way is one of life's great challenges. If doing it was easy, everyone would be good at it—but few of us are. Nevertheless, each of us can significantly improve our ability to sustain our focus in more positive and connected ways. Make this your daily goal. Whenever you are successful, make a note of what you focused on to achieve success. Doing so will help you reach your desired destination.

Changing Focus

Sylvie Bernier, an Olympic champion in diving, began to work seriously on distraction control about one and a half years before she won the Olympics. Previously, she had suffered from distractions that resulted in inferior performances, especially on the last dives of a competition. Sylvie's main distraction was paying attention to the scoreboard (leaderboard) instead of focusing on her own dives.

> I started to shift away from the scoreboard a year and a half before the Olympics because I knew that every time I looked at the scoreboard, my heart went crazy. I couldn't control it. I knew that I dove better if I concentrated on my diving instead of concentrating on everyone else. It was harder to get ready for 10 dives than to get ready for 1 dive, so I decided to stop looking at everyone else, to just be myself and focus on preparing for my next dive. That was the best way for me to concentrate for my event. I knew I could win, but I had to dive

well. I stopped saying, *This diver's doing this, so she's going to miss this one*, or *If she misses one, I'm going to win*.

At the Olympics I really focused on my dives instead of on other divers. That was the biggest change in those two years. Before that, I used to watch the event. I'd watch the Chinese and think, *Oh, how can she do that? She's a great diver*. Then I thought, *I'm as good as anyone else, so let's stop talking about them and focus on my own dives*. That was an important step in my career.

Recovering from Setbacks

Silken Laumann, an Olympic medalist and 1991 world champion in rowing, had the unfortunate experience of having a men's rowing crew run right through her boat, breaking it in half, during her warm-up at an international regatta in Essen, Germany. She sustained a serious injury to her lower leg, and her calf muscle was severed. This happened eight weeks before the 1992 Barcelona Olympics. She flew home for surgery and rehabilitation, and had five reconstructive operations to repair her leg.

Almost everyone assumed that it would be impossible for her to compete in the Barcelona Olympics. She showed up at the Olympics, limping with the help of a cane. Her competitors asked her if she would be commentating as a media person for rowing. She said, "No, I am here to compete." Their mouths dropped open in disbelief. Silken had decided that she didn't really need that leg to row and that she was going to compete anyway, although she had done only limited on-water training over those eight weeks.

Race day came at the Olympics. Silken limped down to her boat and needed help to get in. Nevertheless, she qualified for the Olympic final. In the final race, halfway down the course, she was still with the leading group. At that point in the race she said that she was feeling so tired that she thought she could not pull another stroke. At that instant, she refocused by deciding to pull 10 strokes. *Anyone can pull 10 strokes*, she thought. So she pulled 10 strokes, and then another 10 strokes, and then another 10, all the way to the finish line. When she looked up at the scoreboard after crossing the line, there was her name—Silken Laumann, bronze medal.

After the race, she commented, "I was up for a completely committed effort. . . . I'd come so far and thought that if I could commit just a little more energy, I could win a medal." And she did, by breaking her huge challenge into little pieces—only 10 strokes, an effort that she thought anyone could get through. Four years later at the 1996 Atlanta Olympics, Silken won a silver medal and retired from competitive rowing to pursue other meaningful challenges in life.

Lori Fung, Olympic champion in rhythmic gymnastics, provides another example of recovering from setbacks. Her goal in preparing herself for major competitions was to be consistent in all her performances and not to allow one bad move or one bad routine to affect the next. She discussed the importance of refocusing between events, especially after making an error:

> If you have a bad routine, you've got to get back to zero again. You just have to say, "OK, that's forgotten. It's totally forgotten. That's it." You go out, do the next one, pretend that the next one is the first routine of the day, and it is going to count. Otherwise, you are never going to pull back again. You can't do anything about it. You can't do anything about the score you're getting. You can't do anything about why you dropped that one move or how great it was; it's over and done with. Sometimes it's really hard to make yourself forget it, but the more you try, the better you're going to get at it in the future.

Keeping Your Focus

Laurie Graham, winner of many World Cup races in downhill skiing, discovered that to win at the highest levels she had to focus through the potential distraction of small errors within a downhill race:

> Once I push out at the start, I am focused on where I am at the time. A lot of it is "line" in downhill. You don't go right at the gate. You've got the line that you have been running all week, and you just say, *OK, I've got to stay high here, I have to go direct here, I have to jump this jump*, so that you are aware of each obstacle as it comes. If I make a small mistake, often it doesn't even register for me until the end, when I'm at the bottom. At the time you are still thinking about going forward, about speed, about momentum. You don't carry the mistake down the hill. It is shelved until later. Often those mistakes will mean just running them out, and it really won't cost you that much time if you don't panic, if you just get back on track.

Focusing through distractions is probably the most important skill of all for consistently performing to your potential in important challenges or competitions. Perfecting this skill requires a lot of practice. What focus do you want to carry today? Think about it. Make it clear in your mind. Know that you can make it happen. You have the capacity to live that focus today and everyday. Take control. Make it happen.

CHAPTER 8

Positive Images

Thoughts, images, or feelings run through our minds at some time or another as we draw near significant upcoming events—making or receiving an important call; doing

> *Your images lead your reality. They always have and always will.*

something for the first time; meeting someone new; going out on a date; doing an audition, presentation, or job interview; or preparing for a challenge or competition. Do you run through, or mentally rehearse what you want to do, what you want to say, what you want to project, or how you want to "be" or perform in the specific context that you are about to enter?

In your everyday life and in your performance life, do your thoughts and images help you create the realities that you would like to live? Do your thoughts and images ever interfere with your chances of reaching your goals and living your dreams?

When you begin to guide your focus and mental images in positive ways, you begin to create a better you in many different parts of your life. Through positive imagery you can prepare yourself to perform closer to the way that you would prefer to perform, respond more effectively to expected and unexpected distractions that might arise in a variety of contexts, and become more like the person you would really like to be. You can use your positive thoughts, images, and experiences to guide your performance and your life in positive ways.

Mental imagery provides an opportunity to create a better reality and allows you to deal effectively with problems, challenges, or events in your mind before you confront them in real life. If a challenge that you have prepared for mentally does arise, you are better able to handle it, cope with it, or focus through it. You have already lived the reality, faced the challenge, practiced some means of coping with it, overcome the challenge, or seen it from a different, more positive perspective. You have been successful in your mental reality, if not yet in your physical reality.

By guiding your mental images in positive and creative ways, you can enter a variety of real situations, including performances and competitions, with the feeling that you have been there before. You can enter the situation thinking, *It's no big surprise. There's no reason to panic. I've prepared for this; I can handle it. I choose to be here. I want to be here. There is no place I would rather be. I am ready. I am focused.* The only remaining step is to focus fully on the step in front of you and allow good things to unfold.

Positive Imagery in Performance

In sport and other performance situations, you can use mental imagery primarily to help you get the best out of yourself in training, competitions, or performances, and to open the door to becoming what you can be. Mental imagery is also highly effective when you have limited practice time, are making a comeback, or are recovering from an injury because you can repeat many successful experiences (in your mind) in a relatively short time without the physical risk or fatigue sometimes associated with doing those skills or performances in the real world.

One of the reasons that mental imagery can be so valuable in performance contexts is that the human brain cannot distinguish between an imagined experience and a real experience. Both are equally real for your brain. The same areas of the brain light up in an imagined experience or imagined performance as in a real experience or performance. For that reason, positive performance imagery has enormous potential.

When you repeatedly imagine yourself doing what you want to do, performing the way that you want to perform, and being what you want to become, you are putting yourself on a path to create a more positive future reality. Successfully repeating skills, moves, performances, or experiences in your mind and feeling those experiences in your body is often as good as doing them in your physical reality because you can do them perfectly and your brain views them as real.

You need a certain number of successful experiences to create an integrated net of nerve cells (neuronets) in your brain to perform a skill at a high level with consistency.

> A fundamental rule of neuroscience is the nerve cells that fire together, wire together. If you do something once, a loose collection of neurons will form a network in response, but if you don't repeat the behavior, it will not "carve a track" in the brain. When something is practiced over and over again, those nerve cells develop a stronger and stronger connection, and it gets easier and easier to fire that network (Arntz, Chasse, & Vicente, 2005, 147).

Creating Advantages

Quality mental imagery training provides an opportunity to create mental, physical, technical, and motivational advantages in your preparation and performance. You can create the mind-set, performance, and reality that you would like to live without external interference. In a real sense, positive images lead positive realities.

As far back as the 1984 Olympics, Canadian swimmer Alex Baumann was using imagery to help him win two Olympic gold medals and set two new Olympic and world records in the 200-meter and 400-meter individual medley. In an interview I did with Alex shortly after those races, he spoke about the role that visualization or imagery played in his success:

> The best way I have learned to prepare mentally for competitions is to visualize the race in my mind and to put down a split time. The splits I use in my imagery are determined by my coach and me for each part of the race. For example, in the 200 individual medley, splits are made up for each 50 meters because after 50 meters the stroke changes. These splits are based on training times and what we feel I am capable of doing.
>
> In my imagery I concentrate on attaining the splits I have set out to do. About 15 minutes before the race I always visualize the race in my mind and "see" how it will go. I see where everybody else is, and then I really focus on myself. I do not worry about anybody else. I think about my own race and nothing else. I try to get those splits in my mind, and after that I am ready to go. That is what really got me the world record and Olympic medals. . . . I started visualizing six years before the Olympics. My visualization has been refined more and more as the years went on. I see myself swimming the race before the race really happens, and I try to be on the splits. I am really swimming the race. In my mind I go up and down the pool, rehearsing all parts of the race, visualizing how I actually feel in the water.

The split times that Alex was swimming in his mind in preparation for his Olympic wins were the times that he thought he needed to swim in order to win and to break the Olympic and world records. He never swam those times in a real pool until he swam them at the Olympics.

I have worked with other athletes who have become Olympic champions in other sports (like Alwyn Morris, gold medalist in flatwater kayaking) who have put clocks on their imagery to ensure that their timing and pacing are exactly what they want them to be in major events. They were keen to do it and had fun doing it. Others were not as interested in taking their imagery that far, which is also fine. They looked for other ways to gain an advantage.

Imagining Success

Imagining in your mind and body the feeling of executing the moves that you need to be successful can help you accomplish those moves in the real world. Positive imagery can also enhance your confidence because you are repeating performance skills in your mind and body with focus and precision, exactly the way you would like to do them.

Using video imagery is a great way to make this happen. In 1992 I was part of a 22-week mental imagery study done with 7- to 10-year-old Chinese table tennis (Ping-Pong) players who were attending a sports school in China (Li-Wei, Qi-Wei, Orlick, and Zitzelsberger, 1992). During the study, all the children continued to participate in the same physical, technical, and fitness training that they did before the experiment, and they spent the same total amount of time on training during the course of the study.

The children were divided into three equally skilled groups. Group 1 participated in the experimental mental training program, which included relaxation sessions, video observation sessions, and mental imagery sessions. The video sessions consisted of watching a collection of table tennis techniques executed by 12 top Chinese table tennis players (all of whom were world champions). The children were asked to choose the player they liked best or with whom they felt most compatible. Then, as they watched the videos, they imagined themselves making the same forehand and backhand smashes as their role models. They did this hundreds of times, and then before they physically

► Watching the technique of a great athlete such as Mia Hamm can enhance imagery. Assist your own imagery by watching an outstanding athlete in your sport.

practiced with a real table tennis racket, ball, and table, they recalled the feeling of the moves that they had watched and imagined in the video.

Group 2 watched the same videos as group 1 did, but they were not asked to imagine themselves making the same great moves as the pros. Group 2 also didn't participate in the relaxation sessions. Group 3 did only their normal physical and technical training. The children in group 1 made significant improvements in the quality and accuracy of their shots and performance when compared with the other two groups. Two of the children in this group also placed in the top three in a national table tennis competition held that year against children of the same age from other sports schools in China.

For many years I have witnessed similar kinds of success using video imagery with national team athletes. These athletes used video imagery mostly to improve their performance skills, correct technical errors or unwanted performance habits, or be inspired by the outstanding people they were watching. In one case a national team paddler had a technical problem that had been ongoing for many years. He resolved the problem by watching video of one of the world's best technical paddlers, and while watching he tried to make the same movements in his own mind and body (often getting in his paddling position with a real or imaginary paddle in his hands). This paddler became an Olympic medalist.

In another case a national team skier had been experiencing a technical problem with her approach to gates for many years. She was able to resolve the problem with two weeks of intensive video imagery work. She watched video of a technically great skier (whom she admired), skied gates perfectly in her mind, and felt the perfect technique in her body hundreds of times. This skier became an Olympic medalist.

In another situation an Olympic skier was at a training camp where the weather and lack of snow became a concern. She had many things to work on before the first World Cup race and almost no time for training on snow. So she started to visualize a lot more—taking some time each day to keep skiing in her head, trying to feel the motion through her body, keeping her body alert to the feeling that it should be looking for. For some of her imagery sessions, she put on her ski boots, got herself in her start position (in her hotel room), and focused on feeling the forward pressure on the front of her boots—relaxing her ankles, feeling grounded in her boots, feeling the speed, feeling her skis carving the turns, skiing flawlessly.

She also pulled out some videos of her best races and videos of other great racers so that she could emulate certain parts of their skiing. She skied with them in her mind and body while watching the videos. "It really helped," she said.

Improving Technique

Most athletes who make fast progress and ultimately become their best make extensive use of performance imagery. It leads them where they want to go. Some athletes use it daily as a means of directing what will happen in their day, in their training, and as a way of preexperiencing their best performances. Mental imagery often starts out simply by thinking through your daily goals, your moves, your game plan, and your desired competitive performances. With practice, you will eventually be able to draw on various senses to experience in your mind and body the flawless execution of many of your goals, moves, performances, focus plans, and refocusing strategies.

For many years, an Olympic figure skater had experienced inconsistency with a particular skill. I asked her to try to visualize herself doing it while I was sitting with her. She was unable to imagine herself completing the skill successfully. She would see herself making an error (the same one that she usually made in the real world) and stop at that point, or the image would break up.

After this first attempt, I asked her to practice doing that skill mentally for approximately 10 minutes every night for a week. I suggested that she take it in steps. First, she tried to get past the point where she made the error or the image broke up, without worrying about her form. She needed several nights of mental practice just to get through that point in imagery. Next, she began working on consistently getting through the complete skill in imagery and refining her form. Finally, she focused on feeling herself do the skill perfectly and fluidly several times in a row.

As soon as she began to feel herself performing the skill flawlessly in imagery, she started to do it correctly in real practice situations. Within two weeks of our initial session, she was doing that skill with more quality and consistency than she ever had before.

This skater usually did her mental imagery in the evening just before going to sleep. She would lie in bed, close her eyes, and try to call up the desired feeling. Later she began to run through the skill in imagery just before doing it on the ice. Finally, while standing in the arena at a competition, she was able to look at the ice, map out her program, and feel herself going through it flawlessly; this set the stage for a clean, focused performance.

Sharpening Focus

Many athletes find it helpful to imagine and feel themselves performing certain skills or movements perfectly just before competitive performances. High jumpers feel their ideal jumps, divers their perfect dives, skiers their best runs, gymnasts their perfect routines, and archers their shooting sequence for bull's-eyes. Team sport athletes run through key offensive moves, quick transitions, or great defensive moves and remind themselves where their focus needs to be to perform at their best in the game.

Positive preperformance images strengthen your mental readiness and confidence because they center you on the feeling and focus of your best performances. They get you fully focused on what you need to focus on, usually the task at hand or the step in front of you. They serve as a last-minute or last-second reminder of the focus that you have chosen to carry into this game, race, routine, or performance. They take your thoughts away from worry or self-doubt, boost your confidence, get you focused on doing what you came here to do, and free your mind and body to perform.

A final reminder that you may want use just before performing is to call up the essential image, feeling, rhythm, relaxed power, or pace of the skill, movement, or action that you are about to perform. Then just focus ahead and go. Clear images that are fresh in your mind just before you begin a performance will usually stay with you during your performance.

Mental imagery can also be used after a successful performance to reexperience the successful aspects of your performance while the performance feeling and focus are still fresh in your mind. This routine can help you prepare for your future best performances. Imagery after an unsuccessful performance can also help you improve if you review the parts that you did well, target areas in which you got off track, and draw out positive lessons to act on for your next best performance.

Best Images

The world's best athletes have extremely well-developed imagery skills. They use imagery daily to prepare themselves to get what they want out of training, to perfect skills within training sessions, to make technical corrections, to overcome obstacles, to imagine themselves succeeding in competition, and to strengthen their belief in their capacity to achieve their ultimate goals.

The refined performance imagery that highly successful athletes, astronauts, musicians, surgeons, and actors have developed often involves feeling as if they are actually living the performance and feeling the sensations. Even the best performers, however, typically did not have good control over their mental imagery when they first began using it. They perfected this mental skill through persistent daily use and focused practice.

Picturing the Perfect Dive

I did my dives in my head all the time. At night, before going to sleep, I always did my dives. Ten dives. I started with a front dive, the first one that I had to do at the Olympics, and I did everything as if I was actually there. I saw myself in the pool at the Olympics doing my dives. If the dive was wrong, I went back and started over. For me it was better than a workout. I felt like I was on the board. Sometimes I would take the weekend off and do imagery five times a day. It took me a long time to control my images and perfect my imagery, maybe a year, doing it every day. At first I couldn't see myself. I always saw everyone else, or I would see my dives wrong all the time. I would get an image of hurting myself, or tripping on the board, or I would see something done really badly. As I continued to work at it, I got to the point where I could feel myself on the board doing a perfect dive and hear the crowd yelling at the Olympics. I worked at it so much, it got to the point that I could do all my dives easily. Sometimes I would even be in the middle of a conversation with someone, and I would think of one of my dives and do it (in my mind).

Sylvie Bernier, former Olympic champion in springboard diving

Listening to Your Feelings

My imagery is more just feel. I don't think it is visual at all. I get this internal feeling. When I'm actually doing the skill on the ice, I get the same feeling inside. It is an internal feeling that is hard to explain. You have to experience it, and once you do, then you know what you are going after. I can even get a feeling for an entire program. Sometimes in a practice I get myself psyched into a program that will win. I step on the ice and go to my starting position, and I get this feeling that I'm at the Olympic Games. I get this internal feeling how this program will be. Usually I'm fresh, and usually it will be a perfect program. I don't just step out there in training and say, *Here we go, another program*.

Brian Orser, former world champion and two-time Olympic silver medalist in men's figure skating

Correcting Skills Mentally

Sometimes I think, *Why did I miss that one move? OK, I know what happened, I pulled my body in too close to the apparatus. OK, now how do I avoid that?* Then I try to see myself doing it correctly in imagery. I can actually see the apparatus coming down; I can see the stripe on the club as it rotates, the same way you'd see it when you're doing the routine; that's the best way. Most of the time I look at it from within, because that's the way it's going to be in competition. It is natural because I do the routines so many times that it's drilled into my head, what I see and how I do it. So if I think about a certain part of my club routine, or my ribbon routine, I think of it as the way I've done it so many times, and that's from within my body.

Lori Fung, former Olympic champion in rhythmic gymnastics

The earlier that you begin your imagery training, the better off you'll be. I recall a talented eight-year-old gymnast who was capable of incredibly clear imagery. She began doing mental imagery completely on her own with no knowledge that many great athletes practiced it. She would lie in bed at night running through her routines. For her it seemed a natural thing to do. She was able to see the people around her, feel the moves, and experience the emotions.

I remember a 19-year-old college basketball player who had been experiencing difficulty with a particular play sequence in the heat of the game. I asked her to try to imagine herself executing the play properly and driving in for a successful lay-up. She closed her eyes and sat quietly for a couple of minutes. When I asked what had happened in the imagined scene, she said that she had seen a bunch of Xs and Os on a chalkboard going through the pattern of the play.

Contrast this with the vivid mental imagery that Bill Russell was using when he was 18 years old. Russell became one of the best basketball players ever, winning 11 NBA Championships as leader of the Boston Celtics. He describes his use of mental imagery in his book *Second Wind* (Russell and Branch, 1979, 73–74):

> Something happened that night that opened my eyes and chilled my spine. I was sitting on the bench watching Treu and McKelvey the way I always did. Every time one of them would make one of the moves I liked, I'd close my eyes just afterward and try to see the play in my mind. In other words, I'd try to create an instant replay on the inside of my eyelids. Usually I'd catch only part of a particular move the first time I tried this; I'd miss the headwork or the way the ball was carried or maybe the sequence of steps. But the next time I saw the move I'd catch a little more of it, so that soon I could call up a complete picture.
>
> On this particular night I was working on replays of many plays, including McKelvey's way of taking an offensive rebound and moving quickly to the hoop. It's a fairly simple play for any big man in basketball, but I didn't execute it well and McKelvey did. Since I had an accurate vision of his technique in my head, I started playing with the image right there on the bench, running back the picture several times and each time inserting a part of me for McKelvey. Finally I saw myself making the whole move, and I ran this over and over. When I went in the game, I grabbed an offensive rebound and put it in the basket just the way McKelvey did. It seemed natural, almost as if I were just stepping into a film and following the signs. When the imitation worked and the ball went in, I could barely contain myself. I was so elated I thought I'd float right out of the gym. Now for the first time I had transferred something from my head to my body. It seemed so easy. My first dose of athletic confidence was coming to me when I was 18 years old.

Russell immersed himself in the vivid mental replication of a skilled athlete executing a fast-moving play on the court and driving in for the basket; then he acted out that image and turned it into a living reality. Later he began to create many of his own moves in his mind before ever playing them out on the court.

Developing Imagery Skills

No matter how good or how limited your mental imagery skills are now, you can improve them through daily practice both at home and on-site in your training or performance setting. The more quality imagery you do on-site and off-site, the more quickly your imagery will improve.

If you have never done any systematic imagery training, start with simple, familiar images or skills. For the next week or two set aside five minutes a day, either before going to practice or before going to sleep, to work on your imagery. Let yourself relax. Shut your eyes.

Try to imagine the place where you usually train—what it looks like, how it smells, how it feels when you walk in. Imagine the people there, the first things you do to warm up, the look and feel of the playing surface, and the equipment that you use. Try to imagine and feel yourself doing some basic skills in your sport, such as easy running, skipping, free skiing, skating, dribbling, kicking, passing, throwing, rolling, jumping, swinging, turning, riding, moving freely. Through imagery, gradually increase the complexity of the skills.

As a rule, you should get into a pattern of doing about 10 to 15 minutes of quality imagery every day. Most Olympic and world champions do at least 15 minutes of imagery daily. Many do more because they also watch video and do video imagery sessions, particularly when preparing for major competitions, coming back from an injury, or returning to active sport-specific training after taking some time off. They also use mental imagery to run through their race plans, game plans, focusing plans, distraction control plans, and refocusing plans so what they need is fresh in their minds when they need to draw on it. Finally, before competing, most great performers call up flashes of confidence-enhancing images from past best performances and projected future best performances.

Besides helping you perfect physical and technical skills, mental imagery is itself a great focusing exercise. You must focus to create and control the images or feelings that you want to experience in your mind or body. This mental exercise can sometimes be tiring, especially in the beginning. So take your time and move into it gradually. Doing short periods of high-quality imagery throughout the day is better than doing long periods of low-quality imagery.

Keep in mind that your ultimate objective is to reexperience or preexperience ideal performances using the senses that you use in real performances. When perfecting performance skills through your imagery, try to call up the feeling, not merely something visual. The more vivid and accurate the feeling, and the more effectively that you perform within that image, the greater your chances of replicating the image in the real situation. With daily practice, your imagery skills will improve immensely, and your imagined performances will feel real, in the same way that your nighttime dreams feel real.

A good way to perfect feeling-oriented imagery is to integrate a piece of your sport or performance equipment and actually move your body while doing the imagery. Instead of lying down, get into your normal starting position for executing the skill. For example, a kayak paddler can sit with her knees bent and arms up, either holding a paddle or as if holding a paddle, and then move her arms through a paddling motion as she imagines and feels perfect execution in her mind and body. In the quiet of his apartment or an empty field, a baseball player can stand up, step into the batter's box, see the windup, swing a real or imaginary bat, and feel the pop of the ball as he imagines and feels his perfect swing and contact. A basketball player can move her body (with or without the ball) and feel perfect shots, beautifully handled passes, and perfect execution of a variety of offensive and defensive skills.

An NHL and Canadian Olympic hockey goalie I worked with prepared for each of his games by going up into the stands before each game when no one was in the rink. He sat in the stands behind the goal that he was going to start in with his stick in his hand. He imagined himself focusing on the puck so that he could pick it up early, reading the play, making one awesome save after another, and reacting quickly to stop multiple rebounds off his pads. For key games he anticipated moves that the top scorers on the opposing team would make. He stopped those shots in his mind before the game even started.

When you are learning to do imagery, some physical movement often helps you call up the feelings associated with the skill. A gymnast, skater, or dancer can run through a complete imagined routine on the floor, stage, or ice with feeling by imagining the moves as she walks, skates, or dances across the floor doing slight arm movements, body gestures, turns, and pauses. By combining mental imagery with real movement, you often feel more and this can speed up and enhance the complete learning process. As you become more skilled at feeling imagery, the sensations and emotions associated with best movements will surface more naturally in your imagined performances and real performances.

Most of the world's best athletes use imagery to prepare for training and competition, as well as to improve execution of their skills. Before arriving at the training site, they often mentally run through what they want to accomplish that day and decide what they will focus on to do it. Before performances, they run through key skills or strategies and imagine themselves executing parts of their performance perfectly. They often imagine themselves in the competitive arena—with the sights, sounds, feelings, excitement, spectators, competitors, and coaches—and then focus only on their own best performance.

Imagery can also play a key role in familiarizing yourself with a particular competition venue. In sports like alpine skiing, big-mountain free skiing, mountain bike or road racing, whitewater kayak racing, cross-country skiing, and triathlon, internalizing the course is important. The best performers in such pursuits use imagery extensively to learn the course so that they know exactly what is coming and feel ready to negotiate whatever lies ahead of them, such as when or where to initiate a change in direction, pace, or strategy.

During the course inspection, they memorize the course and run it through their minds over and over. After they know all the critical landmarks, they imagine themselves going through the course or racing certain parts of the course, seeing key markers, and feeling themselves do what they want to do in the race. Without this mental familiarization process, the risk factor, especially in speed sports, would increase dramatically, and competitors in many sports wouldn't have the confidence needed to let it go and give everything.

Mental Imagery for Coping Skills

Mentally preparing yourself to cope effectively with distractions, potentially stressful situations, or negative thinking is an important yet largely overlooked aspect of the mental imagery process. If you can see and feel yourself respond the way that you would prefer to respond to a variety of potential distractions, you will be better prepared to respond effectively in the real world. You can mentally rehearse an effective response to almost any situation that might arise or anything that you would like to approach in a more positive manner, including a competitor staring at you, a coach screaming at you, or a stadium filled with 100,000 people. You just have to imagine the situation and see or feel yourself focusing and responding the way that you would prefer to focus or respond in that context.

Mental rehearsal lets you prepare for and practice effective responses in your mind before you confront a real-life challenge, problem, or distraction. This kind of learning can feel real in your mind, yet it lacks the serious consequences that sometimes occur in the real world. The mental run-through of your preferred response makes it possible to enter a potentially threatening situation feeling better prepared, less fearful, more confident, and more in control. Perhaps even more important, it gives you something positive to focus on to get back on track quickly when you actually face that challenging situation.

When you think about the focus that you want to carry into a game or performance, you are mentally preparing yourself to do what you want to do in this performance. When you decide to carry this focus into the game or performance, you enhance your performance by eliminating potential problems and respecting the focus that works best for you.

Imagine yourself at your performance site feeling positive, staying positive, relaxing, overcoming obstacles, focusing only on the task at hand, stretching your limits, and achieving your goals. Whatever you want to do in your sport or your life, you can turn into reality by imagining yourself doing it, step by step, and then by focusing fully on doing it, step by step.

A world-class water skier became extremely anxious during important competitions when she passed the first buoy on the way to the slalom run. When she passed this buoy she would say to herself, *Oh no, here it comes*, and tenseness would overcome her entire body. She decided to employ mental imagery to practice using the buoy as a signal to relax. She imagined herself skiing by the buoy and saying to herself, *Relax*, at which point she would relax her shoulders and think, *You're ready—just let it happen*. This process helped her alleviate the problem in the real situation and freed her to win the world championships.

A highly ranked figure skater became extremely stressed in important competitions. She was particularly distraught just before starting her program. She tried to imagine herself at the competition site, just as the stress began to rise. As the anxious feelings began to surface, she imagined herself relaxing. She focused on her breathing and said to herself, *Nice and smooth—flow*. She then imagined herself doing her first few moves in a calm, controlled, focused manner. She mentally practiced this refocusing strategy in her mind to feel the effectiveness of her strategy. Later, she used the strategy during her competitions and felt focused and in control.

Many athletes have used mental imagery to change channels, reduce stress, shift focus, cope more effectively, and improve performance in a variety of situations. National team archers attending a national training camp shared with me several creative uses of imagery. The following examples of archers who combined simulation and imagery show how you can be creative in putting together workable strategies and how different approaches work for different people.

A world champion archer spoke about how she used imagery to transport herself to the world championships from her practice site. Instead of seeing the single target that was actually in front of her, she saw targets stretched across the field. She was fully aware of her competitors. On her right was the leading Polish archer, on her left a German. She could see them, hear them, and feel them. She shot her rounds under those conditions in the same sequence as she would shoot in the real competition. She prepared herself for the competition and distractions by creating the world championships in imagery and by shooting under mentally simulated world championship conditions—at practice.

A leading member of the men's national team did just the opposite. In the actual competition he was able to simulate practice conditions mentally. As he prepared to draw his bow to shoot his first arrow at the world championships, his heart was pounding. He glanced down at his tackle box (holding equipment and odds and ends) and noticed the words *Go, go, go*, which one of his hometown buddies had painted in red. That note triggered another reality—a flashback to familiar grounds. From that point on in the competition, he was on his practice range at home, with one small battered target in front of him. He could even hear some of his buddies on the practice field chattering and joking in the background, in place of the chatter of those of different nations who surrounded him. He shot in a steady, collected, and relaxed manner, as if he were at home.

In many cases, mental imagery is a first step that performers take to improve certain skills or overcome anticipated problems. Imagery gets you started. It is not highly time consuming, and you can do it yourself, wherever and whenever you choose. Sometimes mental imagery can itself lead to your overcoming a particular problem or improving your performance. The usual sequence, however, is to begin with mental imagery of what you want to happen, practice the imagined skill or coping strategy in a real-world training situation, introduce the skill or focusing strategy in a simulated competition situation, and finally use it in the real performance event.

CHAPTER 9

Simulation

Simulation training lets you practice your desired performance responses, as well as your focusing and refocusing strategies, in circumstances that are as real as you can make them before you take them into the real situation. Astronauts were among the first to make extensive use of simulation training to improve the quality of their performance and their overall effectiveness in real-time situations.

> *To have been there before and succeeded without ever having been there—that is the goal of simulation.*

In preparation for each mission into space, astronauts simulate every potential condition that they could experience in space, including launch procedures, in-flight and surface activities, and many possible malfunctions, so that they can practice appropriate responses for each. The cost of error is high when human life and billions of dollars are at stake, so no effort is spared to ensure that the astronauts are well prepared for their mission, without their having ventured into space on the specific mission.

Before they leave the launch pad, they feel totally ready, as if they have been there before. They know that they can perform effectively and handle any problems that arise that are within their potential control. Astronauts also do extensive performance debriefs to evaluate every aspect of the performance and draw out lessons for improvement after each simulation and each mission to space. One of NASA's most respected astronauts, Chris Hadfield, described the critical importance of simulation training and performance debriefs for successful space flights:

> We simulate a tremendous amount in preparation for space flight, and we try to make our simulations and our simulators as realistic as possible. We work hard to set up a scenario that is realistic, that is credible, so that the people in the shuttle simulator feel as if they're in a shuttle and the people in mission control feel as if they're controlling a real shuttle. So there's an air of realism to it. Then we will set up the malfunctions so that you drive the system to its edges, try to get into a gray area. What if this failed? Would we know what to do? And so we try to drive ourselves to the edge.

We also debrief in exhaustive detail. The way the debrief runs is that the person who was running the simulation, the flight director or the shuttle commander, has kept major event notes through the whole exercise, whether it's 4 hours or an 8-hour simulation or a 36-hour simulation, whatever. They will hit every single major event during the simulation and what went right, and thank the people who did it right. Or if there was a new way of doing something that worked better, we grab that lesson. Then we definitely get into the details of what went wrong or what was inefficient. Then actions are taken to put that into the flight rules or put that into the training from now on. Let's expand our collective brain power here. Let's learn from this thing.

We've flown the shuttle over 90 times, and we've made it look effortless. That is purely through accurate simulation and then incredible attention to detail in learning every lesson we can from every effort and rolling that back into the training flow so that the next one is even better. We implement things as quickly as possible. If it's something that is critical, we'll turn it around in a day.

For my first mission we did an actual full-crew simulation of the docking (with the space station) about 250 times. And then I simulated stages of it, or complete bits of it, in my head. I couldn't count the number of times I did that. I sat out on my deck at home, at night, and thought through it and practiced with it. When we actually got to do it, it was easy because of our detailed planning and detailed preparation. The most important thing is that you have enough representative training that when you get to the real test you aren't relying on chance and you can just focus down and get the job done.

In sport and many other performance domains, simulation training can help prepare you to perform closer to your capacity and get you ready to meet the challenges that you will likely face in your performance context. Simulation prepares you for the physical, technical, and mental demands through high-quality, high-intensity, focused training that replicates the performance demands of real performances or competition. It helps you prepare mentally for potential distractions so that you are better able to stay focused and get the job done, regardless of the demands of your event or the happenings around you.

Understanding Simulation Benefits

In the 1988 Winter Olympics, figure skater Elizabeth Manley (who subsequently became a professional figure skater and is now a coach) delivered her best-ever international performance, winning the long program and placing second overall. She previously had experienced problems with her long program and often worried before competing about whether she could get through a clean program, especially in major competitions. To perform to her capacity at the Olympics, she needed to be confident that she could skate the whole program with no problems and to know that she could maintain total focus on executing her skills.

To prepare herself fully, Liz did more run-throughs of her program that year than she had ever done before. In her final simulations, which took place in an arena similar in size to the Olympic arena, she imagined that she was skating at the Olympics. Liz was confident going into her long program at the Olympics, and she executed it flawlessly. She believed that the additional simulations had really helped.

Eric Heiden, one of the world's all-time best speed skaters, won five gold medals at the 1980 Winter Olympics. Speed skating is a high-intensity sport that involves lots of pain and discomfort when you are going flat out. To excel in this sport and others like it, you must learn how to relax and push through discomfort barriers. Toward the end of many events, your muscles are hurting, burning, screaming. An athlete can tolerate high levels of discomfort—if you know that you have decided to do this, that your success depends on doing this, that focusing through discomfort is within your capacity, that pushing through discomfort is helping you achieve your goals, and that you can always stop if you really have to. This is a battle that your mind must win over your body because in many sports you must push past discomfort barriers to explore your limits. Your focus definitely rules your body and your results, and your body will obey if you focus on the right things.

Eric often used simulation training to practice pushing forward through personal discomfort barriers. He even included the pain in his mental imagery of races, and he raced beyond the pain. By consistently pushing through discomfort barriers in training, he was well prepared to endure and extend his limits in major competitions. Sometimes he pushed so hard in training that after a hard piece his legs were too shaky to stand on.

Like Eric Heiden, speed skater Gaetan Boucher learned to train with incredible intensity. He used simulation training extensively in preparation for his double gold medal performance at the Olympics, but only after being inspired to step up his training after visiting and training with Heiden. In an interview that I did with Gaetan Boucher, he told me the following story:

> I was second in the world in 1979 and 1980. Heiden was first. I saw him train in the summer when I was with him for a week. He was the guy to beat. When I was second to him at the world championships, I said, "Next year at the Olympic Games I am going to win the 1000 meters, and he will be second." I believed that the whole summer until I went to see him training . . . because his training was so much harder. I thought I was training as hard as I could, and then I saw this guy training even harder. He started with a 10,000-meter warm-up of skating imitations on a small 200-meter track. You are in a skating

position, bent over. To do one lap of skating imitations is about the same as doing 400 meters on a track. He was doing that just as a warm-up, and he was going fast. I stopped after 20 laps. My legs were hurting, and that was just a warm-up. Then he did a 5000, 1500, and 1000 all at maximum speed, just like a race.

We took 5 to 10 minutes to rest after he did the 10,000-meter warm-up, and then he said, "OK, I am doing a 5000." So I followed him and stopped after 3000 meters. After that he did the 1500, fast. This time I did the whole 1500 meters, but he was pulling ahead. Then he did the 1000. I saw him stagger and almost fall from exertion after that interval. It was all in the legs, and it was hard! He said he had started the 5000 too fast, maybe because I was training with him. It was really fast. He was not keeping time. It was just the effort that was so impressive. The 1500 was maximum. The 1000 meters was maximum. Our team would do that same type of training and say, "Well, I have 5 or 10 laps to go. I'll go easier." He was doing the 5000 meters at the same speed I would do a 1500 or 3000. So after that experience I knew I could take more.

A 1500-meter race hurts most because it is almost all maximum. Heiden got ready for the pain through his preparation. I never used to do that. He even put the pain in his imagery for his mental run-through. He would think that it would hurt, and he would be ready to accept the pain, so he knew he could do it. When I raced the 1500 after that, I thought about the fact that it is going to hurt, and I was prepared for it. You have to be mentally ready to accept the pain.

After my training visit with Heiden, it was not my training itself that I changed, but my thoughts on how much I could take when I train. Before that visit I would do an interval that was supposed to be maximum, and I would think I was going maximum, but I could have taken more. So I changed my understanding of what I had to do to go to my maximum. My training method itself was not different, but the intensity I brought to year-round training was.

At his next Olympics in 1984 Gaetan Boucher won gold medals in the 1500- and 1000-meter races and a bronze medal in the 500 meters.

Replicating Performance Demands

If you replicate real performance demands or competition demands in training, you will be much better prepared to perform to your capacity in the real situation. But you must realize that you can't train with that kind intensity every day or every interval. You have to pick your times, pick your runs, pick the pieces when you really go all out and when you don't. Find ways to push your limits or replicate competition demands often enough to know that you can do it when it really counts. Remember that rest and recovery are also essential. Find ways to rest as much as possible, physically and mentally, after major simulations and before big performances.

You can overcome many adverse or unforeseen conditions if you have simulated similar conditions in practice. Performing under simulated adverse conditions is one way of knowing that you can do well in all kinds of circumstances. By anticipating and working through challenges or potential problem situations, you will enter them with less fear, better focus, and more confidence. Simulation helps you do what you are capable of doing in real situations because you know that you can do it and you know how to focus to do it. You also know that you can refocus or adapt to a variety of situations and still perform well. You can perform well if you arrive early or late, if you have a brief warm-up or even a poor warm-up. You can perform well whether you are up or down in points, feeling great or not feeling great, on target or slightly off target. All you have to do is focus on doing it.

Simulation of distractions that occur in your real-world contexts can prepare you to overcome all kinds of potential distractions. Think of the kinds of things that happen or might happen in a big meet or a key game. Consider introducing some of them into a practice or preparation setting. If you cannot replicate certain things in practice or in a preparation context, then simulate

© Reuters/Corbis

▶ Top athletes like Tiger Woods are prepared to perform under adverse conditions. Use simulation training to prepare for the unexpected.

them through your mental imagery so that you have at least worked through some effective responses in your mind. Then, in the real situation, if something does not go perfectly, it isn't a big deal, and you can focus right through it. You can perform well with announcements, interruptions, or distractions going on right in the middle of your performance, presentation, or mission.

Introduce expected competition demands and go through the normal sequence of your competition events in your practice or preparation sessions. For example, enter the gym, arena, or performance setting, warm up, get yourself ready, and then play your game, run through your events, or do your presentation, just as you would in your real-world performance context. Consider including judges, officials, audiences, cameras, and other athletes or adversaries at these simulated performances. Some athletes and teams with whom I have worked found that something as simple as wearing their competition uniforms, racing bibs, or performance costumes during time trials, dress rehearsals, or run-throughs made the simulation feel more real.

Run through your event, program, game, or race in conditions that you might face—in the rain, in the sun, in the heat, in the wind, in the cold, when tired, when fresh, after eating, after missing a meal, in the morning, in the afternoon, and in the evening. Practice overcoming difficult challenges, running different offenses and defenses, responding to false starts, reacting to someone who has passed you late in the race, coming off the bench, or coming on strong toward the final part of the race or game after you have slipped behind. Introduce sounds of applause or PA announcements just when you are beginning to start or are halfway through a routine. Warm up on your own and run through your events on your own, without your coach being there (your coach may be sick, stuck in traffic, or delayed at a meeting). By preparing in some of these ways you can go into almost any challenging situation feeling at ease and knowing that you can perform your best. This is the goal of simulation.

Coaches or team leaders can introduce unexpected changes that athletes or performers must adapt to. For example, the coach (or a friend role-playing the coach) can tell you that you have an hour to warm up but then start the performance or competition in 15 minutes instead (the bus was stuck in traffic, and your team arrived late). The coach can change the lineup, offense, defense, or order of events at the last minute; unexpectedly bring in judges, unfair officials, important evaluators; and so on. You can practice remaining calm and focused under all these simulated conditions. Coaches should openly discuss the reasons for introducing these kinds of simulated distractions before introducing them.

A young figure skater found that while she was waiting to perform in competitions, she often heard other skaters coming off the ice making negative comments like, "It is so hot out there . . . It was hard to get through the program." As she stepped on the ice herself, she worried about the heat and about how it would affect her performance. During the final minute of her last five-minute competition program, she was thinking, *It's so hot . . . my mouth is so dry . . . feels like there's no air . . . I don't think I am going to get through it.* She barely scraped through the last portion of her program and was not at all pleased with her performance. She had never worried about the heat in practice meets or exhibitions; her concern surfaced only in competitions, although the physical setup in exhibitions was basically the same: packed arena, bright lights, and high temperature. This led me to believe that the young skater's anxiety about performing well in competitions resulted more from the other skaters' comments about the heat than from the heat itself.

We discussed the possibility of practicing with an elevated arena temperature. This idea posed some logistical problems, so we decided to increase the skater's body temperature and leave the rink manager's body temperature alone. We agreed that at the next practice she would dress warmly in heavy clothing and try running through her full free program.

She reported back a few days later and said, "I did my program in practice with a big sweater and leg warmers. I was burning hot, but I didn't have a problem with it. I didn't even think about it." From that time on, heat was not a problem for her in competitions. Even if all the other skaters came off the ice complaining about the heat, she was never preoccupied with it. She knew that she had skated well through elevated heat in practice with no problem. She just needed to know that she could handle the situation without a problem—which she could. All she needed to do was focus on her skating, which she did. The simulation merely provided confidence-enhancing proof.

All performers gain from having confidence in their ability to do what they are capable of doing. Almost everyone would like to enter performances or competitions knowing in advance that they will get through their programs or perform to their capacity. Simulation helps build this kind of confidence. Some athletes find it helpful to do more in their simulations than they are required to do in their real performance or competition. For example, if you know that one five-minute performance program is required, do two in a row; if you know that your game will last an hour, play an additional half hour of high-intensity overtime.

To do multiple simulations, you must build up your performance level by setting progressively more challenging goals and by ensuring that you are well rested on the days that you choose to do these kinds of focused simulations. But after you are accustomed to doing more than is required, doing what is required is no big deal. If you are accustomed to playing four or five periods of fully focused high-intensity hockey or six quarters of high-intensity basketball in simulated competitive games, you should be able to enter the competitive arena with full confidence in your ability to maintain your focus and intensity for the mere three periods or four quarters. Top Asian gymnasts have successfully used this approach. I have seen them execute two complete routines in a row before dismounting. This is one reason that their routines are flawless in competition. Knowing that in practice they regularly do more than the competition demands gives them confidence that they can hit clean routines. The single remaining goal is just to focus on doing it.

You, your coach, and your teammates are in the best position to determine what kinds of simulated activities and conditions might be most helpful for you and your team in your sport or performance domain. The important advantage of relevant simulation training is that if you have been exposed to most of the expected and unexpected conditions and distractions that are likely to occur at your major events or competitions, you will be better equipped to stay focused and to perform your best under these conditions. If you have practiced focusing through distractions and doing more than is required, you will feel more prepared. You will know, somewhere deep in the core of your being, that you will do well. No sweat. Well, some sweat, but you'll know that you can nail it if you just keep your focus in the right place.

Simulation gives you some added confidence in knowing that you have the ability to do what you set out to do. Simulation helps you believe in yourself and your focus, which is crucial in all sports, all performance contexts, and on all missions. Your objective is to reach the point where you can face all kinds of challenges or distractions and still have confidence in yourself and your focus to come through. You know that your capabilities are there and your best focus is there with you—no matter what! You are then free to live your potential much more consistently.

Growing Through Others

Deciding to grow better and wiser from positive examples set by others is another effective way to improve yourself and your performance. You can gain greatly from attempting to draw from, act on, or live some of the positive attributes of any performer you respect or person you admire. You can consciously decide to borrow some of the best attributes from that person or performer in an attempt to improve yourself, your focus, or your performance. Often when I see, meet, observe, or get to know someone, I discover in that person some characteristics that I like or admire. That person could be a young child, student, family member, parent, teacher, coach, developing athlete, great athlete, performing artist, musician, surgeon, business executive, or outstanding performer in any field. You can gain from those people who have something that lives within them that you respect or admire. The attributes that you see may be related to their physical skills, technical skills, commitment, focus, connection to what they are engaged in, way of communicating, balance, or just their overall presence and way of being.

You can look for and selectively integrate other people's best qualities and strengths to better yourself technically, physically, mentally, emotionally, or spiritually. You can literally attempt to be that person in certain respects, to see how it feels for you. You can imagine yourself being that great athlete in stance, posture, and execution. You can tell yourself, Today I'm going to pretend I'm so-and-so, from the time I step out the door or onto the floor. I'm going to walk tall, the way he does, and try to execute my moves as gracefully; I'm going to be calm just like him, even if the coach starts yelling. I'm going to work really hard just like he does for the whole practice or game. You can make a conscious decision to be a certain way, or focus in a certain way, for a specified period. If it feels right and helps you, hang on to it. If not, let it slide.

Embracing special qualities that you admire in other people and nurturing the best qualities within yourself opens another path to becoming what you are capable of becoming. On the flip side, you can also learn what you do not want to be or become from observing others. For example, you might see a person or performer engaging in a behavior, technique, action, reaction, lifestyle, or way of being that is contrary to your values or the way that you want to be. You decide at that moment that you are not going to be like that, perform like that, or act that way. And then you do everything in your power to avoid behaving that way or becoming that kind of person or performer. The point is that you can learn valuable lessons from others by looking for their good parts and using those lessons to your advantage, and by noting their less admirable parts and using those lessons as reminders of what you don't want to become.

The quest to become what you want to become, but have not yet become, is important for excelling in many domains. We rarely start where we want to end up in terms of our specific skills, confidence, way of being, and focus. We have to develop those skills to become the confident, focused person that we choose to be.

Applying Simulation

Indonesian athletes were world champions in badminton for many years. They had a history of winning when it counted. When they were the best in the world, I watched them play; talked with them, their coaches, and their former world champions; and visited their training camps. One reason that they were on top of the world at that time was their extensive use of simulation training. They simulated every aspect of the game—their strategy, coming from behind, bad calls, high temperature, crowd effects—particularly for the world championships. You can adapt the basic ideas underlying this specific simulation program to whatever sport or challenge you are facing.

Long before the match, the top Indonesian players knew everything about their opponents—their strengths, weaknesses, playing style, and technical peculiarities. They studied videos of their opponents and gained from the experiences of teammates who had already faced them. They preplanned a strategy and mentally ran through exactly what they would do when their opponents did A, B, or C. Teammates sometimes role-played the actions of opponents in simulated games. The players knew where they should return the shuttle, or bird, for a particular opponent before they played him, and they prepared to place the bird accordingly before it ever reached them in the actual game.

They also practiced anticipating their opponents' returns, which meant knowing beforehand where the bird would likely go and planning to be there. If this strategy worked on 7 out of 10 shots, it was worth targeting the anticipated return area. In a sport like badminton, speed is closely linked to anticipation. The player must anticipate and move toward the return area before the bird is fully hit, particularly for a hard smash. (A hockey goalie or soccer goalie facing a hard shot must react in a similar way. To be successful, the goalkeeper must anticipate where the puck or ball will go and be there before the player makes full contact with the puck or ball. The puck or ball often moves to the goal faster than a goalie can react; correct anticipation is therefore essential.)

By studying where the bird (or ball) usually goes under various conditions and with different opponents, a player can greatly increase the chances of being in the right place at the right time. The top Indonesian players were undoubtedly quick, but they had much more than speed—they knew where and when to move. They were usually in the return area before the bird arrived, even on blistering shots in doubles play. They targeted their speed, anticipated their opponents' shots, and perfected their own strategies through simulation training.

The Indonesian players also used simulation to improve their performance by preparing themselves for the following performance situations:

➤ **Coming from behind.** Top players built confidence in their ability to come from behind and win a game by simulating specific come-from-behind game situations in practice. A game might start at 14 to 3—a stronger player would begin with 3 or 4 points and a weaker player with 13 or 14 points. The objective for the stronger player was to come back and win the game. For the weaker player, the objective was to prevent this from happening, or at least to have some strong rallies. With a proper matchup, both players could play hard and push their limits, and the stronger player would come back to win. This process gave less experienced players a chance to play the champions and the champions practice coming back from behind. For many years in the Thomas Cup championships, whenever the Indonesian players fell behind they were consistently able to come on strong to win. The fact that they were behind did not seem to distract them at all; they had practiced coming back. They knew that they would come back, they focused on doing it, and they did.

➤ **Bad calls.** Poor officiating—for example, calling a shuttle out of bounds when it is obviously in bounds—was simulated in practice to prepare players to overcome the frustration that can follow a bad call. The purpose of this simulation was discussed and then implemented in some practice games and exhibitions. Sometimes the simulating official would make a series of bad calls. The player's goal was to ignore the bad calls and focus on preparing for the next shot, to shift focus from something beyond his control to something within his control. There were no emotional outbursts or even second looks from the Indonesian players after questionable or close calls at the championships. They simply focused on getting ready for the next rally and got on with the game.

➤ **High temperatures.** For many years, the Thomas Cup championships were held in Jakarta under extreme temperature conditions. The outside air temperature in the evening was in the mid-30s Celsius (mid-90s Fahrenheit), and the humidity was in the 90s. The arena was packed with 12,000 sweaty people, and there was no air conditioning. Heat-producing television lights were set up right next to the court, and all windows and doors were closed to prevent drifting of the shuttles. Needless to say, it was hot! The spectators, including me, ended up dripping wet just sitting in the stands.

How did the Indonesian players prepare for those conditions? They prepared by living and playing in the heat and by bringing in large crowds to fill extremely hot and humid arenas for exhibition matches. If visiting teams are to play to their capacity under such extreme temperature conditions, they too must prepare for them. The best preparation is to practice and play exhibition games for a couple of weeks in the same time zone, in a similar climate, under similar conditions, and then rest well before the tournament. This approach prepares an athlete to walk into that arena and be ready to go the distance.

➤ **Crowd effects.** I have rarely heard fans roar as loudly as the crowd did in Jakarta for the badminton championships. The sound was deafening, and the crowd was definitely partisan. They heckled opponents and roared approval for their heroes' every shot. (The fact that badminton was their major sport and that a lot of private betting was associated with those games may explain some of the fans' enthusiasm.) In some countries a crowd of 12,000 people for a badminton match is unheard of; in Indonesia it was normal. The audience would have been much larger had the seating capacity in the halls been greater. Younger players learned to adapt to those crowds by growing up with them. The junior players and national team members traveled throughout the country giving exhibitions to large crowds. They invited the public to the main badminton hall in Jakarta for simulation matches in final preparation for the championships; the free invitation was accepted gratefully, and the hall was full. This final simulation was aimed at readying the athletes to walk onto the championship court feeling totally supported and completely prepared mentally.

➤ **Longer or more challenging games.** The best players often took on more in their training than was required for their championships. For example, they might play one and a half to two hours straight at an extremely fast pace. They might play whole games in which one player was allowed only to lob, or smash, or play defensively, or play to the backhand, while the other player could use all his moves. To keep the pace moving, to work on speed, and to develop anticipation, one player might play against two opponents, or multishuttle games might be introduced. In multishuttle games it is possible to play nonstop badminton, with a shuttle always in play, or to practice reacting to shuttles coming rapid fire from all corners of the court.

As a result of training for more than what was required on the day of the competition, the players were in superb physical condition. They used their fitness to their advantage, particularly in the extreme temperature conditions. They could maintain a very fast pace or deliberately keep a rally or game going for a long time simply to tire out their opponents.

▶ **Taller or different sized players.** When the taller top European players started to play well at the international level, the Indonesians developed a new simulation strategy to train their players to play more effectively against them. They built courts that were higher on one side, so that the players playing on that side were the same height as the taller top European players.

A former world champion and one of badminton's all-time greats believed that following three simple rules, which could easily be applied in practice simulation, gave a player an advantage both strategically and psychologically:

1. Never stop a game to change a shuttle when you are winning. If you lose two points in a row, change the shuttle.
2. Continue to use serves and shots that are working—often—but also use variation in your play. Otherwise, at the higher levels your opponents will anticipate your shots.
3. Never change a winning tactic or strategy.

While still at the top of their game, the Indonesian superstars worked directly with the most promising junior players. The reigning and longtime world champions in both singles and doubles spent about two days a week coaching and playing with younger players. The youthful players had an opportunity to play with their heroes, watch them at close range, learn from them, follow their actions, and be inspired by them. The championship players learned and gained from coaching and working with enthusiastic young players and enjoyed the sessions.

China now has most of the dominant players in badminton and has become a leader in many other sports as well. The Chinese are masters at simulation training, partly because simulation training originated long ago with traditional training in the martial arts and partly because it works. The Chinese are doing everything that the Indonesian players used to do and more. They make extensive use of video imagery training and have a strong central sport development program supporting their efforts.

The only country where I have witnessed in-depth simulation training that surpassed that of Indonesia was China. In table tennis, a sport that they have dominated for many years, the Chinese used simulation extensively and creatively. In the early 1980s Chinese badminton players were using some of the high-quality simulation procedures used by China's best table tennis players. In the latter part of 1980s China became the dominant badminton power in the world. They gained ground in many sports in the 1990s and are still gaining ground in the 2000s. The Chinese have become the masters of repetition and high-quality simulation and use it to their advantage in sports where they excel.

Simulation has played a major role in their tradition in martial arts (wushu, for example) for many years. It has also been applied in contemporary sports in which they excel, such as table tennis, badminton, volleyball, gymnastics, and diving. With their most successful teams, the Chinese went a step beyond what most other countries do with respect to repetition of skills, moves, and programs in training. They prepare their athletes to perform well when fatigued and to play well when competing against their most challenging opponents. For example, some skilled Chinese athletes have been trained to replicate the playing styles of top opponents from other countries to provide realistic simulation training for national team members. This kind of training has helped strengthen their overall readiness to face the challenges of high-level opponents and high-level competition.

When countries such as Malaysia, Korea, Denmark, Sweden, and England began to make extensive use of effective simulation training in badminton, they took a step up and produced some world leaders in the sport. Similarly, when the Europeans, notably the Swedes, began to implement some of the extensive simulation preparation strategies used by the Chinese in table tennis, for a time they became world leaders in that sport. The point is that a well-designed, high-quality simulation training program can prepare performers for the expected and the unexpected, and help them achieve their goals in almost any performance domain.

The one cautionary note about simulation training is to avoid overloading athletes or performers with too much simulation, too much repetition, too many performances, or too many competitions. Oversimulation, like overtraining, overworking, or overperforming, burns people out physically, psychologically, and emotionally. Excessive simulation can take the joy out of the pursuit, injure people physically or psychologically, lower their resistance to common illnesses, and take away the spontaneity that is sometimes needed for a truly great performance. We have to ensure that simulation, competition, and performance schedules work for us and the people with whom we work, not against us. A sense of joy must remain within the pursuit, and performers must have adequate rest and recovery. Individual differences must be respected in determining what works best and how much rest and recovery are required.

CHAPTER 10

Self-Hypnosis

One way to turn more of our life dreams into reality is through self-hypnosis, a state of relaxed receptivity that can release some of the untapped potential within each of us.

> *Belief is the mother of reality. Excellence is a state of mind.*

My father, Dr. Emanuel Orlick, worked in the area of hypnosis and self-directed mind control for over 75 years. At age 90 he was still living on his farm and writing a regular column for the *Journal of Hypnosis*. Two years later he passed away, and I am thankful that before that time he consented to share his perspectives on self-hypnosis by writing this chapter.

My father started doing hypnosis on himself when he was 12 years old after reading everything he could find about it in books available at that time. As a child I remember my father sitting down with the whole family in the living room and taking us through the basic relaxation script presented in this chapter (page 131). It always included positive suggestions like "Day by day you are getting better and better in every way."

The hypnosis that my father did had no resemblance to the hypnosis that you sometimes see stage performers do. They snap their fingers, and people fall into a trance and do bizarre things. The goal in stage hypnosis is entertainment. His goal and his process for reaching it were completely different.

He followed a similar procedure regardless of whom he worked with or what goal they were hoping to achieve. First, people had to relax completely. They then had to focus on seeing themselves, feeling themselves, and imagining themselves being the way that they wanted to be. From my perspective the process that he was engaged in was not scary or magical. The process involved relaxing, clearing the mind of clutter or negative interference, and focusing on good things and positive possibilities. Whenever you are able to do this, you increase your chances of having good things happen. My father used hypnosis as a way to enhance life and performance. In this chapter, he shares some simple guidelines on how you can apply this approach to your life.

The Power Within

Humans everywhere are looking both inside and outside themselves for ways to develop or use talents, abilities, or powers that they feel they possess. No matter how accomplished you are, you can be better. This is true for all your mind–body attributes, talents, and abilities. No matter how good any of these may be now, they can be better—much better.

All of us have within us amazing mind–body powers that sometimes come into play when we face life-or-death situations. Almost every newspaper has on file eyewitness accounts of people who have performed incredible feats of strength in dire situations. For example, all major news media carried reports of a 110-pound mother who lifted the back of a station wagon off the crushed legs of her screaming 17-year-old son after a jack slipped and he was trapped beneath the vehicle.

We all live and function far below our maximum mental and physical limits until something of sufficient importance triggers the use of our dormant mental and physical powers. Somehow, self-hypnosis can act as this triggering mechanism, thus enabling ordinary humans to perform superhuman mental and physical feats. With practice, each of us can significantly boost our normal, everyday mind–body levels.

Vasili Alexeev, one of the greatest Russian weightlifters of all time, was able to tap into his mind–body potential. Before each lift he appeared to enter a trancelike hypnotic state. Observers could feel his intense concentration as he stood over the ponderous barbell at his feet, preparing himself mentally to thrust it over his head. Spectators had the feeling that it was not only muscle power but some form of psychic energy that enabled Alexeev to lift those enormous weights and break one record after another.

Self-hypnosis substitutes one powerful, positive, dominating thought for a number of distracting, competing, negative thoughts; it substitutes one powerful, positive belief for a number of competing negative beliefs; it substitutes one powerful "I can" for a number of competing "I can'ts"; it suspends a host of critical, doubting, restraining, and interfering thoughts to focus all relevant mind–body faculties on accomplishing one goal to the exclusion of all others. Perhaps the simplest way to describe the focusing aspect of hypnosis is to compare it to a magnifying glass that can concentrate ordinary, harmless sun rays into one narrow point that can burn a hole through a piece of paper.

Performance Enhancement Techniques

Self-hypnosis and autosuggestion have the capacity to enhance your performance. In self-hypnosis you put yourself into a relaxed, receptive state. In this state the normal critical faculties of the conscious mind are temporarily suspended. Thus, you become receptive to any strong or repetitive suggestions that you make to yourself, either directly or indirectly. Under self-hypnosis you may talk to yourself, read previously prepared scripts, listen to prerecorded scripts, or listen to another person read scripts. In self-hypnosis you control everything, from start to finish, in each session.

In autosuggestion you directly or indirectly influence your thoughts or actions in the conscious, waking state. Autosuggestion can be intentional or unintentional and may have positive or negative effects. An example of positive autosuggestion can be seen in Muhammad Ali's constant repetition of the phrase "I am the greatest." His use of this phrase and his subconscious belief in himself played a major role in his rise to become one of the greatest boxers ever and to stay at the top over an extended period.

Both positive autosuggestion and self-hypnosis can help you in your performance activities. You can use autosuggestion by reading short scripts over and over; by repeating positive phrases to yourself; and by playing recorded suggestions to yourself as you drive to school, work, or training, or at any other time.

Think of your brain as a highly sophisticated computer that you program to direct your body in a certain way, just as the space center computers direct an unmanned vehicle to land on Mars. Your body is the vehicle; your brain is the computer. After your brain is programmed, your body must follow its commands, seek out the goals that you have established, and strive constantly to achieve them. You are the programmer, and you determine what you will feed into your brain.

Think of your ultimate goal. You must etch this goal deeply into your neuron pattern so that you will do everything in your power to achieve it. You must believe not only that you can achieve it but also that you will achieve it. I have never met a person who was a success at anything who did not believe in his or her ability to succeed. Unfortunately, most people around us, including our families and coaches, spend more time telling us what we cannot do than what we can do. Therefore, your first step is to instill in yourself an unshakable belief.

Through self-hypnosis your normal critical, judgmental, or negative thinking can be suspended temporarily so that you can more rapidly internalize the highest possible degree of absolute belief. After the belief becomes a permanent part of your subconscious thought process, you will automatically behave in accordance with it.

The secret of self-hypnosis is twofold:

1. You must fixate your conscious attention.
2. You must relax your body.

The moment that you do these two things, you are in self-hypnosis. Pick a spot on the wall in front of you right now and stare at it while you let your body become limp and relaxed. If you keep staring and relaxing for a few moments, you will feel yourself sinking deeper and deeper into self-hypnosis.

That is all there is to it. Even in this light hypnotic state, you can begin to program yourself with beneficial positive suggestions. Anyone can put himself into self-hypnosis simply by fixating his conscious attention and relaxing. With practice, you can go deeper and deeper, and the programming will become more and more effective. Even in the lightest state of hypnosis you can accomplish remarkable things, such as eliminating the pain of a throbbing headache, curing insomnia, improving your concentration, and so on.

Components of Hypnosis

Effective self-hypnosis involves fixation, relaxation, receptivity, and repetitive suggestion. Learning about each of these components will help you fixate your conscious attention, relax your body, and make your subconscious mind more receptive to the beneficial positive suggestions that you will make to yourself. After you are in a relaxed, receptive state, the most important thing is repetition. Whether you are programming yourself for the first time, reprogramming yourself, or reinforcing past programming, you should repeat each positive suggestion many times to implant it deeply and firmly in your subconscious mind.

Fixation

Although you can fixate your conscious attention on almost any external object, one of the most effective objects is a candle or a black dot in the middle of a piece of white paper. Any piece of white paper will do, and the black dot can be any size you wish. I usually use an index card on which I draw a circle with the help of a dime or other small coin. I then fill in the circle with a black marking pen. I have found that I get the best results when I place this card about 12 inches (30 centimeters) away from my eyes and a little above them. Also, I prefer to face a blank wall, preferably dark, with the light coming from somewhere behind me.

Relaxation

Over the years I have developed my own method of relaxation, which I believe is most effective for use in hypnosis. I call it the think-into method because you must think into your various body parts to make it work. You may have some difficulty thinking into some body parts the first time you try it, but after a few attempts the process will become easy.

To facilitate relaxation when you are about to induce self-hypnosis, you should follow a specific sequence. For example, you can start with your toes, work your way up your body, and end with your fingers. At first it will take a few minutes as you read and think into the body parts listed, but before long you will do it in a matter of seconds. After a few practice sessions you will be able to do the whole procedure from memory, without referring to the instructions that follow:

1. Think into your toes. Let your mind scan your toes as if it were an X-ray machine. With your mind, command your toes to relax, relax, relax.

2. Think into your feet. Let your mind scan your feet as if it were an X-ray machine. With your mind, command your feet to relax, relax, relax.

3. Think into your calves. Let your mind scan your calves as if it were an X-ray machine. With your mind, command your calves to relax, relax, relax.

4. Repeat the same think-into sequence for your thighs, buttocks, abdomen, lower back, chest, upper back, shoulders, neck, face, arms, hands, and fingers.

After you have followed these instructions three or four times, close your eyes and do the sequence from memory. Start with your toes, work up your body as described, and finish with your fingers. You do not have to think into every body part I mentioned. The important point is to reach the major segments of your body and the muscle groups that activate them.

Receptivity

Fixation and deep relaxation lead to a state of receptivity for positive suggestion. Receptivity involves having an open mind or giving something a chance to work before deciding that it does not or cannot work. Try to free yourself to give it a chance to work for you. With practice you will be able to enter this state more completely and more quickly, until the time comes when you will be able to relax instantly just by saying to yourself, *Relax, relax, relax*. Having this ability will not only increase your receptivity to self-hypnosis but also help you eliminate undesirable stress and tension whenever the need arises.

Repetitive Suggestion

To develop the greatest possible control over your body and yourself, prepare a short script to read, to think to yourself, or to play back on tape a number of times when you have put yourself into the relaxed, receptive hypnotic state. Your self-suggestions can relate to any area that you would like to improve. Your script should be short, powerful, and positive. Repeat the script three times. The most effective procedure is to use repetitive self-suggestions during self-hypnosis and to follow up with autosuggestion during the event itself. Following are three sample scripts, with pointers for their use.

Sample 1. My tremendously powerful brain has absolute control over all the cells, tissues, and organs that make up my body. It has complete control over all my feelings, emotions, and reactions. If I feel the jitters coming on, I will simply say to myself, *Relax, relax,* and the jitters will vanish.

Repeat this script to yourself a number of times during each self-hypnosis session until it becomes implanted deeply in your subconscious mind. Then, whenever you feel the jitters coming on and want to control them, repeat the words *relax, relax,* and the jitters will vanish.

Sample 2. I am an outstanding player. I have everything it takes to achieve my goals. I will remain focused in the present. Whenever I shoot I will focus directly on the open space and shoot directly into that space. I will shoot and score. I will shoot and score. I will shoot and score.

When sitting on the bench, during a practice or a game, you can reinforce the script through autosuggestion. Repeat to yourself, *I am a skilled player. I have everything I need to achieve my goals. I will think and look and shoot at the best open space. I will score goals. I will stay focused on the step in front of me.*

Sample 3. I love running. I am in great physical condition, and I am improving every day. I have a powerful brain and body. When I run, my brain and body combine their power to speed the flow of oxygen and nutrients to my hard-working muscles. They work in complete harmony to speed the removal of waste products from my muscles. I am strong and efficient.

While running, visualize the oxygen and nutrients flowing to your working muscles and the waste products being removed from your working muscles. While running, also repeat the words *relax, relax* to yourself, thinking into your arms, legs, and other working body parts. This will encourage better relaxation between the vigorous contractions and speed recovery between each thrust, thereby helping you run more efficiently. As you begin to feel your body extending itself, say over and over to yourself, *Strong and efficient . . . strong and efficient . . . I could run forever.*

Steps for Hypnosis

You now have the information that you need to put yourself in self-hypnosis and begin to use this power to draw out and develop your mental and physical capabilities. Select a quiet room where you can complete your entire self-hypnosis session without being disturbed. Place your focus object—a candle or a white card with a black dot—in front of the place where you will sit, making sure that it is about 12 inches (30 centimeters) away from your eyes and a little above them.

Place your scripts or other self-programming materials (for example, audio tape or CD and player) on a table just in front of your chair. If you have memorized your script or know exactly what you want to program into yourself, so much the better. Sit down on a fairly comfortable chair facing your focus point. Put yourself into a receptive state. Place your forearms on the table with the palms of your hands facing down.

Think relaxation. Think of every muscle in your entire body becoming soft and limp.

Stare at the focus object. Take a fairly deep breath, hold it for a moment, and then let it out slowly. As you exhale, say to yourself, *Relax, relax, relax.* Repeat this breathing and exhaling process seven times, letting your entire body become more limp and more relaxed each time.

Your eyes will begin to water. Then they will blink, and your eyelids will become heavier and heavier until it is all you can do to keep them open. The moment that your eyes begin to blink, water, or close, you will know that you are sinking into the receptive state of self-hypnosis. A tingling sensation in your hands or fingers is another indication. Don't worry about being sure that you are under or how deep you are under. If you follow the steps outlined here, you will be receptive to your own positive self-suggestions.

If you want to sink still deeper, say to yourself, *I am sinking, sinking, sinking, deeper, deeper, and deeper.* Repeat this a number of times and then say to yourself, *I am now in a deep, deep, deep state of self-hypnosis, and I am sinking deeper and deeper and deeper.* You must see yourself sinking deeper and deeper, you must feel yourself sinking deeper and deeper, you must really believe that you are sinking deeper and deeper, and then you will sink deeper and deeper.

After taking your seven fairly deep breaths, start your thinking-into sequence, beginning with your toes and ending with your fingers, as described earlier. Do this mentally with your eyes closed; command each body part, as you scan it with your mind, to relax, relax, relax.

By the time you reach your fingers, you should be in a relaxed, self-hypnotized, receptive state, and you may proceed to feed any desired suggestions directly into your powerful subconscious mind. Do this by opening your eyes and reading your prepared script. Before doing so, be sure to tell yourself that you will remain in the relaxed, receptive hypnotic state even after you open your eyes. If you have taped your script, you may open your eyes, switch on your audio player, and then close your eyes again. Or you can have a close, trusted friend or teammate turn on your audio player or read the script to you when you are in the hypnotic state. If you are alone without an audio recording, the best method may be to memorize your script beforehand and then simply repeat the suggestions to yourself as you fall into the hypnotic state.

At the completion of each self-hypnosis session, while you are still in the relaxed, receptive state, say to yourself, *When I hold my next self-hypnosis session, I will be able to enter a deep state of self-hypnosis quickly and easily.*

Finally, just before you are ready to wake up, say to yourself, *When I count three I will wake up, and when I wake up I will feel great, I will feel terrific, I will feel better than I have ever felt before.* Then count one, two, three and wake up feeling rejuvenated.

If you go to bed immediately after your self-hypnosis session, sleep will come rapidly, and the powerful suggestions that you have just given yourself will become even more deeply entrenched in your subconscious mind.

When you awake next morning, say to yourself, *I feel great, I feel terrific,* and you really will. Think it! Believe it! And act accordingly.

CHAPTER 11

Zen Experiences

What does it mean to be in the moment, to be fully here, to be focused with every fiber of your being, to be in the zone? Those terms means everything to someone and nothing to someone else. Words are just words. They have different meanings for different people in different contexts, cultures, languages, and times. What is the "way," the Zen way, the river of life, the fully focused connection? The terms probably mean different things to you at different times in your life as they have to others at different times of human life on earth.

Childlikeness has to be restored with long years of training in the art of self-forgetfulness. When this is attained, man does his great works. He thinks yet he does not think.

Daisetz T. Suzuki

The origins of Zen were first presented in ancient Chinese characters (or ideograms). Each character represents more than just one word; each denotes a concept or way of seeing or perceiving things. So we might never be sure of the essence of ancient Chinese characters that paint the philosophy of Zen. Only when we experience it ourselves do the characters take on personal meaning. We then know the Zen connection from the inside as an experience, from experience, through experience. We get to know the Zen connection by experimenting with our own performances, focus, and life.

Much of what has been written about Zen originates with a little book titled *Tao Te Ching* (The Book of the Way), written by Lao-tzu in China over 2,500 years ago. Originally written in ancient Chinese characters, the book has been translated by many authors into English and translated into many other languages, each presenting a slightly different interpretation of Lao-tzu's original meaning. The book really makes you think about the importance of connecting and not thinking.

You get to know Zen on an internal level by just being in the moment and going with your feelings, intuitions, and simple connections. Zen can never be forced, but it can always become a way of being or a way of connecting every day—in every piece of your life and within every performance context. Zen can also be elusive if you push it too hard, chase it, or try to apply force to it.

The Zen connection, or the way, lives within you. You experienced it many times as a child and sometimes fleetingly in parts of your adult life.

One of the intriguing aspects of sports, martial arts, fine arts, and performing arts as they were originally practiced in Asia thousands of years ago was their focus on training the mind. Zen was developed and experienced through sport, martial arts, and fine arts, but its ultimate purpose was to enhance the living of life itself.

Interpreting Zen

For me, the most important lesson of ancient and modern Zen practice is the concept of oneness, a concept that was also embraced by many North American aboriginal people, including Native American Indians and the Inuit people (Eskimos) who inhabited the Canadian Arctic and Alaska. Entering the Zen zone means becoming one with and inseparable from the essence of what you are doing during the moment that you are doing it. Being in the Zen zone means being all here; being totally present; absorbing yourself in, connecting yourself to, and becoming one with your body, your task, your performance, your experience, nature, the tree that you are looking at, the child you are playing with, the person you are speaking with.

When you are totally engaged in the process of doing, you become what you are doing. For those moments nothing else in the world exists for you. You suspend all thoughts or judgments about yourself, others, or your performance. You simply connect fully and absolutely with what you are doing or experiencing.

If you begin to reflect, deliberate, question, condemn, or judge along the way, you lose the pure connection or become disconnected, apart from, separate, tentative, distracted. The original natural childlike bond between mind and mind, mind and body, mind and task, mind and creation, or mind and nature is broken. There are times for thinking and reflection, but there are also times for connecting totally with what you are doing and leaving your conscious thinking behind. Performance is a time for connection rather than reflection. Pure experience is made possible through pure connection.

Some of my personal thoughts to get you thinking about not thinking and to get you doing by not doing are presented here. You might feel that some of my reflections are a little out there, especially at first glance, but they can become grounded in your performance and in your life if you give them a chance. Then again, they might not. This is the way of Zen—it is for everyone, and then again it is not. The positive, hopeful attraction about a Zen connection is that everyone has experienced it and everyone can experience it more often. Zen is grounded in what I call a focused connection—being completely where you are when you are there, being completely absorbed in your performance when you are performing, without any interfering thoughts.

Your challenge is to discover or rediscover what this absolute connection is for you, how you can be with it and let it be part of you more often, and in what situations it can help you most. For me a Zen connection is little bit like the wind: You can't grab it in your hand, but you can breathe it in and feel it and let it become part of you. To enter the Zen zone,

- ➤ let go of forcing things;
- ➤ let go of outcomes;
- ➤ let go of your thoughts about outcomes;
- ➤ connect only to the doing;
- ➤ focus on doing the doing, being the being, being all here, being completely present, and being fully connected; and
- ➤ become your performance by being inseparable from what you are doing.

The goal is always pure connection. When you are fully connected no separation exists between you and your performance, you and your experience, you and the person with whom you are interacting, you and nature. You are pure and connected as one.

"When nothing is done, nothing is left undone." Nothing done means nothing forced and nothing thought that takes you away from the experience or breaks the connection. You may feel as though "nothing is done" because you become the performance, because you become what you are doing or are engaged in. The connection is so strong that nothing else needs to be done; the doing takes care of itself. "Nothing" in this context is really the purity of the connection and has everything to do with a great performance or a great connection in any part of your life.

Lao-tzu spoke about softness or suppleness as opposed to rigidity, hardness, or inflexibility. I view this as relaxed power, free-flowing power, and pure connection. The Tao, or, as I see it, the truth or the way, is really all about the connection—which we are all capable of experiencing. The way to what you want or are seeking is made possible by connecting and made impossible by disconnecting. Finding your way revolves around how deeply you connect (and what you connect to) as well as when and how often you disconnect. Connection and disconnection lead the way of your life and your performance. The connection lives within you and within me. It lives within all of us. All we have to do is embrace it. When you lose the connection or let obstacles get in the way of your fully connected focus, the effect is like a cloud blocking the sun so that the rays no longer shine through. By removing the obstacles in your mind, you allow the pure connection to shine through.

Nurturing Pure Connection

Entering a state of pure connection, or your personal Zen zone, does not have to be difficult and mysterious. You can do it every day, in any context. Accessibility is the beauty and the real benefit of Zen, which is as fluid as water in terms of application. Pure connection is the "way" to enhance your performance and enrich your life. Here are some pointers to reflect on that might help you nurture a purer connection within different contexts of your life.

➤ Seek moments of pure connection every day.
➤ Practice trying by not trying.
➤ Connect with the connection.
➤ Practice connecting without thinking.
➤ Practice doing by connecting.
➤ Absorb yourself in the doing.
➤ Absorb yourself in each experience.
➤ Trust your body and intuition to lead you wisely to your destination.
➤ Trust your connection to lead the way.

What do you think is possible for you in your performance, schoolwork, profession, or life with a pure and absolute connection? What is your potential with a positive, sustained focus? With focused connection, everything is possible and all things are possible. Focus rules your life, your performance, my life, my performance. Focus rules the world because it directly affects every person, every experience, every performance, every family, every community, society, and the world—for better or worse.

What is there without positive focus? What is there without connection? In the absence of pure focused connection, there is nothing—no meaningful learning, no performing to your potential, no feeling or experiencing the moment, and no possibility of living to your full potential.

One of the greatest lessons that I have learned from great performers is the oneness or absolute connection that they have with what they are doing, seeing, feeling, or creating. They have learned to become one with their performance (through a Zen-like connection), and nothing else in the world exists for them during those moments in time. To live life to the fullest, it is not enough to enter this fully connected state only in your performance or professional life and then live without pure connection at home, in relationships, with children, or with nature. The way to life fulfillment is to bring this kind of connected focus into all parts of your life. Great performers and great connectors do not allow thinking or distractions to get in the way of doing or experiencing. When they are thinking, they are usually thinking about how to enhance or sustain their connection.

Let your connection lead you.

Let your focus lead you.

Lead by feel and not by thought.

Let go of anything outside or beyond the connection itself.

Some of my favorite quotes from Lao-tzu's original work are presented here. Following each quote I have noted the practical reminder, lesson, or meaning that I have drawn from it. Think about what each quote means to you and how you might act on it.

➤ "Keep sharpening your knife and it will become blunt." My reminder: There is a point beyond which more gives you less. Discover that point to perform your best and live more joyfully.

➤ "Care about people's approval and you will be their prisoner." My reminder: Don't let other people's thoughts rule your life or your day.

➤ "Do your work, then step back. The only path to serenity." My reminder: Take time to relax, regenerate, and spend time in the serenity of nature.

➤ "Coax your mind from its wandering and keep to the original oneness." My lesson: Stay connected—be one with your mission.

➤ "Cleanse your inner vision until you see nothing but light." My lesson: Stay focused on the positives and let the negatives go.

➤ "Deal with the most vital matters by letting events take their course." My lesson: Control what you can control and let go of the things that you cannot control.

➤ "Giving birth and nourishing, having without possessing, acting with no expectations, leading and not trying to control: This is the supreme virtue." My lesson: Let simple, worthy wisdom guide each day.

Zen is centered in connecting, experiencing, and doing good things. You may be thinking about being more positive, more complete, or more connected in the present moment, but not acting on being more positive or more completely connected in what you are doing or living. When you move from saying to doing, from thinking to acting, and from reflecting to connecting, you enter the Zen zone and everything else will follow.

Transcending Technique

I often wondered how the great fencing masters prepared for duels in the old days, before touches were recorded on an electronic scoreboard. How did the great swordsmen prevent themselves from becoming distracted by outcomes and suffering a fatal performance flaw when the stakes were literally life or death? Many overanxious swordsmen did not live to tell their tales, but what of those who survived and continued to excel?

Daisetz T. Suzuki (1993), in his excellent book *Zen and Japanese Culture*, touched eloquently on this question. Suzuki discussed the connection between Zen and the ancient art of swordsmanship:

> If one really wishes to be master of an art, technical knowledge is not enough. One has to transcend technique so that the art grows out of the unconscious. . . . You must let the unconscious come

forward. In such cases, you cease to be your own conscious master but become an instrument in the hands of the unknown. The unknown has no ego-consciousness and consequently no thought of winning the contest. . . . It is for this reason that the sword moves where it ought to move and makes the contest end victoriously. This is the practical application of the Lao-tzu doctrine of doing by not doing. (Suzuki, 1993, 94, 96)

To excel or even to survive, a swordsman had to free himself from all ideas of life and death, gain and loss, right and wrong, and give himself up to a power that lives deep within him. In essence he had to clear his mind of all irrelevant thoughts, follow his trained instincts, and trust his body to lead. The swordsman who performed at the highest level of excellence was likened to a scarecrow that "is not endowed with a mind, but still scares the deer" (Suzuki, 1993, 100).

Suzuki continued, "A mind unconscious of itself is a mind that is not at all disturbed by effects of any kind. . . . It fills the whole body, pervading every part of the body . . . flowing like a stream filling each corner." If it should find a resting place anywhere, it is a state of "no thinking," "emptiness," "no-mind-ness," or "the mind of no mind" (Suzuki, 1993, 111).

Freeing Mind and Body

All at once I forgot the public, the other bullfighters, myself, and even the bull; I began to fight as I had so often by myself at night in the corrals and pastures, as precisely as if I had been drawing a design on a blackboard. They say that my passes with the cape and my work with the muleta that afternoon were a revelation of the art of bullfighting. I don't know, and I'm not competent to judge. I simply fought as I believe one ought to fight, without a thought, outside of my own faith in what I was doing. With the last bull I succeeded for the first time in my life in delivering myself and my soul to the pure joy of fighting without being consciously aware of an audience.

Juan Belmonte, the great Spanish bullfighter, reflecting on the moment when he first freed his body and mind to dance within a performance

Reacting Naturally

For me it was a feeling of separating my body from my conscious mind and letting my body do what came naturally. When this happened things always went surprisingly well, almost as if my mind would look at what my body was doing and say, *Hey, you're good*, but at the same time not making any judgments on what I was doing because it was not "me" that was doing it; it was my body. This way, by not making any judgments, it was easy to stay in the present.

Canadian Olympian Kim Alleston speaking of a similar phenomenon

Professional figure skater Charlene Wong and Olympic downhill skier Kellie Casey became exceptionally good at drawing on the Zen perspective to free themselves in their quests for personal excellence. When Charlene "turned on her autopilot," a wonderful program unfolded. When Kellie suspended conscious thinking and "let her body lead," she had a great run. For the duration of their best performances, they both suspended critical evaluation and trusted the mind–body connection to work without interference from conscious thought.

In the ancient art of swordsmanship, focusing was intimately connected with life. In Suzuki's words, "When a stroke is missed, all is lost eternally; no idle thinking could enter here." A consciousness occupied with irrelevant thoughts and feelings stands in the way of "successfully carry-

©Barry Gossage/Getty Images

The performance of a great athlete like Diana Taurasi transcends technique to reach a pure mind–body connection.

ing out the momentous business of life and death, and the best way to cope with the situation is to clear the field of all useless rubbish and to turn the consciousness into an automaton in the hands of the unconscious" (Suzuki, 1993, 117).

Distracting thoughts or emotions could result in a swordsman's failing to see or detect "the movements of the enemy's sword with the immediacy of the moon casting its reflection on the water" (Suzuki, 1993, 133). Seeing and instantaneous action of body and limbs are essential. This is no place for minds obscured by irrelevant thought or clouded by anxiety. No obstruction should come between mind and movement. As one Japanese Zen master pointed out, you can read the environment much more clearly when you are calm internally, just as you can see the reflection more clearly on a calm lake than on a disturbed one. Stress is like wind that disturbs the image on a calm lake.

Suzuki pointed out that the perfect swordsman takes no cognizance of the enemy's personality, no more than of his own. He is an indifferent onlooker of the fatal drama of life and death in which he himself is the most active participant. The swordsman's unconscious is free from the notion of self. As soon as his mind "stops" with an object of whatever nature, the swordsman ceases to be master of himself and is sure to fall victim to the enemy's sword (Suzuki, 1993, 96–97).

Suzuki went on to say that an idea, no matter how worthy and desirable in itself, becomes a disease when the mind is obsessed with it. The obsessions that the swordsman has to get rid of are

1. the desire for victory,
2. the desire to resort to technical cunning,
3. the desire to display all that he has learned,
4. the desire to overawe the enemy,
5. the desire to play a passive role, and
6. the obsession to get rid of whatever obsession he is likely to be infected with (Suzuki, 1993, 153–154).

"When any one of these obsesses him, he becomes its slave, as it makes him lose all the freedom he is entitled to as a swordsman." Whenever and wherever the mind is obsessed with anything, "make haste to detach yourself from it" (Suzuki, 1993, 154). The primary reason that these obsessions can interfere with pure performance or excellence is that they interfere with gaining the purest connection with your performance.

The following quotations from Yagyu Tajima, the great 16th-century Japanese swordsman, provide some Eastern visions to reflect on (Suzuki, 1993, 114–115):

➤   "Emptiness is one-mind-ness, one-mind-ness is no-mind-ness, and it is no-mind-ness that achieves wonders."

➤   "Give up thinking as though not giving it up. Observe the technique as though not observing."

➤   "Have nothing left in your mind, keep it thoroughly cleansed of its contents, and then the mirror will reflect the images in their 'isness.'"

➤   "Turn yourself into a doll made of wood: it has no ego, it thinks nothing; and let the body and limbs work themselves out in accordance with the discipline they have undergone. This is the way to win."

A fencer with whom I worked stimulated my thinking about performing without thinking and without thinking about not thinking. He combined some aspects of Eastern and Western approaches to improve his fencing performance. He developed a precompetition plan that helped him start in a calmer, more relaxed state. What he wanted most was to compete in a Zen mind-set. In the beginning he wrote out a list of quotations that triggered in him the primary feelings of a Zen perspective. They included the following:

> ➤ Zen is against conceptualization. The experience is the thing. Verbalism often becomes an empty abstraction.

> ➤ If you want to see, see right at once. When you think, you miss the point.

> ➤ When I look at a tree, I perceive that one of the leaves is red, and my mind stops with this leaf. When this happens, I see just one leaf and fail to take cognizance of the innumerable other leaves of the tree. If instead of this I look at the tree without any preconceived ideas, I shall see all the leaves. One leaf effectively stops my mind from seeing all the rest. When the mind moves on without stopping, it takes up hundreds of leaves without fail.

> ➤ To think that I am not going to think of you anymore is still thinking of you. Let me then try not to think that I am not going to think of you.

> ➤ Do not rely on others, or on the readings of the masters. Be your own lamp.

> ➤ You have mastered the art when the body and limbs perform by themselves what is assigned to them to do with no interference from the mind.

The fencer read these quotations to himself several times before competing, as a reminder of the state of mind that he sought. He had some initial success but also some subsequent difficulties in maintaining this approach throughout his most crucial bouts. He refined his approach into a series of key words (for example, *It, it . . . be with it* or *Be here . . . be all here*), which he plugged in whenever he experienced too many thoughts or too much stress. As he went out to compete he began to tell himself, *You're here to fence, and nothing beyond the experience of fencing really matters . . . just go out and fence and enjoy yourself.* When he was able to follow these simple reminders, his body took over and he moved in an incredibly fluid way—sometimes making touch after touch without thought. After bouts like that he occasionally found himself wondering where all those great moves came from.

The fencer could not always enter this state, but it began to happen more frequently with less thought in more tournaments. He began searching for competitions to practice improving his focused connection and letting his performance flow. Improving his overall perspective toward competition was his primary goal, but he also found help in backup strategies such as verbal reminders and relaxation when he ran into problems. A Zen orientation is not something that can be accomplished hurriedly, but it is certainly responsive to nurturing, as the fencer's comments make clear:

For the first few competitions, after reading and talking and thinking, I realized that I was too focused on what was wrong in the bout. I paid attention to what was wrong. To turn that around, I got back into the doing. I went into one tournament thinking, *There's nothing that says I have to be tied up in a competition.* The first two bouts were great. Then I started to tie up. I couldn't let go of the feeling. I was first able to turn it around by becoming interested in what I was doing and experiencing, instead of being so worried about the expectations of others. This took a bit of time. I had to "be in" the competition. With each subsequent competition I had better and better focus control for more and more of the time. The coach stayed away and let me work things out for myself. Telling me technical things at the last minute, or after I'd blown something, just made things worse. I thanked him for staying quiet.

When speaking about his last competition, the fencer said,

As I stepped up for the bout, I thought, I am here for the fencing . . . nothing else matters . . . get into the experience. At no time did the thought of winning or losing enter the picture. I got into the finals, which was my goal, and we won the team competition. The "pressure situation" didn't faze me. On one occasion one guy did upset me emotionally. I went into the corner, did some relaxation, read my Zen reminders, came back, and won a key match 5 to 0. My primary strategy worked fine, and I gave myself reminders in the bout if I felt I needed them (for example, *I'm here to experience it*). Many people commented on how relaxed I was. I really enjoyed myself and beat four very good fencers. I was there to fence—that's all.

He ended our discussion by saying, "The event is the focus. If I focus on the event, the feeling comes automatically. So I just let my interest get absorbed in the event. I relax and enjoy it. Lots of hits are unintentional. The guy just runs into my point."

Certain things cannot be forced. You must free yourself to let them happen. You don't have to try to be happy. You simply live, connect with your experiences, and embrace the simple joys of life; happiness comes as a by-product. In a similar vein, you don't have to try consciously to focus on winning during a performance in order to win. During the contest you simply become absorbed in the experience. By being in the present, trusting your body, and allowing the performance program that has been ingrained in your mind and body to unfold, the winning takes care of itself.

Before every performance, decide what you really want to do and know that you are fully capable of doing it. To be the best that you can be, your only goal is to connect fully and to free yourself to perform. When you are totally engaged in the process of doing, you become what you are doing. You, your focus, and your performance are one—this is the Zen zone.

Here are some focus reminders that will free you to connect fully with your performance. Choose the ones that feel best for you. Before you enter your next performance, remind yourself to carry this focus.

- ➤ Focus by feeling, not forcing.
- ➤ Let your intuition lead you.
- ➤ Stop judging along the way. Focus on the doing.
- ➤ Trust what is already living deep within your body and soul.
- ➤ Become one with your performance.
- ➤ Win by removing all thoughts of winning.
- ➤ Simply connect and trust the connection.
- ➤ Relax. Attack by relaxing.
- ➤ Pure focus is pure connection—this is the only place to be.
- ➤ With pure focus nothing gets between you and your performance.
- ➤ Enter the Zen zone.

PART III

Building Toward Excellence

CHAPTER 12

Perspectives

The key to living closer to your potential in both your performance pursuits and the rest of your life lies in developing your ability to focus in ways that allow you to carry a positive perspective and view the challenges that you face in a constructive way.

One thing over which you have the potential to exert absolute control is your own focus. This gives you the opportunity to control your own perspective and much of your own destiny.

What does having a positive perspective mean to you? Who are the most positive people you know? What do they do or say that makes you believe that they are positive? When they are positive, how does that make you feel when you are in their presence?

A positive perspective becomes possible when you start to focus on the good things in yourself, in your day, in your life, in others, and in the world around you. A negative perspective becomes your reality when you focus on finding bad or negative things in yourself, in your day, in your life, in others, and in the world around you. A positive perspective comes from focusing on opportunities instead of obstacles, solutions instead of problems, positives instead of negatives, good things instead of bad things. Here is a simple example. If you have a shopping list or a to-do list (for your day at home, at work, at school, at practice, or in your performance setting) and you tick off 19 out of 20 things as successfully completed, do you focus on being happy about accomplishing those 19 things or on being upset about the 1 thing that you did not accomplish?

A hundred good things (little highlights) and one bad thing (a little low-light) might happen during your day. Do you appreciate and remember all the good things, or do you focus only on the bad things? People do billions of good things for each other every day in every corner of the world. When you watch television or listen to the daily news, how often do you hear about those good things? In your own life how often do you focus on the positives and not the negatives, on the opportunities and not the obstacles? How skilled are you at finding the positives in the negatives?

Embracing a Positive Perspective

In some ways, living with a positive perspective is like becoming your own best friend. You choose to support yourself, help yourself and others get through difficult times, encourage yourself and others to do the good things that you each want to do, remind yourself of your good qualities, remind others of their good qualities, remind yourself and others to embrace the special moments that you now have together and alone, remind yourself and others of what you each have the potential to be, and remind yourself and loved ones to embrace opportunities and simple things that lift you. This will free you to enjoy parts of every day and every pursuit, even when facing extremely difficult challenges. Living with a positive perspective becomes possible when you

- decide to find good things in you and your life,
- decide to find good things in others and their lives,
- acknowledge good things in you and your life,
- acknowledge good things in others and their lives,
- appreciate the good things in you and your life,
- appreciate the good things in others and their lives,
- rejoice in the good parts of you and your life, and
- rejoice in the good parts of others and their lives.

To move more rapidly along the path with positive perspective, respect and follow these practices:

- Look for the good things, the highlights, in each day and each situation.
- Look for the opportunities in each situation, every day.
- Embrace the positive in positive situations.
- Find the positives in negative situations.
- Focus on why you can do what you want to do (for example, attain your goals, accomplish your mission, or live more positively).
- See the possibilities within the obstacles and see what lies beyond the obstacles.
- Focus on why you can rise to the challenge or get through the setback and then focus on how you will move forward in a positive direction.
- Recognize that everyone faces adversity at some time in his or her life. Challenge yourself to find a positive path through the adversity.
- Recognize that it is OK not to be perfect, because no one is perfect.
- Focus on putting yourself up instead of putting yourself down.
- When you start to get down on yourself, hit the emergency brake and shift your focus to something more positive.

➤ Remember that there is no advantage in putting yourself down and many advantages in lifting yourself up.

➤ Continue to appreciate the good things that you have, the good things that you have done, and the good things still to come.

➤ Continue to find and appreciate the good things in others—past, present, and future.

Choosing Your Perspective

Whenever you participate in an important performance or event, or even a not-so-important event, thoughts will run through your head before the event (and sometimes during and after the event). You may say certain things to yourself about what you think might happen and begin to feel strong emotions related to those thoughts. Are the thoughts running through your head going to help or hurt your perspective and your performance? Are they going to help or hurt your experiences and your life? Are your thoughts making you worry or freeing you from worry? Are they helping you feel confident or shattering your confidence? Are they helping you focus on the right things or leading you to focus on the wrong things?

What triggers your emotional reaction to an event is the way that you perceive the event, or what you say to yourself about yourself in relation to it, rather than the event itself. A simple shift in your perspective about the importance or meaning of a particular event, or a shift in your belief about your capacity to cope with it positively, can change your focus and your emotional reality. Nothing changes except the way that you perceive yourself, interpret the event, or view your capacity to cope with it, yet that simple positive change in focus can give you inner strength and confidence, release you from stress, and free you to live, perform, and contribute more joyfully. You can choose the perspective that you carry into your daily life and your performances.

Let's take performance stress as an example. If you take some sportscasters seriously, you might begin to believe that stress is external and inescapable, like rain pouring down from a dark cloud: "You can almost hear the tension out there . . . this is it . . . do or die . . . the world is watching . . . there's real pressure on these athletes here today." Yet some performers are able to enter those situations and stay focused on doing their jobs without becoming overstressed. They perform extremely well and may even feed off challenging situations to raise the level of their performance. How is that possible?

The explanation lies in two reasons. First, these athletes are focused on preparing themselves to do what they came to do and then focused on doing what they came to do. Nothing outside that focus shapes their day. Second, stress or anxiety doesn't float around out there waiting to pounce on the performer like some kind of bogeyman. Stress is strictly internal; it does not exist outside the person's mind. Certain performance situations may tend to get the adrenaline flowing, but the person is not required to become anxious in

► A top performer like Martin Brodeur is able to maintain control even in challenging circumstances.

those situations. And even if the performer begins to feel anxious, he or she can regain composure by shifting focus back to the simple steps of executing the performance or game plan.

Situations do not become anxious; people do. We are anxious when we accept a situation as stressful or when we become too concerned with outcomes or consequences of failing or falling short of our goals. Performers who enter the performance arena feeling excited and fully focused on the right things remain in control. They repaint the anxiety-filled picture that others may have painted for them. Successful performers create a picture that is positive, focused, and filled with opportunity.

We experience stress and frustration in performance situations and other areas of life largely because we want to be perfect at everything we do. We expect the performance situations that we enter to be perfect, which of course they almost never are. We also want our partners, children, parents, coaches, teachers, athletes, colleagues, bosses, and others to be perfect. Sometimes we set ourselves up for stress or frustration because we have impossible expectations of ongoing perfection for ourselves and others.

Ellis and Harper (1976, 25) identified several perspectives or beliefs that can interfere with your capacity to perform to your potential and live a joyful life:

1. The belief that you must always have love and approval from all the people you find significant
2. The belief that you must always prove to be thoroughly competent, adequate, and achieving
3. The belief that emotional misery comes from external pressures and that you have little ability to control or change your feelings
4. The belief that if something seems fearsome or threatening, you must preoccupy yourself with it and make yourself anxious about it
5. The belief that your past remains all important and that because something once strongly influenced your life, it has to keep determining your feelings and behavior today

You cannot have the love and approval of all people at all times, no matter what you do or how much you give of yourself; nor can you always be thoroughly competent at all things. None of us is, or ever will be, perfect at all things. We all screw up sometimes, and that's OK. That's being human.

We all have the capacity to change our perspectives, improve our focus, and directly influence our feelings. We are not locked into the limitations of our experiences. This ongoing capacity to change and improve is what makes sport and life such a wonderful adventure. We all have room to grow and to engage continually in the process of becoming.

The excessive worry that destroys skilled performance usually comes from exaggerating the importance of the outcome of an event, from viewing it as if your physical or emotional life is at stake, or from thinking that your entire meaning on earth rests in the balance. We know that this is not really the case in most performance situations, but we sometimes act as if it were. On rare occasions, in some high-risk events, a physical life may hang in the balance (and even in this case, a full focus on the task is your best way through it). But never is our emotional life or overall meaning on the line in other kinds of performances, no matter how much we may tell ourselves or how much others may lead us to believe that it is.

If you approach a performance as if it is the only important event in the world, as if your life will be useless unless you do well, then you set yourself up for needless stress. If you incessantly worry about your performance or about appearing incompetent, you are probably too focused on negative possibilities or too concerned with what others might think and not focused enough on the positives or not focused fully on the task at hand. The worry is usually worse than the event itself. Your performance (and people's reaction to it) rarely turns out to be as terrible as you might have imagined. And it would turn out a lot better if you did not dwell on the negatives in the first place.

Shifting Your Perspective

You can lessen your worries and improve your performance by shifting your perspective to something positive that is within your control and by viewing yourself, the event, and your performance in a more positive light. Consistent high-level performers approach their performances by being physically and mentally ready: *I've got a job to do; I'm capable of doing it; I'll focus fully on doing it the best I can—step by step. Beyond that, I'm not going to worry about it.* If they have a great performance, they rejoice in it briefly, draw out the positive lessons, and move on. If they have a disappointing performance, they soak in the disappointment briefly, draw out the positive lessons, and move on. They have learned to refocus quickly and to keep things in perspective because if they don't do this, they waste a lot of emotional energy and become an obstacle on the path to achieving their goals.

Think about your own situation. At one time you had limited skills in your performance domain—in fact, you hadn't even begun to participate in it. Yet you were a valued person, and those close to you loved you. Now that you are much more skilled, is it really so disastrous to achieve a little less than perfection? You are still a skilled performer and a worthy human being, and you will continue to be acceptable and worthy long after you stop working, performing, or competing in this domain.

There are lots of physical skills that I can no longer do since I stopped competing and performing in gymnastics. For example, I can no longer do a quadruple twisting back somersault on a trampoline; it's been over 10 years since I've done a double. But I can now do many other things in other sports and in other fields that I could never do when I was a competitive athlete. Does my decline in gymnastics skills mean that I am half as good, half as worthy a person, as I used to be? Do the gymnastics skills that I still possess mean that I'm twice as good a person as someone who cannot do even a single somersault? Thinking that my overall value as a person depends on my performance in any given field on any given night would be ridiculous, but we sometimes treat our performance as if it carries that kind of importance. We sometimes confuse the outcome of a performance with our overall worth as a human being. When this happens, we need to regain a more positive and balanced perspective. Our human essence extends far beyond our performance in a given task at a given time. It always has and it always will.

Reducing Stress

Some effective techniques for on-site stress control include changing channels or choosing to make positive shifts in perspective, making your focus stronger than the fear, relaxing your breathing, and channeling your focus into the step-by-step process of your performance. These strategies are effective in most performance situations, but you may not need them if you can get to the root of the issue, which is whether you view a situation as necessarily stressful. Your first line of stress prevention and control lies in keeping your own worth in perspective and knowing that your value as a human being remains intact regardless of whether you meet the expectations of others or achieve a particular performance goal.

The best way to achieve a permanent reduction in unwanted and unproductive stress is to set realistic performance goals, focus fully on executing your task, and know in your heart that you remain a valued person regardless of the performance outcome. If you can approach potentially stress-provoking situations with a more positive and focused perspective, then debilitating stress will not surface. You will become positively energized and your heart will be thumping because you are excited and need a certain level of positive intensity to perform your best in this situation. But you will not become stressed to the point that anxiety will jeopardize your performance focus or your well-being.

How can you shift to a more positive perspective and become less stressed? Perhaps you can begin by questioning some of your thoughts—the ones that may create stress for you in the first place. The next time that you start to become negative or feel stressed out, stop and ask yourself, *Why am I getting negative? Why am I getting stressed out? What am I thinking or saying to myself about this situation, this person, myself, my performance, or other people, that is making me feel negative or stressed? Do I have to see it this way, do I have to think this way, and do I have to feel this way? Do I have to get stressed out over this? Is it going to help me or my situation? Is it really worth continuing to be stressed or negative about this? Is it doing me or anyone else any good?* If the answer is no, set a personal goal to stop doing things or focusing on things that are likely to make you feel negative or worried, and focus more in ways that will uplift you and others. Choose to do it and act on that choice.

Look for legitimate reasons to believe in your capacity to meet the challenges that you are facing, whatever they may be. You are fully capable of getting through this and growing from it. Remind yourself of your strengths. Remind yourself to focus on the step in front of you and nothing else. Remember the power of your fully connected focus. You are fully capable of achieving your goals. You are fully capable of carrying a positive perspective. Decide to act in ways that are positive and focus fully on executing your mission or performance—nothing more, nothing less.

Deciding to be more positive and more focused before you enter the performance context will help you make the positive changes that you are seeking. Think about how you would prefer to enter, focus, and respond to various situations within your performance arena and other arenas of your life. Imagine yourself responding more effectively to situations that may have upset you unnecessarily in the past. Visualize yourself in future performance situations—thinking, focusing, believing, and acting in more positive and constructive ways. Then focus on bringing this more positive vision of yourself to life in your real-world performance context. With persistence and focus, you'll win this one.

Sometimes a simple shift in focus so that you see things from a slightly different perspective, or as they could be, leads to a big change in the way that you view a situation, your performance, or yourself. As soon as you start to believe what you really want to believe before a performance—*Hey, I'm ready, I can do this; I own my focus; I control my actions and reactions; just focus, focus, focus, and execute my game plan*—your feelings, focus, and performance will nearly always improve immediately. As soon as you start to believe what you would really want to believe after a less-than-best performance—*Hey, this doesn't really matter in the big picture; there's no reason to get upset about this; I have the strength, focus, and balance to deal with this, learn from this, and get better from this*—your feelings, focus, and performance will nearly always improve immediately.

Whenever you are able to make a positive change in your focus, perspective, or performance, think about what you did, focused on, or said to yourself to bring it about. Hang on to those positive memories for future use. Also, try to be aware of self-imposed obstacles to positive change, such as focusing on things that distract you or saying things to yourself that block your progress, for example, things like *I don't feel ready, This will never work, I can't do this, I'm not good enough to do this, I'll probably mess it up*, and the like.

What are you saying to yourself right now about your capacity to improve your focus and make the positive changes that you need to make to achieve your goals? This is a good place to start establishing a strong positive focus. Decide right now to move forward with a powerful positive perspective.

Building Confidence

Virtually every athlete or performer you have ever seen or competed against, including the best athletes in the world, experiences a rush of excitement, a feeling of being fully alive, before an important event. This feeling shows that they care and want to excel. They make the feeling work for them by recognizing its positive elements and by channeling their focus into their performance.

Sometimes simply reinterpreting your physical sensations is enough to keep you in control or put you back in control within a performance context. Let's say that you get a knot in your stomach or your heart starts to thump hard just before a performance begins. You could say to yourself, *Oh man, I'm so nervous . . . I don't know what I'm going to do. . . . I'll probably blow it.* Or you could interpret these physical signals in a positive manner and say, *The feeling in my stomach is the result of positive adrenaline, which acts as a stimulant. My body is telling me that I'm ready and I'm focused. Let's go!*

A certain amount of intensity is necessary for quality performances in mind–body endeavors. You wouldn't do well if you were half asleep, but you don't want to be bouncing off the walls either. You are seeking that optimal amount of "upness," the place where your readiness feels just right. If you find yourself feeling too pumped up, you can make that feeling work for you by using it as a signal to bring yourself down a bit, perhaps by shifting your focus to deliberate relaxed breathing or by refocusing on connecting fully with your warm-up or performance.

Remember that no matter how you may have viewed yourself in the past, you are not obligated to keep viewing yourself in the same light. You may have thought of yourself as being negative, anxious, or overreactive in certain situations in the past, but you can change and control how you react in any situation by changing what you focus on in that situation. By thinking about how you would prefer to focus and planning to do it, you can enter most situations focused and in control, even situations that previously caused stress or performance problems. A positive focus plan for performances can help you get your focus where you want it and keep it where it does you the most good.

Suppose that at your performance site your thoughts start to drift to such things as how nervous you are or how terrible it would be if you blew it. What can you do about it? You can use these thoughts as a reminder to shift your focus to something more constructive that puts you back in control. For example, at that moment, remind yourself that you are fully capable of executing this performance; recall your simple goal of just doing the best that you can do today; focus on your preparation or warm-up and then connect fully with executing your performance. Just before you begin, focus on the first thing that you will do—your start, your beginning, your opening statement, or your first action. For the remainder of the performance stay focused on doing your job, one move at a time, one step at a time, a task that is totally within your control. Remind yourself of your best performance focus, your good recent practices, your best-ever performances, and your capacity to focus and perform well. Remember also that your overall value as a person remains intact no matter what happens that day. Focus on your preparation, your readiness, your commitment, your capacity, and your best focus. Just go out there and focus fully on doing your job. Everything else will take care of itself.

The most important parts of you, including your performance focus and your life perspective, are within your control. When you accept that you can effect positive change in these areas, you will, precisely because they are within your control. These changes depend on what you choose to do and what you decide to focus on. At times, important things in life are beyond your control. It is self-defeating to take responsibility or feel guilty for things that happen to you or those close to you over which you have no direct control. You cannot control things that are impossible to control, no matter how hard you try or how much responsibility you assume for doing so. You cannot control the past; you cannot control things that occur strictly by chance; you cannot control the actions, reactions, or incompetence of the people around you. But you can control how you see the past, what you learn from the past, how you view things that are truly beyond your control, and how to control what is within your control. This realization alone can put you back in control.

You best serve yourself, your teammates, your goals, and the people closest to you when you focus on positive things within your potential control. Your thoughts are within your control. Your focus is within your control. Your focus leads your confidence, your perspective, and your performance. If you focus on failure, you become stressed. If you focus on errors, they are yours. If you focus on your strengths, you are strong. If you focus on why you can and how you will, your confidence grows. If you focus on the doing, the doing will become your reality. Consider some of the following positive focus reminders to help you in your ongoing pursuit of personal excellence:

➤ I am in control of my thinking, my focus, my life.

➤ I am a good, valued person in my own right.

➤ I control my focus and therein direct the whole pattern of my performance, health, and life.

➤ I am fully capable of achieving the goals that I set for myself. They are within my control.

➤ I control the step in front of me by focusing fully on that step.

➤ I am fully capable of focusing through adversity and staying on a positive path.

➤ I learn from setbacks and turn them into positive opportunities for personal growth.

➤ I embrace the lessons from my experiences and act on those lessons.

➤ My powerful mind and body are one. I free them to excel.

➤ Every day in some way I am better, wiser, more adaptable, more focused, more confident, and more in control.

➤ I choose to live my life fully.

➤ I choose to excel.

➤ What I decide, I become.

After many years of working with students, athletes, teams, and people in all life contexts, I realized that they wanted bottom-line reminders of what they could do each day to come closer to living their dreams in their performance domains and life pursuits. I developed the following positive reminders specifically for that purpose. I often photocopy these reminders and give them to the people I work with. They stick the positive reminder list on a wall where they can see it daily. Their feedback on these reminders has been extremely positive, especially for bringing them back to a positive perspective when they begin to drift away.

Positive Reminders for Excelling

➤ **Always positive thoughts**. Only positive thoughts help you do the things that you really want to do. So think to yourself, talk to yourself, and focus only in ways that will help you live and perform to your true capacity.

➤ **Always positive images**. Only positive images of the things that you want to do or hope to accomplish will help you to accomplish them. So imagine yourself being the way you want to be, achieving the things that you want to achieve and doing the things that you want to do exactly the way that you would like to do them—with full focus, precision, and total confidence.

➤ **Always I can**. There is no advantage in approaching performance or life situations thinking *I can't* or *I won't be able to do this*. Approach all challenges and opportunities thinking only *I can* or *We can*. Act as if you can, even if you are not sure that you can. This perspective will give you your best chance of achieving your goals and living your dreams.

➤ **Always opportunities**. Opportunities are present in everything—to learn, to grow, to find something positive or of personal value, to know yourself better, to overcome challenges, to become stronger, wiser, more focused, more balanced, more joyful, or more consistent. Find the opportunities in everything.

➤ **Always focused**. Only when you are fully focused on connecting with each step, each experience, each interaction, each opportunity, or each performance can you live and perform to your true potential. So stay focused on the little things that free you to feel your best, be your best, and perform your best. Seek the pure connection, it will give you your best chance of living and performing to your ultimate capacity.

➤ **Always lessons**. In every practice, performance, and life experience there are lessons. Look for the good things that you have done, draw out the positive lessons from each experience, and live those lessons. Doing this will ensure that you continue to improve, grow, live, and excel in positive ways.

➤ **Always step-by-step**. You can accomplish great things by taking tiny steps forward each day. The step in front of you is all that matters. You are always capable of taking that one little step. Take that step, and then the next, and the next. This is the only path to your desired destination.

CHAPTER 13

Goals

I've had frustrated students and athletes come to me and say that they can't seem to meet their goals. Sometimes discussions about goals go something like this:

> *A journey of a lifetime begins with a single goal or vision that you commit to act on—one step at a time.*

Terry:	Did you set specific goals for yourself?
Student/athlete:	Oh, yes—I tried it and it didn't work, so I stopped setting goals.
Terry:	What were your goals?
Student/athlete:	To make my dream team, to compete in the Olympics. (Or "To finish my thesis by the summer," "To get an A in this class"; you get the idea.)
Terry:	Oh, I see. Did you set short-term goals, every day, that were totally within your control—like what you are going to do today, in the next hour, that will bring you one step closer to being your best?
Student/athlete:	No, not really.
Terry:	Do you have any specific goals for how you are going to get better tomorrow?
Student/athlete:	No, not really.

People often set long-term, far-off goals without focusing enough on the present. But it is the present that gets us to the future in the way that we wish to get there. Long-term goals can help motivate and guide you, but you also need lots of modest or achievable daily goals that take you progressively closer to your desired destination. In your journey to personal excellence, the best approach is to focus your energy on taking small steps that are within your control—to improve your skills, your preparation, your focus, your execution, your routines—and to prepare yourself mentally to be the best that you can be that day. Some outcomes in performances or competitive situations are not within your direct control because you do not control competitors, teammates, judges, officials, playing conditions, the weather, or chance occurrences—all of which can influence outcomes. When you set goals to control elements that are beyond your control, you set yourself up for frustration and needless stress. Controlling what is within your control—your focus and your best performance—is challenging enough. My advice is to stay focused on what you can do to be your best every day. Every day ask yourself, *What am I going to focus on doing today to take myself one step closer to my goal?*

Accomplishing Everyday Goals

To get where you want to go, set specific, relevant, daily goals and then focus fully on pursuing them, one step at a time. Encourage yourself, compliment yourself, and enjoy yourself as you achieve each short-term goal and move toward long-term ones. You want to get from point A to point B efficiently and joyfully, and focusing on the little steps gets you there. Let's say that you want to become the best performer that you can be, or that you want to write a book. Great! What are you going to do about it in the next five minutes, hour, day, week, month, year? Setting specific daily goals and pursuing them in a systematic, focused way separates those who want to meet challenges and excel from those who actually do.

Let's take the writing of the fourth edition of this book as an example. I could simply write whenever I feel like it, or whenever I have free time, and finish whenever the book is complete (if ever). Or I could commit to accomplish specific, concrete goals for myself, within a specific time frame, saying that I want to finish this section today, before eating supper; write the following section by the end of the week; finish the next chapter by the end of the month; complete the book by the end of the summer. I've tried the "do it when I feel like it" approach, but I never seem to advance very quickly toward my goal—not because I don't want to but because a hundred other things pull on my time. When I commit to specific times to write and set specific short-term goals that will take me to my long-term goals, things begin to roll along nicely.

For me, the process goes something like this. First, I think about whether completing a fourth edition of this book is important to me or anyone else. This first step is critical, because only if I have a meaningful reason to do it will I be truly committed to the goal and have a realistic chance of achieving it with quality. I decide that this goal is important to me because I like writing, creating, and reflecting, and I want to share my thoughts with you and others in hopes of helping you achieve some of your goals. I know more now than I did when I completed the third edition of this book eight years ago. I know that this book will be a much improved edition because the experiences that I have gained over these past years have crystallized the essence of excellence for me. Sharing meaningful and practical ideas that help people improve their performance and enhance their lives makes me feel that I am doing something worthwhile. Also, I love to see the visions in my mind become a bunch of roughly typed pages and then be transformed into a real book. It's concrete: I can see what I'm accomplishing, and in the end I can feel it and touch it. Thinking about the outcome and why it is important to me inspires me to do the work required to make it a reality. But achieving the outcome always comes back to focusing on the doing—which means acting on the day-by-day, step-by-step goals.

The concreteness of progress in most sports is readily obvious. New tricks, better technique, faster times, higher jumps, better plays, improved rankings—all can be seen and felt. You know exactly where you are, and you can see progress in a way that is often not possible in other aspects of life. When I teach a class or make a presentation to a group, for example, I rarely know whether I've really accomplished anything. I don't have anything concrete that tells me that I have effected any change in the lives of the members of the audience. On the other hand, sport, some performing arts, and my one-on-one consulting work with athletes offer indisputable proof of progress and influence, which can yield much personal meaning and add joy to life.

Let me return to my example of writing this book. Having determined at the outset that writing the book is important to me and to others, I begin to set some goals that are realistic in terms of my time, abilities, and motivation. Just the process of thinking about specific goals gets my mind moving. Writing my goals and projected completion dates on paper usually helps even more. During the process, some things take longer to finish than expected, but that is no reason to panic. I simply readjust the goals to bring them in line with my reality. At times I move ahead of my stated goals, usually when I am totally focused—in a zone—and things just seem to flow along by themselves. Some days I really need a break from writing. I take that break because it allows me to return refreshed with a clearer mind. The next day I usually work twice as well—particularly if I know that my goal is to complete a certain amount by the end of the week. I also take short breaks every day when I am writing—to run or paddle or exercise or play because doing so helps me feel better, be better, focus better, and write better.

I gain great satisfaction from fulfilling my goals, even the small ones. Meeting my goals makes me feel more alive. It shows me that I can decide to do something that is important to me and then do it. Reaching a goal feels good, even if it is only a short-term one. Often this feeling is enough to keep me moving toward the next goal, as long as I believe that it is a worthy one. If the goal has been difficult to meet or if I'm tired or need a lift, I take a few days off, go to nature, spend more time with my family or friends, run, ski, kayak, see a movie, or just relax. I treat myself well when I think I need or deserve a treat. We all need and deserve an occasional extravagance.

When you decide that something is worth pursuing, you can apply your mental skills to reach a high level in virtually any area of life. Whether you want to improve your focus; win a championship; excel in school, business, or the performing arts; enhance your health; improve a relationship; or balance your life, the basic procedures are the same. You need commitment, focus, a positive mind-set, and specific goals that are relevant to your pursuit.

Choosing Commitment

We all start with one constant: Each day has 24 hours! If I'm training or working toward a specific goal for a limited period of time, I might as well dig in and do as much quality work as I can during the time that I'm there. If I mentally prepare myself to complete every task as efficiently as I can, with high-quality focus and effort, I can meet my goals and still have time for myself, my family, and my friends. By organizing your time—planning your work or workout, setting specific daily goals, and focusing fully on executing those goals—you can accomplish more with quality while you are working or training. This approach leaves time for adequate rest and other joys in life. You can even schedule some relaxation time, some fun time, some free time. I believe in the importance of quality focus, quality work, and quality rest.

Three of my students observed some local gymnasts at practice. They recorded the time that each gymnast spent actually performing on the apparatus during a 2-hour workout. The average time was 15 to 20 minutes. How much time do you spend committed to focused, high-quality training or work during a practice or work session? Could you be using your time more effectively? Probably. But you have to be careful not to go overboard. You can't push your limits every second. You need time to breathe, to reflect, to evaluate previous performances, to prepare mentally for the next high-quality effort, to focus, to rest, to interact with others, and sometimes to just have fun.

It all boils down to what you want at different stages and within different contexts of your life. If it doesn't really matter to you whether you use your time more efficiently or whether you improve in a particular area, forget the performance goals and the striving for excellence. Focus on getting what you want out of the experience—fun, fitness, social interaction, the wind and sun on your face, or whatever you are seeking. Making that decision is perfectly OK. But if you want to excel or be your best in a particular field, then you need to make a major commitment, set specific goals, and maintain a fully connected focus.

When making this kind of focused commitment, you should be quite sure that the goal, and the overall process of striving to reach it, is sufficiently important to you to warrant your focus and commitment. Often we know intuitively whether something is worth pursuing with commitment. At other times we may want to ask ourselves some questions or discuss our feelings with people close to us. If you think about each of the following questions and respond to them honestly (perhaps in writing), the choice may become clear in your mind and you will probably be in a better position to make a decision that is right for you:

➤ Are you doing it because you really want to do it, or because someone else wants you to do it?

➤ Is this something in which you can find ongoing joy and satisfaction?

➤ Why do you want to do this?

➤ What do you expect to gain?

➤ What do you expect to lose?

➤ Do you think that the effort will be worth it when there are no guarantees of the outcome?

When you recognize that you have a choice and make a conscious decision in either direction, you can often approach things in a positive light. If you decide to go for it and are dedicated to the choice, you will have a greater capacity to endure the demands that follow. Friedrich Nietzsche wrote, "He who has a reason why can bear with almost any how." If your decision is to let it go, then you are free to pursue other, perhaps more meaningful, pursuits.

Setting Short-Term and Long-Term Goals

A respected coach or seasoned performer may be able to assist you in establishing realistic but challenging goals by helping you translate your overall aims into specific actions, moves, plays, times, programs, routines, scores, or performance requirements. Establish a series of short-term goals, with specific target dates for achievement, that are directly relevant to your long-term goals. Achieving a goal, even a short-term one, makes you feel competent and inspires you to pursue your next goal, thereby helping you maintain commitment and build self-confidence.

Short-term goals might include mastering a certain skill, focusing on quality work or quality execution, getting adequate rest, or completing a certain number of moves, plays, programs, or assignments—today, by the end of the week, by the end of the month. Your short-term goals can help you improve not only physically, technically, and tactically but also mentally; thus you should set daily goals for mental readiness, positive imagery, focusing, distraction control, relaxation, positive thinking, and drawing out lessons from your experiences.

Long-term goals may include becoming more positive with your overall attitude, less stressed, or more consistent with your best focus; reaching your highest level of excellence in your sport or performance domain; mastering a particular routine, program, race plan, or game plan; deciding on the speed, distance, time, or performance level that you want to attain by the end of the current year and in the following year; or achieving a personal best in an important assignment, performance, or competition.

©Tim Shaffer/Reuters/Corbis

► Annika Sorenstam didn't achieve success overnight. Great performers use short-term as well as long-term goals to achieve their dreams and you can too.

By writing down your goals in concrete terms (I will accomplish this by this time), you have a greater chance of accomplishing your objectives more quickly than you otherwise would. How many preparation days remain before your next performance, presentation, trials, audition, assignment, championship, or event? Write down your goals and the number of days remaining before your next key event. This simple activity is often enough to stimulate positive action.

Many top performers keep daily logbooks for training and performances to direct, monitor, and improve their performance. They list goals set and met, record their training programs, and keep track of their focus during best and less-than-best practices and performances. This routine speeds up their learning and makes their best performances more consistent because they learn more from each of their experiences and act on the lessons learned.

Think about tomorrow's goals tonight before you go to sleep or first thing in the morning before you get out of bed. Just lie there for a few minutes and run through your mind what you want to accomplish that day. This simple action sets the stage for doing the good things that you want to do every day.

Ultimately, you must set or commit to your own goals rather than have someone else dictate them for you. When you make the decision or completely agree with the decision, your commitment to go after that goal increases. Shared goal setting—between you and your coach, between you and your trainer or supervisor, between you and your parents, between you and your partner—is valuable as long as you have personally weighed the situation and feel that the goal is what you really want.

For many people, identifying their own goals and having input into their preparation or training program is the most effective means for reaching their potential. I know that this is true for most high-performance athletes with whom I work, and the same is probably true for you. You know better than anyone else what you have done and what you want to do. You also know better than others what will help you and what you need at a particular moment. You know yourself better than anyone else does.

You can sometimes strengthen your commitment to a goal by talking with family members, fellow performers, coaches, or friends about your reasons for making a particular commitment or pursuing a specific mission. Some athletes go so far as to make a public statement about their goals in an attempt to increase their commitment to pursue them. Many of us do not gain from making our goals public, but we can all gain from the support and encouragement of important people in our lives as we pursue our personal goals.

Support or guidance from others can be meaningful if it is constructive and on target. Still, you are unique. No one else is exactly like you. If you are to become your best, you and those around you must respect your unique qualities. Those special qualities are often what lead to greatness.

Pursuing meaningful goals helps you know yourself better, extend your limits, and give what you are capable of giving to yourself and others. If you really want to explore and embrace your potential, set individualized goals that you believe will take you where you want to go. The goal-setting process will likely become less formal as you become more experienced, but goals will still be there in your mind to guide you.

Making Adjustments

When you fall short of the goals that you set, remember that unmet goals, plateaus, times of seemingly little or no progress, and even periods of backsliding are natural. Everyone faces these experiences at some point. Progress is a series of ups and downs; it is not all clear sailing. Even when you see no obvious signs of improvement, you may still be laying the groundwork for future progress. Think of the best performer in your discipline. He has been discouraged at times. She has had to overcome problems and has failed to meet some of her goals. But somehow these performers persist through the setbacks and overcome the obstacles. Such trials are part of the path to excellence, part of the path of day-to-day living.

Falling short of a particular goal is not a tragedy. You grow from the experience and learn from it. Refine your focus, adjust your goal, and stick some short-term goals or intermediate steps in front of it. A temporary setback doesn't mean that you have to quit or give up on your goals. Instead, you draw out the lessons, work on setting additional short-term goals or more appropriate goals, improve your focus, and readjust goals as you come to know yourself and your situation better. Your goal may simply be to do, or cope, the best that you can on that day.

When I was younger, I used goal setting in a haphazard way. Now that I am more knowledgeable in this area, I am better able to set specific goals and adjust unmet goals by bringing them into line with myself, rather than trying to force myself into line with them. When a discrepancy exists, the goals are usually off target. I am being who I am. I am doing the best that I can at this moment, given the complexities of life. Goal setting doesn't provide all the answers, but when used properly it nudges you in the direction that you want to go. Regardless of what you want to accomplish, setting goals, being positive with yourself, and focusing on the step in front of you are important. Set some short-term goals to work on today, tomorrow, and every day. Put your goals up on the wall as a reminder. Try it. You've got nothing to lose and a lot to gain in terms of living closer to your potential.

Believing in Yourself

Your performance is a result of your visions and expectations for yourself, which you can bring to life through your focus. If you see yourself as having something of value to offer, as having a contribution to make, as having great potential, then this will be your reality. If you view yourself as having little or nothing to offer, then this will likewise be reflected in your performance, unless you change your perspective. Don't sell yourself short! You have much more to offer than you or most people recognize. How can I say that? I don't even know you, right? Well, if you are anything like other members of the human species whom I have encountered, you have all kinds of untapped potential. And if you are reading this book, you probably have visions of realizing some of that potential.

Excellence in any field depends largely on

➤ knowing where you want to go (having a vision),

➤ wanting to get there (making a commitment),

➤ believing in your ability to arrive at your desired destination (believing in your capacity), and

➤ connecting with the step in front of you (having a fully focused connection).

I once worked with a cross-country skier who was overflowing with natural talent. But he didn't think that he could be a great athlete because he had no "proof"—that was the word he used to describe what he needed before he could believe in himself. One way of securing the proof of your potential is to chart your progress systematically so that you can see your improvement. Another way is to work, train, or compete with some highly respected performers so that you realize that they too are human and that you can hang in there with them at least for certain pieces, assignments, or parts of training or competition.

Start looking for the good things in yourself and in your performances instead of always looking for what is lacking. Remind yourself of what you do well and give yourself suggestions for improvement in a positive and constructive manner. Walk out there and try to be positive with yourself. Act as if you can do anything. You will feel better, work better, and perform better; your approach might even rub off on those around you.

On many development teams, national teams, and professional teams with whom I have worked, I have asked athletes and coaches to respond in writing to questions about three key goals. I ask these questions to inspire personal excellence (the dream), to target realistic goals, and to address the critical issue of personal acceptance. The dream goal opens the door to your stretched potential, the realistic goal keeps you grounded and focused in reality, and the goal of self-acceptance helps create awareness that you are a valued human being and will continue to be one quite apart from your performance.

Goal Questions

➤ Dream goal. What is your dream goal? What would you really love to accomplish? What is potentially possible in the long run if you remove all barriers and stretch all your limits?

➤ Realistic goal. What do you feel is a realistic best performance goal that you can accomplish this year (based on your present skill level, your current motivation, and your commitment to focus on improvement)?

➤ Goal of self-acceptance. Can you make a commitment to accept yourself as a worthy human being and grow from the experience, regardless of whether you achieve your dream goal or realistic performance goal for this year?

Follow these three key goals. Dream big so you keep the door open for doing big things, focus fully on attaining a realistic best performance goal this year, and accept yourself as a valuable and worthy human being regardless of whether you attain those goals.

I remember inviting Alwyn Morris, an Olympic gold and silver medalist in flatwater kayaking, to speak at an international sport psychology conference that I was hosting. I had worked with Alwyn for many years through the ups and downs of his journey to excellence, and we had become good friends. He mentioned in his talk that he first started to believe that he could be an Olympic champion (and set it as a goal) when he met me and the national canoe–kayak team training camp in Florida. He specifically mentioned that writing down his dream goal on paper—Olympic champion—had somehow made it seem possible. He also mentioned that because he had a dream goal, a realistic goal, and a goal of self-acceptance, he had all the bases covered no mattered what happened. After you have the big three goals in place, everything else revolves around daily goals for mental readiness, best focus, and best effort to build the physical, technical, tactical, and mental skills that you need to be your best.

CHAPTER 14

Commitments

When Beckie Scott decided to become an Olympic champion in cross-country skiing and be the best she could possibly be, she made the choice that many other great performers make. She described it as "putting your heart and soul into doing everything it takes to accomplish that goal." That is the kind of focus and commitment required to excel at the highest levels.

My greatest power in life is my power to choose. I am the final authority over me. I make me.

Long before the Olympic Games, diver Sylvie Bernier, like many Olympic champions, decided that she was going to win the Olympics. As the Games approached, she often dreamed of achieving her goal, in her own words, "like flashes all the time. Every day I would see myself doing perfect dives, walking down and getting the medal. When it actually happened, it felt like I had already done it before."

To achieve your potential or live your real possibilities, somewhere deep in your core you have to choose to go after your dreams. You also have to create an underlying belief that you can do it. When you dream big dreams and focus on the little daily steps that will take you there, you nourish your long-term commitment, your focus, your confidence, and your belief in your mission.

Even if you fall short of attaining your ultimate goal, your dream of getting there inspires you to become far better and draw far closer to your dream than you otherwise would have. Great human accomplishments begin with some kind of vision or dream. Every great feat flashes through someone's mind before it surfaces as concrete reality, whether it be flying to the moon or Mars; becoming a great student, artist, or performer; making a positive difference in the world; healing yourself; excelling in a relationship; building a dynasty or a dream house. Dreams precede reality; they nourish it, even create it.

Our dreams of excellence or personal accomplishments are reflections into a future in which we are doing the things that we want to do, being the way that we want to be, and getting to the places we want to go. Visions of excellence, creative accomplishment, or harmonious relationships are themselves stimulating and uplifting. They provide us with meaningful direction and positive energy. Dreams of excellence often become memories of the future, waiting to unfold, for those who choose to push beyond the boundaries of past and present experiences.

All people who have excelled at anything had a dream of making a meaningful contribution, stretching their limits, accomplishing things that were important to them, becoming their best, or reaching the top. Those who excel dream big and go after their dreams. They begin with a dream and end up living a better reality—not because they are inherently better than others but because they have a dream and act in concrete ways that take them to their dreams. That is their essential advantage.

Some people dream big and stop with the dream. They remain stuck where they are because they do not act in concrete ways that lead them to their dream. That is their essential disadvantage. Dreams do not become a reality unless people act in ways that make them a reality.

Some people have no dreams of what they can be, what they can do, or what they can accomplish. They remain stuck where they are because they don't dream of a better way, or a better life, and they don't act because they don't see or believe in the possibility of a better way. This is a tragedy. But people can turn this situation around by beginning to see and accept the possibilities in undertakings they previously viewed as impossible. Few things are impossible for those who believe strongly enough in the possibilities and focus fully on making them positive realities.

Think about your own dreams. Visit them often in your mind. Decide to go after your dreams—large and small. Let them lead you. Following your dreams is the only chance you have of moving along your path of self-fulfillment, joy, and excellence. One life, many opportunities. Seize these opportunities now. Make them your reality now rather than looking back later and wishing that you had.

Identifying Qualities of Excellence

Why is it that two runners with identical physical capacities (percentage of fast- and slow-twitch muscle fiber, reaction time, limb size, aerobic capacity, and so on) run vastly different times? One becomes a world champion, and the other is a mediocre runner. Why do some athletes with all the right physical attributes never really excel? How do athletes with relatively little going for them physically meet world-class standards in extremely demanding events? The answer lies in using what one has to the fullest capacity.

Excellence is housed in a variety of shapes, sizes, shades, and cultures. Many great performers emerge from highly systematic training or educational programs, whereas others emerge from places or countries that lack any kind of organized system. Personal excellence is largely a question of believing in your capabilities and fully committing yourself to your development. Success is often based on finding a way to make it happen—regardless of where you come from or what kind of support system you have. If you want it badly enough, there is a way.

I have interviewed some of the world's best performers and coaches to get their views on the ingredients necessary to make it to the highest levels in their sports or performance disciplines. Commitment and focus were identified as the essential keys to excellence. To excel in any field, you must become highly committed and develop a sustained focus that allows you to perform your best under a variety of distracting or stressful circumstances.

Excellence in sport, school, the performing arts, business, or your profession begins with a dream or goal to which you bring commitment, intensity, and focus. At some point you have to say to yourself, *Hey, I want to be really great at this; I am going to do everything I can to be as good as I can be; I am making this a priority in my life*. To be your best, you must live this commitment and continue to focus on stretching your current limits. Commitment and focus guarantee improvement, and a lack of commitment or focus guarantees that you'll fall short of your potential.

©Jessica Rinaldi/Stringer/Reuters/Corbis

▶ Tom Brady exemplifies the kind of commitment and focus needed to make success happen.

The solid leaders in every sport and every performance discipline—for example, Michael Jordan, Wayne Gretzky, Tiger Woods, Mia Hamm, and Chris McCormack and Olympic champions Larry Cain, Kerrin Lee Gartner, Beckie Scott, Bonnie Blair, and Clara Hughes—are great examples of the kind of commitment and focus required to become the best that one can be. Their commitment and focus is or was reflected in the incredible focus and intensity that they brought to practice and competition. When they trained, they were there for a reason—to do their best and to accomplish their goals—and their goal was to be fully focused every second out there. In competition, they were energized and super focused. Nothing less than their best focus was enough. Their minds were on the right channel, and they were determined to perform their best, no matter what.

Making a Personal Commitment

Your personal level of commitment is something that you must work out for yourself. No one can tell you how important something is in your life; that is your decision. But it is clear that people who excel are extremely committed people. Achieving a high level of excellence without a high level of personal commitment is impossible.

At this point you may want to rate the importance of excelling in your sport, performance domain, or other meaningful pursuit on a scale from 1 to 10. A rating of 10 indicates that the activity is the most important thing in your life (very high commitment), a 1 indicates that it is not important at all (very low commitment), and a 5 indicates a middle position between the two.

How important is it for you to excel in your sport or performance domain?

1   2   3   4   5   6   7   8   9   10

Not very   Most important
important   focus in my life

When a large group of marathon runners responded to this commitment scale, it became evident that those with the highest commitment (scores of 9 and 10) became the fastest runners. As the commitment scores decreased, the performance levels decreased proportionally. The same was true for performers in a variety of other disciplines.

When members of national teams were asked what the main difference was between them and others who did not make the national team, their first response was commitment ("wanting it more," "being willing to train harder or smarter," "training and competing with more focus"). These committed athletes sometimes stayed after practice, focused on learning by watching the best athletes play or perform, practiced with more focus, and did extra work when required. They were willing to make sacrifices, and they believed that they would one day be excellent performers. Most important was their commitment to be totally focused within the practice and performance arenas.

In a study with the National Hockey League (NHL), we interviewed top NHL coaches and scouts. We asked them what they looked for when drafting a player into the NHL and why they thought that some players who were selected didn't do well. Commitment (desire, determination, attitude, heart, self-motivation) and focus were the crucial ingredients that tilted the balance between making it and not making it at the professional level. Making their hockey careers a top priority, maintaining personal pride, constantly trying to improve, and always investing maximum focus and effort were named as the key indicators of the kind of commitment necessary to succeed. The chief scout for one of the NHL's top teams expressed it this way: "The main thing is that the player is willing to give that little extra when it's needed. . . . He's preparing himself to give that little bit more . . . even when he might be dead tired. . . . This separates the great hockey player from the good hockey player."

Physically talented athletes who do not make it in the major leagues are described as lacking in the area of commitment, focus, or distraction control; unable to cope with the stress of the pro situation on or off the field, court, or ice ("could not cope with pro demands," "choked under pressure"). The difference between making it and not making it was highlighted in a discussion of the drafting of one of the NHL's most celebrated players—Bobby Clarke, former team captain and general manager of the Philadelphia Flyers hockey club.

> We drafted Bobby Clarke on our second round, but there was a boy we drafted on our first round who was bigger and stronger, could skate and shoot better than Clarke, but Clarke made it and he didn't. He never had the heart for the game. He wasn't willing to sacrifice that little bit extra that you need to be a professional hockey player. In practice, Clarke would be there 10 minutes longer and he would work harder. In a game, he got himself mentally prepared to give the extra effort. . . . The other player didn't do that. Result—one went ahead, the other fell behind. Clarke did extra work on the ice, where he had to give a little more to check the man, where he had to bear down. Where it showed more than any place is coming back. . . . Gotta give a little more. If you lose possession of the puck, now you have to dig down to your bootstraps for extra adrenaline to come back and check the man. Bobby Clarke would always show that. The other boy would put his head down and sort of give up. That's the difference between the two.

A commitment to do quality work is a prerequisite for excellence at any level in every discipline, but unless you also master the art of focus control you will continue to fall short of your goals or dreams. Excellence requires the development of a strong, fully connected focus, as well as an openness to learn from others.

Scotty Bowman, a highly respected NHL coach who guided his teams to many Stanley Cup NHL championships, offered some interesting advice in this regard:

➤ **Accept criticism**. "Our superstars can handle constructive criticism. . . . They can even handle unfair criticism. . . . If they make a mistake, they acknowledge it and do everything in their power to not make it again. . . . A person with star potential will not become a star if, when I criticize him or point out a mistake, he tries to fight me."

➤ **Don't be afraid to fail**. "If a superstar ever sees a slight opening, zip, he has the courage to go for the small hole. He won't hold back because he's afraid to fail."

➤ **Maintain composure**. "The best players maintain their composure . . . when there's a call that goes against them, maybe even a bad call. They stay cool, look to correct, and try to calm down the other players."

Being Your Best

To become the best you can possibly be, the first essential ingredient is your commitment to focus on doing the right things. It takes commitment and focus to train and rest your body so that you can perform under demanding conditions. It takes commitment to train your focus so that you can focus totally on executing your best performance skills under the most demanding or distracting circumstances. If you really want to become your best, acting on the following basic guidelines will help immensely:

➤ **Set specific daily goals**. You need to know what you want to accomplish every day, every practice, or every work session. Before you begin, take some time to prepare yourself mentally so that you actually do what you want to do and get the most out of yourself during that practice, work, or performance session. Commit yourself to execute your skills with full focus. In practice sessions, simulate what you want to do in the performance setting. Run through complete, clean routines, programs, plays, moves, races, or events on a regular basis. During work sessions, scrimmages, or run-throughs, focus 100 percent, every step of the way. Positive imagery can help you prepare your mind and body to perform closer to your potential. Imagine and feel yourself successfully executing the skills that you are trying to perfect, and then focus fully on executing those skills.

➤ **Listen to your body**. When preparing for an important competition, series, or performance, rest well and avoid overworking or overtraining so that you go in rested, strong, and healthy. The commitment to rest well is as important as the commitment to train well. Without proper rest, the mind–body system falters and eventually breaks down.

➤ **Discover your best focus**. Discover what focus works best for you in different high-performance contexts. Where is your focus when you perform best? Respect this focus. If it drifts away, click back to your best focus. Remind yourself to activate or reactivate your best focus in preparation sessions, during performances, and whenever you encounter obstacles or distractions.

➤ **Decide to remain positive**. Practice overcoming distractions on a daily basis. Avoid wasting energy on things beyond your control. Staying positive will lead to higher-quality training, better performances, and more joyful living. Before important events, remind yourself of the focus that works best for you. Mentally prepare yourself to connect fully with your task for the entire performance and be prepared to refocus through the distractions in the heat of the moment. Follow the preevent preparation patterns that have resulted in your best performances. Imagine and feel yourself executing your perfect performance or key parts of your performance. Doing so will ensure that the best performance program is fresh in your mind and body. Then close off your thinking and connect totally with your performance.

Draw the lessons out of every event. What went well? What needs refining? Were you able to maintain your best focus for the whole performance? Were you able to refocus quickly if you got off track? What do you want to do in the same way next time? What do you want to change for your next performance? How do you want to focus in your next performance, game, race, event, or competition? What reminders might help you respect the focus that works best for you? Make a note of these key points and work on them so that you are better prepared—mentally, physically and emotionally—for your next challenge.

The following prerequisites for excellence are quotes drawn from interviews with NHL coaches and scouts. Think of ways that you can apply them to your situation or sport.

Prerequisites for Excellence

➤ Do constant work on the ice; be in on the action, always after the puck, the check, or the goal; make things happen; give a little extra when it is important.

➤ After a mistake, goal against, or a coach's criticism, come back with a strong shift, make the right moves, stay in the play or game, and try harder to correct or make up for the mistake.

➤ Never give up (for example, take a check, get back into the play quickly, try and try again).

➤ Plan, evaluate, and correct with linemates on the bench; encourage others; pass to better-positioned players on the ice.

➤ Take tips, ask questions, listen, admit errors and correct them without excuses, and show that you want to continue to learn.

- ➤ Pursue activities both in and out of season to maintain conditioning and improve skills (for example, by fitness training and power skating).

- ➤ Learn how to perform in a big game as well as in a normal game; come through in tight situations or close games; make the big play when needed.

- ➤ Learn how to stay motivated, come back, and play well after a setback, mistake, missed chance, call against you or your team, or bad penalty.

- ➤ Learn to control your temper (for example, do not needlessly retaliate after a hit or setback). Learn to react to referees, coaches, teammates, and fans in a mature and positive way, particularly in big games.

- ➤ Learn to adapt to the stress of success, travel, and playing with different players (for example, line switching) without negative effects on your attitude or play.

- ➤ Learn to stay cool, confident, and focused under pressure (for example, avoid being moody or worrying excessively; maintain focus on getting the job done in pressure situations).

Lessons with Chris McCormack

Chris McCormack is one of the world's best Ironman triathletes. Chris has won over 130 triathlon races globally, at all distances. In July 2004 and 2005 he accomplished two sub-eight-hour Ironman races, and in July 2006 he placed second in the world championships in Hawaii. In this interview he sheds light on the commitment and focus required to bring the highest level of excellence to this extremely demanding sport. My graduate student, Karine Grand'Maison, conducted interviews with Chris and a number of other leading Ironman triathletes for her master's thesis. I extracted portions of Karine's interview with Chris to share an excellent example of commitment to excellence.

Commitment to Training

I guess the biggest challenge for Ironman racers is the volume of work, the training, the time that needs to be committed to the sport for the three disciplines. The volume of work uses up a lot of time. I'm a very hard trainer. I think anyone who trains with me knows that. I have four or five training partners, and I recycle them. I like standing at the start line thinking, *There's not a person here who's trained harder than me.* So for me that's a positive, when I'm standing at the start line, in there swimming, fighting in the water, going, *OK, we've got eight hours of pain, but no one here has been through what I've been through.* Everything I need to do for every race, I do. It gives me confidence, and it gives me the edge when I'm meeting those obstacles during the race. If there's someone up the road, I can remind myself, *I've hurt like this a thousand times before, and he hasn't trained as hard as I did. You're ready for this, don't be soft.*

When I've had good training, I'm standing on that start line and going, *OK, there's nothing more I could have done to be more ready for this phase, and physically I think I'm the best in the world. So there's no one here who should beat me.* So anyone who's in front of me shouldn't be there, and the only person who's stopping me from winning is me. When I have an obstacle I deal with it; I deal with this thing. Otherwise, this guy is going to beat me, and he doesn't deserve to beat me because he's not as good as I am. That's how I deal with things. Self-doubt is the biggest killer for anyone. That's why I like to start every race feeling that I've done everything I can to be ready for it. Self-doubt can kill you and take away a win.

Commitment to Your Plan

The swim. I'll place myself among the good swimmers and get ready to go. Once the gun goes, it's long strokes, like I've done so many times in training. That's all I think about. I'll pick up my rate [turnover of the arms] and think, *Long strokes, long swim strokes, come on.* The first part is fast. I'll usually position myself next to the best swimmer. He's going to be the first out of the water, so all I have to concentrate on is his suit. Obviously, I look up every 10 or 15 strokes, but I just focus on swimming next to him. So I don't look up for maybe the first three or four minutes. We start to get into clear water, and then he might start to pull away because he's a bit stronger. The group starts to establish itself, and then my focus is just staying where I am, staying with the front guys. My aim is just to keep my tempo, the things that I've trained, the pace I've trained at, which is usually in the front group.

Two hundred meters out from the transition, I'm starting to think about the bike. I might be kicking a bit more to get some blood into the legs, and I'm thinking, *OK, where's my bike.* I picture where it is. And I'll start to look at who's around me then, what competitors are there. Then I'm concentrating on the bike, getting out, getting my wetsuit off. You've walked the transition chute so you know where stuff is. You get out of the water and just follow your path that you've done in training.

The bike. My thoughts getting on the bike are, *Let's go! Now we're on the land, this is where I'm good.* So boom, I'm immediately shoes on and ready to rock 'n' roll. I set a really good tempo, and I try to draw people into my pace, especially the younger guys, because I want to have people with me if I can. When you're solo all day for hours on the bike, it's just lonely. It's good to have other people around. Also, if they tend to have bad patches, you drop them. You take their energy and you feel good about it. You sort of steal their energy. I like having people around me and battling with people. I draw from that; I get energy from that.

On the 180-kilometer ride I keep repeating the circle. For me, it's like 500 calories in per hour. I'm going to have a Clif Shot every 15 minutes; I'm going to drink that bidden [bottle] of water within this hour. Every 15 minutes you're riding along and you're like, *OK, there's an aid station: Clif Shot, drink.* And then it's 120 calories, and when you start counting calories it's amazing how quick that part goes, because you're thinking in small increments all the time. You're like, *OK, there's an hour, have I got 500 calories in? Yep, boom, start again. Have I got enough water? What gear am I pushing? Is the pace good?* You're thinking so many things. In my first Ironman, I remember thinking, *What am I going to think of for 8 1/2 hours? How boring!* And I was absolutely amazed how quickly it went.

The run. I'm a runner. But the run still intimidates me. Every Ironman I've done, I have led off the bike. So the two where I've failed, I failed on the run. So in the last five kilometers on the bike I always think, *OK, that felt good.* I get off the bike, and the first thing I'm thinking about is how the legs are feeling. Then my whole race for the run is structured around my watch. I go, *OK, boom, start the watch.* Now I'm going to run four minutes a kilometer. I've done it one million times in training, I know I can do it comfortably, I know I won't be in any trouble, and if I run four minutes a kilometer, no one will catch me. A 2:48 marathon will win it for me, no matter what, because the guys who can run quicker will be too far behind. So I start my watch. After the first kilometer I ask myself, *Too fast or too slow?* And usually it's too fast, because of the hype, so I just adjust my pace and take my fuel in. The run is quite easy for the first 10 miles. I focus on staying controlled, staying on the pace, and staying relaxed.

I want to know where my competitors are, but I'll never look back for them. I always try to think, *I'm in the lead; everyone is feeling equally as uncomfortable as I am.* I consider myself one of the best guys in the world at this, so anyone who is behind me is behind me because they're not as good as me. And they're feeling just as bad as I am. So to catch me, they've got to run quicker than I am running right now and they can't do it. These are the things that I think to myself.

Sometimes you get to a turnaround point and you'll see your competitors for the first time. You always try to look good. And you just keep saying to yourself, *OK, they're four minutes back. OK, we're*

20 kilometers from home. He has to take one minute out of me every 5 kilometers, and he can't do it, man! If I'm hanging on to this pace, he can't do it.

I'll never think about my competitors when I have a bad patch. I'm thinking, *How am I going to get out of this? OK, fuel, caffeine. I need sugar. OK, let's slow it down a bit, slow the pace, and I'm in the circle, I'm expecting it to happen.* I'm not going into this race expecting not to have any bad patch. It's going to happen. You just think, *OK, this is a bad patch, I expected this to happen. I've done this 50 times before in races, and I wonder how long this is going to last.* And sometimes you think, *Oh, here we go, 5 or probably 10 minutes of this, so it will probably be that bridge down there.* You're like, *I'll probably feel uncomfortable up to that bridge; let's just run to that bridge.* Your body will adjust, and you'll come out of it. It's amazing how it does it! When you show your body that you're not going to stop, it says, *OK,* and goes back to being good again. You have to avoid giving in to your body, because if your body senses that your mind is going to be weak and give in to it, it will shut down! When you're feeling good, you capitalize on it, and when you're feeling bad, you can slow it down. If you're capitalizing when your competitors are going through a bad patch, it ends up helping you out. At the end of the day, it's the person who has the fewest bad patches who wins the race.

Commitment to Staying Positive

In the Ironman at the elite level, everyone's physically well conditioned. Your mind is important, and not just in the race. It's the whole package—the training too because it is such a monotonous sport, with monotonous workloads. Mentally, I look at my Ironman failures and successes and try to determine the causes. In the ones that went bad, I allowed outside sources of negativity to move into my race. Things weren't going my way, I went for hard sections, the pace was fast, it was hot and windy, it wasn't what I expected, and I allowed those things to influence my race. Once you start down that path, it's like the dark side of the force in *Star Wars*. Once you start with the negative, it's easy to quit mentally. If you switch off mentally in the Ironman, it's over.

In an Ironman, especially when it gets hard and tough, it's important to be mentally tough. You have to remain positive. The way I try to think of it is this: In my perfect scenario, I lead out of the swim by 5 minutes, I have a 10-minute lead out of the bike, I run great, and I win. That's a perfect scenario, but it's not going to happen. So I think of it like a circle, no matter where I am in that circle I'm going to have obstacles, and I deal with those obstacles as they arise. So if I'm swimming and I'm behind, I deal with it: *OK, I have to make up the distance and focus on the now, not the future or the past.*

In the swim, my plan is to swim off and go with the front people. If that's working, great; I focus on that. If it's not, then when I am in "the now," I think, *OK, let's lengthen my stroke. How can I get back to where I want to be,* and I focus on those things and meet those obstacles as they arise. I look at those races where I did badly, and I didn't deal with "the now." I was like, *Ahhhhh, it's over, it's finished,* instead of focusing on meeting the challenge in front of me. I think many people do that. That's where the mental side as opposed to the physical side is more important, because I think in those bad races, physically I could have been successful, but I allowed the negatives and those obstacles to stop my progress. Instead of meeting the obstacles and fixing them or dealing with them by going, *OK, this has happened, so let's focus on what we're doing and deal with this*, I allowed the obstacles to become an issue so I couldn't get past them. I never completed the circle (back to the positive action focus).

You either deal with the problem in the race now, or you don't. And if you don't it's going to finish you. The race is going to finish, and there's nothing worse than being in the car driving home after the race thinking, *If only I'd sprinted earlier, if only I'd eaten that food, if only . . . .* I never like to have "if onlys."

To complete the circle and not let the negativity affect my performance, if I'm on the bike and I'm behind, I look at my pace and my gear and think, *OK, this is my pace. This guy is going well; maybe he's going too fast.* Obviously, you have to revert to what you're physically capable of doing. If I'm behind on the bike and everything is going well, then I just reassure myself that this is good: *He's going too fast for me at the moment. It's a long day. We have eight or nine hours. Maybe he's pushing too hard.* So I deal with what I can control, my variables. If I'm going for a bad section, if it's tough and I'm losing because it's tough, then I'm constantly saying, *It's OK.* Your body is not too smart, but your mind is amazing. Your body starts to do what you tell it to do. If you start thinking that you're tired and it's hot, your body will react so as to make you tired. It's actually lazy, I think. It wants to stop, and it doesn't want to be there, so it constantly sends these messages that it's uncomfortable. So you keep telling yourself, *I feel good. This is a problem, but we'll deal with it. It's OK.*

Your body is not the smartest thing. It will do anything your mind tells it to do. You've seen these athletes start wobbling during a race. They're physically shutting down, but their minds keep telling them, *Everything is good, everything is good, keep moving forward, keep going forward.* You're still mentally alert. You know what's going on.

If I am tired and I'm losing time, the first thing I can control is fuel. *Let's get some fuel, let's drink, let's shift the gears. Maybe I'm pushing too big a gear. Rest the back.* Just control the things you can control and ride out the storm. When you're tired, you might be running out of fuel. You need to get out of the saddle and change gears. You try to control the things within that environment to take your mind off what isn't helping you. You keep telling yourself, *It's normal, this is normal, this is an Ironman. It's a long day, eight hours.* It's biorhythms. You're going to have good times and bad times, and you expect that. You think, *I'm going through a rough patch at the moment. I'll come out OK.* Maybe you get some caffeine in and spark yourself up, and 9 times out of 10 you ride out the storm. Boom! You're back!

I've been in some races where I truly think I'm going to die and then 10 minutes later, I am Superman again; my body is OK. You just have to remain in a positive frame of mind. And positive is not just saying, *Great, I feel great, I feel great,* because you're not stupid. You don't feel great. Positive is like, *OK, it's an obstacle, but I'm going to make it. I've felt great all day, and suddenly I'm starting to feel tired. Let's deal with this problem now.* Sometimes it could be 10 minutes or 20 minutes. Sometimes it could be a hill, 30 seconds. And after you've ridden that out, you actually feel stronger because you think, *Wow, I just dealt with that. OK. I'm back! Now let's get back in our race plan,* which is to pick up the intensity, pick up the pace.

I'll start riding to pick up the tempo, and I'll work. When I feel good, I capitalize on it. When I feel bad, I'll deal with the problem. I'm prepared to lose time when I feel bad. When I feel good, I'm on the attack, I'm racing my race. I'm an aggressive racer. I think that's why I'm successful. Bang! From the start I'm aggressive. Go! Catch me if you can. I'm usually leading all the time. I always like to be in the front of the race, always in control, putting the pressure on everyone else.

When you race with that mind-set, there's only two ways of thinking: You're on the attack or you're on defense, and the only time that you're on defense is when you're feeling bad. And you're going to feel bad because you're pushing a lot harder than the guys who start out slowly. They're not going to have a bad patch until very late in the race, maybe 10 kilometers from home on the run.

Commitment Through Pain

I think anyone doing an Ironman knows that it's going to be uncomfortable. You know that you're going to get sore, it's going to be painful, but you're going to be close to the finish. That's how I always think. When the pain is coming, the day is nearly done. Honestly, in the Ironman 70 percent of it is comfortable. The swim is easy. The first half of the bike is controlled—you can talk and you feel good. Then the pain starts to come, but you're halfway through the race. I always think, *OK, I'm here in the circle. I have to complete the circle. I've done so much. I only have a little bit to go.* That pain I actually enjoy. I like that part of the race. That's sort of the whole reason you start doing it, to push yourself. You can be in pain or uncomfortable but still in control, and that's different from a bad patch where you can be feeling great and then suddenly feel terrible. You just have to deal with it and take fuel.

At the later part of the races you have painful periods, but you can be in pain and still be in control. The greatest part of the race is when you're on this line and you push yourself and push yourself and push yourself, but you're somewhat in control of it. The endorphins are flowing. It's like a high—that's the buzz of Ironman racing. Mentally, that's not tough. Mentally, it's tough when it's painful and you have one of those bad patches. That's the toughest combination you can have later in the race, maybe on the run 5 kilometers from home. Your legs are very tired, you're physically exhausted, you've been pushing yourself and pushing yourself, and suddenly you run out of glycogen. You have no fuel left, and suddenly you feel terrible, absolutely terrible—weak and tired as well as in pain.

I always tend to suffer the last 30 minutes, because I'm so aggressive early in the race. A lot of the time you're so tired physically, mentally, and emotionally at this point of the race that everything becomes sort of a blur. Because I'm close to the finish I just think, *It's nearly home, it's nearly home, it's nearly home.* I'm thinking, *It's 15 minutes, 15 more minutes and this is over, we've finished this.* I'm always saying that to myself. *Complete the circle, complete the circle, finish the circle, 15 more minutes and we're done. We'll pack it up, go home, it's done.* And if it's half an hour from home, it's a Seinfeld episode. Or 30 minutes from home I might picture my favorite training runs, where I always do my long runs in Sydney. I always say to myself, *You're at the Springs, 30 minutes from home. How many times have you run home from the Springs?* I visualize that run from the Springs: *I'm at the Springs. I've done this a million times. Today it sucks. I don't feel good but just run home from the Springs. Put one foot in front of the other.* And bang, bang, bang—it's like a trance.

Commitment to Finishing Strong

In a race in Germany, I had my toughest competitor (Lothar) right beside me for the whole latter part of the race. I'm always trying to think, *Come on, let's get home, let's get home, you're at the Springs.*

But my competitive instincts are there. I'm looking across at him, and the whole time it was a really strange sensation because it was a real cat and mouse game. I was trying to look great even though I felt terrible. Speaking to Lothar after the race, he said the same thing; he was absolutely destroyed. He said that with eight kilometers to go, he had nothing left, but at the time I thought he looked great. During the race, I just put my chest out, and it was a big mind game between the two of us. I remember thinking, *OK, when we get four kilometers from home, that's it.* I took my belt off. *I'm racing, I don't care how much this hurts.* And for me that last four kilometers was just a blur. I don't remember anything. I just put my head down and ran. All that I remember is seeing Lothar's arm side by side with me the whole time. I just focused on the run. I don't remember the people coming the other way. I just kept running and running.

I remember, like in flashes, coming down the hill and working together side by side. The hill went to the left, and Lothar had the inside. I remember immediately thinking to myself, *It's because it turned left and I was on the right-hand side. I guess it's because he raced there so many times.* We came out of the corner, and he had one step in front. It stayed like that the whole last 500 meters, one step in front. The whole way to the finish. At that point, I remember I was looking, pumping my arms, thinking, *Just run past him, run past him. Come on, run past him, just go, run past him!* But I couldn't catch him, and he's just one step ahead the whole way. All the people were going nuts. I learned some things from that race that made me a better Ironman racer.

Commitment to Learn From Every Race

I always do evaluations of my races and my preparation. I like to write everything down—all my training, my races, what works, what doesn't. For the successful races I can look back at the good things. If I have a bad race, I look at what went wrong, why, and when I felt bad, just so I can replicate good things. You form the model for your training and competitions, so you're always trying to find what works and what doesn't. Your body is an amazing instrument.

If mentally you know that something worked in the past, replicate it. I have done that in my short-course career. Through my whole career, people have asked, "How are you so successful?" I won a race doing something, and I did it again. I won again, just did it again, and did it again. It's simple, and some people and coaches try to complicate things. Find something that works for you and just replicate it. You obviously adjust your training and your focus, but you stick to the patterns that work.

Commitment to Pushing Your Limits

I've had some races where I've got the wobbles a lot. And you're alert, even though it may not look like it. I see this as a mental and physical challenge. I enjoy putting myself in that position and pushing myself. I get immense satisfaction out of it. I don't know why. I get a buzz, I think. If I was going to do these Ironmans and it didn't hurt, I don't think I'd do it. There would be no buzz to it.

All the winners, all the people who have been successful in Hawaii, have taken a chance. They've gone, *You know what, it's the world's championship, and I want this more than you, and I'm going to ride and race like that.* So a lot of people have "died" trying, and they don't become stars, but I respect them more than the guy who is racing for fifth. The person who wants to win Hawaii, the person who ultimately wins Hawaii, arrives thinking that he can. And I think there's only a handful of guys that turn up in Hawaii each year thinking that they can win. I think that of the 100 pros competing, only 10 think that they can win. The rest are there for fifth place.

I would never do that. I'd rather die trying than never try at all. It's just the way I am, and I guess in Hawaii I've blown up the last two years trying. The first one I had a 10-minute lead off the bike, first ever in Hawaii, but I blew the pace in the marathon. Last year, I attacked the last half of the bike. And I got away, took my chance, and blew up six miles away. And everyone keeps saying, "You should wait, you should relax, you have to pay your dues. You need to come in 10th, 5th." Forget that! I don't want to come in 10th. I'm a competitor. I'm a racer. It's in me. I don't train as I do, and go without spending time with my family, and live this harsh lifestyle to come in 10th, you know!

The big obstacle that I'll be working on for Hawaii will be having no doubts. I'll be ready to race. I'll be doing everything I can. I'll be training in the heat. I'm going to Hawaii on a training block for 10 days to race the course, run the course, learn the course, and know the course. I'm going to have rough patches and challenges in that race, and these are the issues that I'm going to deal with. It's all about preparation, visualization, and convincing yourself that everything is good.

Commitment to Be the Best

I'm hard on myself because I think I'm physically good enough to win. If I were riding the Tour de France against Lance Armstrong, I wouldn't be hard on myself if he rode 20 minutes faster than I did. But in this sport I'm hard on myself because I think I'm good enough to win. If I don't win it's because I've done something wrong, or the other person was better and I need to adjust and make changes so that it doesn't happen again. There's no one in the sport I have seen yet who scares me, about whom I think, *You're better than me*.

In short course (Olympic distance), Simon Whitfield is a better runner than I am. I've trained with him, he's one of my best friends, and I know that if we ever came together off the bike and had to run side by side, he would beat me every single time. It's a hard thing to swallow as an athlete. It's the first time ever in my sport where I've had to acknowledge that someone is better than me. I cannot beat him in the run. But in the Ironman if I was racing Simon, I would never let myself be in that position. In Ironman, there's no one I've seen whom I cannot swim with, I cannot bike with, and I cannot run with. So for me it's a big positive, and I try to start the race thinking that way. It's something I take with me every day in training.

Commitment to Achieving Goals

When I first started triathlon I had a list of all the things I wanted to do. I wrote down that I wanted to be a world champion, win the World Cup series, win the national championships, and win the French Iron Tour (Iron Tour is like the Tour de France for triathlon in seven days). I wanted to win Chicago, win Wildflower, and win Alcatraz. I wanted to win the Hawaiian Ironman, and I wanted to break eight hours. That was it. And I ticked them off. I won the worlds, I won the World Cup, I won Alcatraz, I won Wildflower, and the only two left for me are Hawaii and eight hours. I still have the list on a piece of paper in an old training diary. It keeps me motivated.

Until I achieve those goals, I will continue to be hard on myself. I will continue to assess races, continue to learn from what I am doing wrong. I will continue to fly to training camps, go to different places to meet with sport scientists, and spend time away from my family. I think that when I'm done, I will have accomplished things that I can be really proud of. It's better to die trying than never to try at all. That's how I like to think. Catch me if you can. And if you do, well done!

Since this interview, Chris won a silver medal at the Hawaii Ironman World Championships in 2006, ran two sub-8-hour Ironmans to win the Quelle Challenge in Roth, Germany, in 2004 (7:57:50) and 2005 (7:58:45), and won the Australia Ironman in 2005 and 2006.

CHAPTER 15

Connections

One night as I was driving down a little dirt road in the countryside near my home, something darted out of the darkness onto the road right in front of me. My heart pounded as I lurched for the

> Where your mind goes, everything follows.

brakes. A large rust-colored cat was in pursuit of a little gray field mouse. The cat focused on that mouse as if nothing else in the world existed, as if some kind of radiant energy beam connected the cat to the mouse. If I had not hit the brakes, I would have run over the cat—but she pursued that mouse as if I didn't exist. Only after she had the mouse firmly clenched in her teeth did she acknowledge my existence and saunter off into the woods. This is an example of full focusing, the uninterrupted connection between two things. It could be a cat and a mouse, or a performer and his performance, or an athlete and her goal.

Have you ever closely observed young children at play? If you watch pre-school children playing, you will notice that the only thing that exists in their world at that time is the action, interaction, or movement that they are engaged in at that moment. They are totally unhindered by the chaos around them. You can call out their names, yell at them, or drop something on the floor next to them, and they don't even notice. The intensity and connection of their focus is similar to the connection of the cat with the mouse or a great performer with a great performance. If you could focus that completely as a child, you are capable of doing it now.

Focused connection is the most important skill in life because it affects everything—all learning, all performance, all relationships, all joy in life. With a focused connection (see figure 15.1), everything is possible. Without a focused connection, nothing of value is possible. A focused connection is the difference between a great performance and a poor performance, between really living your life and just dragging yourself through another day. Many opportunities are lost because people are present physically but not mentally. They are not taking advantage of learning opportunities, performance opportunities, relationship opportunities, or opportunities to live simple joys

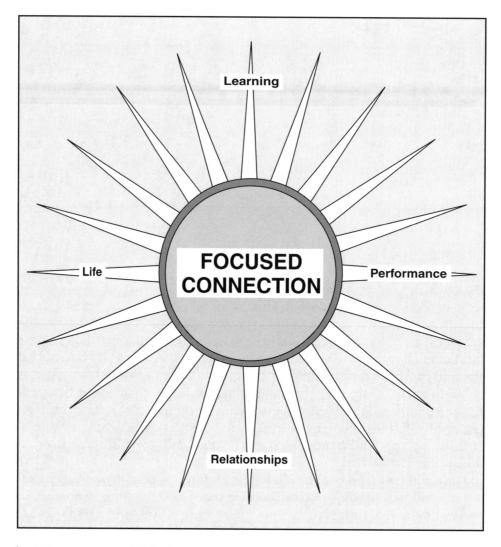

▶ **Figure 15.1**   A fully focused connection is the center of learning, performing, enhancing relationships, and experiencing joy in life. The more connected you are, the more fulfilling your life will be.

every day because they do not bring a fully focused connection into their daily experiences, daily performances, and daily opportunities.

In reality, focus is everything—in life and in performance pursuits. A positive, absorbing focus channels your commitment into a series of positive actions, thereby making your personal journey to excellence possible. A fully connected focus releases you from everything irrelevant and connects you firmly with your experience or performance. Focus is a state of mind where nothing exists apart from your connection with what you are engaged in or experiencing at that moment. Focusing is the most important skill associated with ongoing learning and consistent high-level performance. Your challenge is to discover and perfect a focus that frees you to learn and perform your best and to live that fully connected focus while you are engaged in every task, activity, or performance.

The quality of your focus, or the depth of your focused connection, affects every learning, performance, and relationship situation you have. It determines your rate of learning, quality of learning, quality of performance, and quality of life. By guiding your focused connection in positive ways, you control the intensity, direction, duration, consistency, and joyfulness of your experiences, actions, and reactions. Your focus is the leader. Where your focus goes, everything else follows. Let it lead wisely.

Tuning Out External Worries

If a 2-year-old child who is playing begins to think about being assessed on her movements by all the big people around her, do you think that her focused connection will remain the same or be broken? A 14-year-old competitive figure skater came to see me a few years ago precisely because she had lost this focused connection. She had entered her first major competition when she was 11 years old. At that time, she just went out and let it happen. She skated in the same way that young children play, totally absorbed in her performance and oblivious to the outside world.

Only later, when she started to think about judges, other skaters, the audience, results, and evaluation, did she start to become uptight and lose her focused connection: "When people said I was expected to win, the feeling of pressure started." Her thoughts began to drift to others' expectations of her. She began to worry about her performance and about how it would affect her acceptance by others: "What if I fall or screw something up?" Her stress began to rise, and her performance began to slide. At this moment, she lost her focus—her natural connection. As she attempted to regain this connection, what worked best for her was to try to re-create the focus and feelings that she had taken into her sport in her earlier years, to focus only on connecting with her own performance and forget about everything else.

When you free yourself from dwelling on outside expectations or thoughts of possible failure, when you focus on the step in front of you and know that you will continue to be a valuable human being regardless of numerical outcomes, worry is less likely to intrude on your performance or your life. Your focus will be free to flow more naturally. Worry is one of the greatest inhibitors of skilled performance because it breaks the focused connection that frees you to perform naturally. If you can view your performances as pure opportunities and connect with your performance in a way that is more absorbing than the worry, you will be on your way to consistent performance at your optimum level.

Focusing is an internal process—something that you experience from the inside out. A focused connection is something that you feel and experience within your mind, body, spirit, and soul. It is something that you initiate and have the power to direct or control. Focus is also something that extends beyond you, creating an inseparable connection between you and what you are doing or between you and people around you. A fully connected focus is something that others in your presence can feel and sometimes see. Feeling the presence of that kind of connection, feeling the power of that focus, feeding off the power of that kind of focus is inspiring for you and for others.

An interview that I did with Chris Hadfield, former fighter pilot, test pilot, engineer, and one of the world's most respected astronauts, offers a great example of the value of a fully focused connection. Chris provided the following insights:

> When you're flying an airplane at 500 miles an hour, there's all kinds of things that don't matter, and there's a few things that really, really matter. What's in front of you for the next kilometer really matters because you're going to be there in a few seconds. The whole rest of your world doesn't matter; what's going on with your car or at home, or what just happened 30 seconds ago, or whatever. What really matters is what's going to have the biggest impact on you in the next 30 seconds. In a high-performance airplane things happen quickly, especially when you're flying down low or flying with another aircraft. So you need to completely compartmentalize and just be ready to disregard things that don't matter and worry about them later. Even though it may be life or death later, for now it doesn't matter and you can't pay attention to it. You need to focus fully on what is in front of you right now.
>
> There are times when if you don't focus right down to the critical items right there, you don't give yourself a chance to succeed. So you've got to learn to put things into their boxes and drawers and compartments to be able to succeed. I think I learned to focus that way incrementally over my whole life. I was a downhill ski racer as a teenager, and there's a lot of focus required in that. In downhill racing, you have the next 30 seconds to do it right—either you're getting a medal or you're falling and maybe breaking your leg. So that's a good opportunity to focus. You can begin by doing it on a very small scale. Focus for this length of time to get something done that's difficult. Challenge yourself to do something that you can just barely do, and then learn how to focus on it until you can do it well. Then slowly expand that.

Did you ever wonder why we spend time worrying when all it does is interfere with our effectiveness? Worry creates stress, drains energy, and takes us away from our best performance focus. To close the door on unproductive worry, shift your focus to concrete positive actions that will prepare you to do something constructive or connect you to your performance.

Most performers find that once they are actively engaged in doing things that fully absorb them, such as a preperformance routine or execution of the performance itself, the worry disappears. They have successfully shifted their focus away from worry to a more productive, absorbing focus. If your focus is fully connected to something other than worry, you cannot be worrying at the same time.

You can shift your focus away from worry by refocusing on something more constructive that you would prefer to be doing or thinking about, such as running through a specific move, strategy, or technique that you want to use; reviewing your game plan or race plan; thinking of a previous best performance; remembering a positive life experience, thought, or image; focusing on relaxing your shoulders or relaxing your breathing; or remembering that you are fully capable of executing this performance and reminding yourself of your best focus. This shift in focus will help you stop worrying about what is beyond your control at this moment and get you focused on what is within your control. The goal is to stop comparing, doubting, evaluating yourself, thinking negatively, putting yourself down, thinking about outcomes, or projecting into the future. The goal is to support yourself, remind yourself of your readiness, and then completely absorb yourself in the process of doing what you want to do.

To shift to a more productive focus, absorb yourself in thinking about what you would prefer to be thinking, and focus on doing what you would prefer to be doing at this moment. Let your focus absorb itself in the good things that you have done, the good things that you are doing now, and the good things that you are going to do next. Then focus fully on doing it. If you practice focusing this way in a variety of settings, you will strengthen your focused connection and increase your effectiveness.

When one of my daughters, Skye, was five years old, she asked me, "Daddy, when will I be grown up?" Her question made me reflect on what being grown up actually means. Physically, we are grown up relatively early in life, but mentally and emotionally, and in terms of our focus, we can continue to be in the process of growing up for our entire life. You can choose to improve the depth and quality of your focus in different parts of your life. You can choose to become more positive, to feel less stressed, to deal better with stress, to get better at not wasting your emotions, and to live everyday with a healthier life perspective. There is no end line for growing up mentally and emotionally or for growing your focus.

Focusing for Total Connection

The goal of a world-class archer is to hit the center of the target with each arrow. He trains himself to find the middle of the middle, to see only one center. Genge (1976) described the process that the archer uses:

> In this state of full focus, he could be anywhere in the world and remain undistracted. He shoots each arrow as a separate entity,

concentrating fully for the short period required to release that shot. The periods between are times to relax, in which all tension, muscular and mental, is dissipated and the mind is freed from the last arrow in preparation for the next one-arrow effort.

One world champion archer described focusing in the following way:

> I block out everything in my world, except me and my target. The bow becomes an extension of me. All attention is focused on lining up my pin [sight] with the center of the target. At this point in time, that is all I see, hear, or feel. With the bow drawn and sight on target, a quick body scan can tell me if anything is off. If everything feels right, I hold focus and simply let the arrow fly. It will find the target. If something feels off, I lower the bow and draw again.

When a person has trained her muscles and nervous system to shoot an arrow into the middle of a target, theoretically she should be able to put it into the center every time. What prevents her from doing this? As with most performers, worry, distracting thoughts, and a loss of that totally connected focus with the target prevent archers from achieving their true potential. They have the program in their mind and body to perform the skill flawlessly. They can do it without thinking. Their challenge, like yours, is to free the body and mind to connect totally with the goal—for every shot, for every move, from start to finish.

What all the world's best performers seek, and work to perfect, is a fully connected focus. They clear the mind of irrelevant thoughts and focus only on what is important at that moment. Outside distractions are absent. The focus is centered on a specific target—first the preparation, then the doing—a total connection with one's body and one's performance.

When you are focused in any sport, you are totally connected to what you are engaged in to the exclusion of everything else. In a real sense, you and your performance become one, and nothing else in the world exists for that time. In many individual sports, best performances occur when athletes are totally connected or riveted to their performance, trusting their bodies and their preparation, often to the point of performing on autopilot and letting their bodies lead without conscious interference. In some circumstances they may use conscious reminders to maintain good technique or push through discomfort, pain, or adversity and then reconnect to their performance.

In team sports, best performances likewise occur when players are totally focused and absorbed in the crucial aspects of their performance. They are aware of the flow of relevant play around them, completely trusting in their capacity to automatically read and react to that awareness, and totally connected to executing their moves. Their focus remains adaptable, like the zoom lens on a camera, capable of zooming in and zooming out quickly. For example, a point guard in basketball, a quarterback in American football, or a ball carrier in soccer (World Cup football) needs a wide-angle perspective to

▶ James Blake and other great athletes possess the ability to tune out their surroundings and fully connect with their performance.

read the field for an open player and then must zoom in on the open player and make a crisp, accurate pass. For best performances a total connection to your task is required through the constantly changing demands of the game or performance.

You must discover what kind of focus works best for you and in various circumstances. Initially, you may experience a completely connected focus (on the right things) for only short periods. Work on allowing your best focus to become a natural part of how you connect your focus during practices and performances.

If you want to perform your best, you cannot afford to focus on things or thoughts that interfere with your best performance. Discover what kinds of focus or thoughts get in the way of your best performances and replace them with something that will help you.

A fully connected focus is absorbing, natural, free flowing, and intense. It is simple and magical—a focus that you lived often as a young child. The ultimate goal is to enter this fully connected focus on a consistent basis. Connect fully, trust your connection, and free yourself to let outside worries go so that you can live and perform closer to your capacity in everyday interactions and in situations that count. The key to accomplishing this lies in absorbing yourself in the present, in the here and now, and gradually increasing the consistency, quality, and duration of your connected focus.

Developing Your Best Focus

Your best focus may at times feel like a nonfocus because you are letting a performance unfold automatically and freely—often free from conscious thought, directives, or self-evaluation. In many contexts, connecting to your focus just means tuning in to your body, trusting your body, connecting to the step in front of you, and remaining totally connected to your experience or task. Training to improve your focus involves learning to stay connected to what you are doing, discovering the feelings that free you to perform your best, not letting irrelevant or distracting thoughts interfere with the natural performance program in your mind and body, trusting your mind or body to do what you have trained it to do without forcing, and directing your mind or body when it begins to tire or deviate from an effective performance.

To improve your focusing skills and make your best focus more consistent, set some goals to allow your best focus to surface more regularly. Here are some practical tips to choose from to help make this happen:

1. When you walk into the gym or onto the field or when you step into your practice setting, performance context, or work arena, leave everything else behind. Nothing that happened before you got there matters. During this time, be totally there and totally focused. Make the best of this opportunity.

2. Use focused imagery to feel yourself execute your best actions, reactions, skills, moves, programs, plays, or performances in your mind and body. Then focus on executing some of those key skills, actions, or reactions in your practice, work, or performance setting. Let them unfold freely and naturally, without any negative or interfering thoughts. Remember also that focused, positive imagery is itself a great focusing exercise.

3. When you train, practice, interact, work, or perform, focus on being totally connected to whatever you are doing or trying to do. Think about what you want to do or what you want to accomplish today (physically, technically, tactically, or mentally) and then focus fully on doing it.

4. If your sport, work, or performance domain requires awareness of your teammates (with whom you work or play) or other players to whom you must connect, respond, or react effectively, practice focusing on relevant things that are going on around you in that context. Then totally connect your focus to your target, your moves, your best actions, or your preferred actions and reactions. Practice reading and reacting fluidly and naturally.

5. Free yourself to execute some actions, reactions, skills, moves, or tasks without conscious thought or evaluation. Just do it, let it go, be totally in that moment, and see what happens. Go by feel. Go by instinct. Free yourself to let the moves flow freely and naturally. Don't question. Don't evaluate. Just be totally in the doing. See what it feels like. See where it takes you.

6. When training, working, and performing, decide to respect the focus that allowed you to perform your best in the past and the focus that is likely to free you to perform your best in the future.

7. Find some crisp, powerful focus reminders that can help you enter or reenter your best performance focus and use them every day, in every interaction, in every performance.

8. Practice maintaining your best, most connected focus for as long as you can—even if you start by doing it only for very short periods. Commit to achieving a gradual increase in the time that you are fully connected. The ultimate goal is to be able to sustain your best focus, your absolute connection, throughout your entire performance—every move, every step, or every stroke of the way, from start to finish.

9. When you step out of your performance arena or work space, leave it behind. Shift focus to connecting with something less demanding, more relaxing, or simply joyful. This shift will free you to enter nonperformance contexts with a positive, connected focus and allow you to return to your performance arena feeling more refreshed.

10. Tonight, before you go to sleep, when you are lying quietly in your bed, decide what you are going to do tomorrow. Think of a couple of key things that you want to accomplish tomorrow. When you wake up in the morning, while you are still lying quietly in your bed, think of those key things that you decided to do. Then get up and do them, with a fully connected focus. Make this part of your regular presleep and early morning routine.

Using Focused Actions

The following focused actions grow out of what you have already read about developing your best focus. Act on these suggestions to improve your focused connection within your performance setting:

➤ Stand or sit quietly, let your shoulders relax, and think about doing a particular skill or movement. Try to imagine and feel the perfect execution of that skill. Then perform the skill, letting your body perform automatically.

➤ Seek the feel of the movement. If the feel is right, everything else will be right.

➤ When you are feeling stressed before an event, try hitting the slow-motion button to slow everything down. Move slowly, talk slowly, and stretch slowly; breathe in a slow, deep, relaxed way.

➤ When you are feeling distracted, try clearing the distractions from your mind by thinking about little things that you can focus on that free you to perform your best. Everything else is unimportant.

➤ If you make a mistake, breathe and quickly shift focus to the next move, which is within your control. This refocusing will help you get back on track quickly.

➤ Prepare yourself to stay focused in the moment—one shot, one stroke, one swing, one step, one move at a time, disregarding past and future. Only the present moment counts. Seek this connected focus every day, every opportunity.

➤ Use simple reminders to keep your focus on target (for example, *focus, connect, forward, smooth, relax, be here, be all here, decide*). Find a powerful image or effective reminder that will get you back to your best focus if you drift away.

➤ Embrace the simple joys in your pursuit.

If you experience difficulties with maintaining a fully connected focus, sometimes the best approach is to try easier: Relax your body, relax your focus, lighten your load, and move forward deliberately without forcing anything. Liken your efforts to this ancient Chinese saying: "Sitting quietly, doing nothing, spring comes, the grass grows by itself." A calm mind gives the clearest focus, just as a tranquil lake casts the clearest reflection. A simple connected focus that fully absorbs your awareness frees your body to perform and to follow the visions of your mind.

The world's top performers achieve their best results when they connect fully with their performances and clear their minds of thoughts about outcomes during performances. It is not that they never think about outcomes, but thinking about results, scores, or outcomes during a performance often interferes with their best performance focus. A top Olympic shooter offered this perspective:

> For my best performances, I'm thinking about how to shoot correctly, letting shooting sequences run through my head, seeing myself in control, confident. It is very important for me not to start adding the score and projecting what the score might be. If during the last few ends [rounds] I become nervous and start to worry about blowing it, I have to work hard to keep my shooting sequence in mind (*form, form, form*) and not the glory of shooting a high score.

Another top Olympic athlete maintained, "I'm not nervous in a negative sense in advance, because I remain who I am, myself, so that it is impossible for other competitors to have a harmful effect on me." She doesn't go through a big comparison scene, worrying about how well others are performing. She simply does her own thing.

> For my best performances, I empty my mind and I feel as though it isn't me performing, but at the same time I feel totally connected with the feelings in my body. It's as if my subconscious is doing the performance. I imagine the perfect movement in my head, and the rest follows automatically.

After the event, she evaluates why her performance was good or bad. If it was good, she asks herself, *How did I get my mind and focus working that way, how can I duplicate it the next time.* If her performance was not up to par, she draws out the lessons and moves on. In her own words, "I probably work harder and learn more when something goes wrong."

Regaining Focus

The difference between best and less-than-best performances lies within your focus. In poor performances, you allow negative or distracting thoughts (about other performers, your preparation, doubts, others' expectations, fatigue, a bad warm-up, a mistake, a previous performance, the weather, or final placing) to interfere with a fully connected focus. In best performances, you are able to stay in the moment, which is the only moment that you can influence anyway. If you find yourself losing your best focus, try one of the strategies that I have already discussed or use one of the following strategies:

- Return to basics; go with the focus that has worked best for you.
- Focus on following your game plan, race plan, shot plan, or performance plan.
- Break your challenge into manageable parts—one section, one shift, one rush, one shot, one hurdle, one stroke, one step, one piece, one inch, one day at a time.
- Focus only on the step immediately in front of you. Then focus on the next step, and then on the next.
- If you have trained or prepared well, reassure yourself that you have trained well and are ready (for example, say to yourself, *I have done this skill a thousand times before—I am fully capable of doing it well*).
- If you have not trained or prepared as well as you had hoped, remind yourself that anything is possible if you focus fully on bringing out the best that you have to give: *I am fully capable of doing well if I focus fully on doing it.*
- Remind yourself of your best past performances and recall the feelings and focus that allowed you to perform well.
- Remember that your goals are realistic. All you want to do is perform as you are capable of performing.
- Focus on doing what is right for you rather than worrying about what is wrong.
- Imagine the perfect execution of your skills or game plan; then focus on doing what you are fully capable of doing.
- Remind yourself to stay in the moment. Forget the past, the other athletes or performers, and the final score. Focus only on doing your job.
- Connect your focus to the little steps, one step at a time.
- Remind yourself that it's just another game or performance. It's just you and your performance.

➤ Remind yourself that anything is possible if you focus on the doing. Let your focus lead you.

➤ Do a careful postperformance analysis after every performance (best and less-than-best performances). Reflect closely on where your focus was and where you want it to be. This process is extremely valuable, even two or three days afterward.

➤ Keep some joy in your training and performing. Embrace the good parts. Focus through the tough parts. If you hate it, look closely for the good parts, then focus on finding more good parts; if you can't find any good parts after looking diligently, leave it and do something else.

Practicing Focus

Developing your ability to connect fully with the important little steps in your performance and hold it there is critical to consistent high-level performance. Fully connected focusing is a learned skill that you must practice to achieve perfection. You can find many opportunities to practice improving your focusing skill outside your performance setting. Taking advantage of these opportunities is important for two reasons. First, you will connect more fully in your life outside your performance domain, and second you will improve your focus within your performance domain. Here are some general focusing exercises that you can try:

➤ When you are sitting in a classroom, talking with someone, or listening to a person speak, try to clear your mind of everything else and connect fully with what that person is saying. See how long you can hold a fully connected focus. If you drift away, see how quickly you can refocus or regain a fully focused connection.

➤ When you are reading, studying, writing, doing puzzles, watching TV, hammering nails, doing homework, or performing some other task, practice focusing fully only on what you are doing. You can also try this when other people are watching, making noise, or talking. Breathe, relax, and then focus fully. If you lose focus, see how quickly you can regain a fully connected focus.

➤ Look at the page that is in front of you now. Pick the third word from the end of this sentence and focus on it. Focus on this word until it stands out more than anything else on the page. Then back up your focus so that you become aware of the sentence. Good!

➤ When you are doing something physically active, see how it feels to focus on different kinds of thoughts or feelings. Have a run today, and as you extend your leg, think *stretch* or *float*. Do this about 10 times in a row. See what happens. Then try thinking *power* when your left foot hits the ground and again when your right foot touches the ground. Do this about 10 times in a row. See what happens.

➤ Do some body scans during the day. Focus on the sensations in different parts of your body. How does your back feel right now as you sit here reading? Are you sitting up straight? You are now! Are your hips forward, in line with your shoulders? How do the soles of your feet feel right now? Are they warm? Are your calves relaxed? What does your behind feel like right now? Now focus on your shoulders. Are they relaxed? Let them drop a little. Think relaxation into your shoulders. Wiggle them a bit. Roll your head. Relax.

➤ Sit quietly, relax your breathing, and focus on looking at something in front of you, such as what is on the table, a pen, a flower, a painting, a piece of fruit, a leaf, the bark of a tree, a friend's hand or face, a cloud. Really focus on it; look closely at its shape, texture, design, and feel; get absorbed in it to the point that everything around it disappears.

➤ Sit quietly, breathe in slowly, breathe out slowly, and let yourself relax. Focus on listening to something like the voices of people, the sounds in the room, the sounds outside in the street, the sounds of nature—birds, the wind, the leaves—or other sounds that you hear around you right now. Get absorbed in one of those sounds; then let it fade away by absorbing yourself in another sound or another focus.

➤ Line up several targets or objects. Become aware of all the targets. Then begin to narrow your focus until you are aware of only one target, then the center of that target, and finally the center of the center of the target. Let all other visions blur into the background; let all external sounds disappear. Connect fully with that target.

➤ Close your eyes and focus on a specific positive thought, image, or action that you would like to become your reality. Repeat the thought to yourself or try to make the image or action clear in your mind, then stop thinking about it for about five slow breaths. Then refocus on feeling that specific positive thought, image, or action.

The key to high-quality performance and high-quality living centers on positive connections and fully focused connections. Let those connections lead you to your potential.

CHAPTER 16

Challenges

When you face challenges in which the stakes are higher, the scrutiny is more intense, and the outcome is more important than anything you have done up to that point in your life, you are essentially performing in an Olympic context. As one seasoned professional athlete said of his recent Olympic experience, "It doesn't get any bigger than this."

When you enter your greatest challenges, you have a choice either to get caught up in all the irrelevant things that surround you or to focus fully on executing your best performance.

You have probably faced challenges in your life that felt enormous, or overwhelming, or almost insurmountable at that time, and you will certainly face other challenges like that in the future. How well did you respond to those challenges? Ultimately, if you worked through those challenges successfully, you probably did it by shifting to a positive perspective and by focusing on the step in front of you.

Few of us have experienced the enormous challenge of performing within an Olympic Games context, but most of us have had, or will have, our own Olympic moments. Two factors—perspective and focus—determine how well we perform within those challenges. How prepared are you to accept big challenges as opportunities? How skilled are you at remaining positive and fully focused on the step-by-step process of engaging yourself in the experience or performance? Excelling or performing your best in your Olympic context, whatever that may be at this point in your life, depends almost entirely on your perspective and your focus.

We falter or fail to reach our goals in what is for us an Olympic context for two main reasons. First, we fail to respect the focusing patterns that work best for us. We do this by changing or not respecting the focus that has worked well for us in the past. This failure to respect our best focus results in our performing below our capacity. Second, we fail to prepare ourselves to deal effectively with distractions. Every crucial context that we enter during our lives includes distractions that can take us away from our best performance focus. Problems often surface in this context when we allow ourselves to shift focus away from fully connecting with our performance and begin to focus on doubts, concerns about outcomes, or consequences of failure. Distractions in any challenging context can take you places where you don't want to go, so you must prepare yourself to deal with them effectively.

When facing certain challenges, sometimes we fail to do our best because we don't try hard enough, but in a high-stakes context we often try too hard. At a recent Olympics one of the world's best long-track speed skaters, who was favored to win, faltered in his Olympic races and finished far off the podium. In a subsequent World Cup race shortly after the Olympics, he was back on track as a world leader. What was different? He returned to familiar territory, took the load off his shoulders, and followed patterns of thinking, focusing, and performing that work best for him—not too much and not too little. His beam was focused back on the ground and he was fully connected with the right things.

Your Olympic Context

When you enter your Olympic context, the important event that you are about to participate in, what do you think will be the same and what do you think will be different from other events that you have participated in? What do you think you will have to focus on to have your best results? What do you think might interfere with having your best results? The performance demands in your Olympic context are no different from the performance demands at any other competition, but many things that surround the performance are different.

Have you ever walked across a wooden beam that is lying on the ground or along a train track? Imagine what it would be like to walk across that beam or along that train track if it were suspended between two buildings 100 stories in the air. The performance task is exactly the same. If you can do it on the ground, you can do it on a beam suspended 10 feet or 100 stories in the air. You can do it if you believe that you can do it and if you fully connect with putting one foot in front of the other—step by step. The consequences of failure, however, are dramatically different. If you lose your focus and your balance at extreme heights, even momentarily, the fall will be long and hard.

The raising of the beam gives a little flavor of what some athletes and other performers might feel when walking in to perform within their Olympic context. The task is the same, but the context and consequences are not. When you have dreamed of this moment or trained extremely hard for this moment, and the expectations are high, and many people are watching, including everyone important to you, the consequences may feel different.

When consequences feel critically important and you feel that you have to perform well, focus fully on executing the task before you and on nothing else. Doing this is not always easy, but it is possible if you are able to keep things in perspective and prepare yourself mentally to bring your focus only where it needs to be at that moment.

At some levels and in some sports, the hopes and dreams of nations and sponsors ride on the backs of athletes. For example, at the 2002 Winter Olympics in Salt Lake City the powerful Swedish ice hockey team was unexpectedly eliminated after a strong showing in the preliminary round. The Swedish media tore into the players and described their loss as one of the most devastating events in Swedish history. On the other hand, Canadians were ecstatic when they won the gold medal after a poor showing in the preliminary round. More Canadians watched that game than any other televised event in Canadian history.

Some differences that may surface in your Olympic context include the number of spectators, the crowds around the venue, noise, media presence, security checks, travel time, traffic, delays, crowded restaurants, noisy or uncomfortable lodgings, and reduced training time. If you are prepared to deal with these kinds of distractions and let your positive focusing and refocusing skills lead you, your chances of performing your best within your Olympic context are greatly enhanced. When you are well prepared for the kinds of realities that you will likely face in your Olympic context, they are not a big deal. You plan for them, focus through them, and move on to do what you came to do.

To perform your best in contexts like this, one of the first things that you should do, perhaps after being at least momentarily stunned by the environment, or in awe of the people, or feeling somewhat intimidated, is to take control. This can begin with a simple step—plan your day! How do you want your day to unfold? How much can you do and still respect your primary reason for being here?

When do you want to get up, eat, sleep, practice, rest, take a break, or find some quiet time for yourself? When do you want to make yourself available to other people or other demands and when do you want to restrict access? When do you want to eat together as a team, and when do you want to eat on your own or with a friend, family member, coach, or couple of teammates?

In one Olympic context, a team of basketball players who were accustomed to eating as a team reported that never eating together as an entire team at the Olympics took away from their sense of team unity and hurt their performance. This highlights the importance of respecting familiar patterns that have worked well for you and your team in the past. Decide what you want to do each day as a human being, as an athlete, as a teammate, and as a person who wants to perform your best. What will help you feel your best, focus your best, and perform your best?

Athletes and coaches who do not perform to their potential at the Olympic Games usually fall short not because the performance demands are different but because they have not prepared well enough to deal effectively with the Olympic environment, the Olympic expectations, and the many distractions surrounding their performance. Those who perform to their capacity plan their own best path, commit themselves to staying positive through the

© Ronald Martinez/Getty Images

▶ Successful athletes like Dwyane Wade prepare themselves for dealing with the pressure of high stakes competitions.

many challenges, and focus fully on executing their best performance. Anything is possible when you prepare well, see the challenge as a great opportunity, draw positive energy from your Olympic context, and channel your focus into connecting totally with your performance.

When you are in your high-stakes context, your performance outcome will depend almost entirely on how well you maintain your best performance focus. Your simple goal should be to connect fully with your performance, your game plan, or your race plan to the exclusion of everything else. Focus fully on each stride, each stroke, each move, each shift, each little step. Let your on-site performance focus rivet you to executing your best performance, step by step. Give everything you have so that you leave with no regrets. Nothing else matters.

Phases of Preparation

Preparing to be your best in your Olympic context spans three distinct but interrelated phases: (1) the preparation phase leading up to the event, (2) the on-site familiarization phase, which includes adapting to the new environment and dealing with multiple distractions, and (3) the on-site performance phase. In addition, the important postperformance transition phase allows you to draw out lessons and move on in a positive way. Each of the preparation phases affects the quality of your focus and the quality of your performance. If you are well prepared and focused for each of these phases, you greatly increase your chances of performing to your capacity in your Olympic context. If you ignore these phases of preparation, you heighten the risk of falling short of your dreams, goals, and potential.

1. Preevent Preparation Phase

Within a relatively short period you will be in the midst of the excitement of performing or competing at your big event. To perform your best, plan your preparation phase so that you are at your best when it is time to compete. Respect the training and rest patterns that work best for you in the time leading up to the event. Prepare yourself to remain positive and to focus fully on the right things at the right time at the event. Your goal in the final preparation phase is to do everything that you can to be at your best physically, mentally, technically, and emotionally, without feeling overloaded.

Leading into this performance, fine-tune what already works for you rather than trying to overhaul your training or performance program. Remember what got you where you are now. Keep doing the things that have worked for you and refine the things that will make you even better.

Focus on quality training and quality rest. Avoid overworking or overtraining. Trying to do too much within the limited period before big events is an error that has led to many disappointing performances. Go in rested and ready, knowing that you can give your absolute best. Being well rested and mentally ready for the demands is a critical part of excelling in your big event.

2. On-Site Familiarization Phase

The more familiar you are with the environment in which you will be performing or competing, the more comfortable, relaxed, or normal you will feel within it. Talking with athletes, coaches, or sport psychology consultants who have experience in big events like the one in which you will be competing can be extremely helpful. Ask them for details about what to expect, their own experiences, and their suggestions for preparing to perform in this context. I often ask former Olympic athletes to share their Olympic experiences with athletes, coaches, and teams that I am working with. Their stories help the athletes and coaches prepare themselves for their biggest challenges. These kinds of mental preparation meetings have always been an empowering experience for everyone involved.

Many events or championships have Web sites that provide photos and updates about facilities, competition venues, and so on. In other cases you can request updated information from your coaches, team leaders, former athletes, and sport federations or associations. They may be able to provide answers to your specific questions, requests, or concerns. Every championship venue is unique in certain ways, but there are many common challenges, distractions, and opportunities that athletes and coaches can prepare themselves for.

If you have been through an event similar to the one that you are facing now, be sure to draw out the important lessons from your previous experiences. Carefully reflect on what you did well, what you were focused on when you were doing your best, and what you can improve or do differently to be better prepared and more focused for your upcoming performance.

If possible, go to the competition venue to train or compete sometime before the actual competition. Many athletes with whom I have worked have had personal best performances and won medals at the Olympic Games after visiting, training on, or competing on their Olympic course or in their Olympic arena before doing it under the lights in the real Olympic Games. Their experience made them feel more in control and more comfortable, as if the venue was their place. In addition, they could continue to prepare mentally for competing at that venue when they were away from it. For example, they could recall details of what it looked like, think through their race plans or game plans, and imagine themselves performing their best on that specific course or in that particular arena.

After you arrive on-site for your big event, gradually familiarize or refamiliarize yourself with the various areas where you will be staying, training, and performing. Make sure that you know the location of everything important to you (for example, transportation options, food, drinks, bathrooms, warm-up areas). After you settle into your lodgings, become familiar and comfortable with your competition venue. Even if you have trained or competed in that venue previously, check it out carefully. Some changes in the course or venue may have been made for the current event. For example, for the triathlon event at the 1996 Sydney Olympics, large concrete barriers were erected to restrain the many spectators who lined the course. These barriers dramatically narrowed the course in some sections, resulting in a number of crashes in the bicycle portion of the race. You should be aware of and prepared for these kinds of changes rather than be disappointed by a circumstance that you might have been able to avoid or manage. The more prepared you are for everything that you will face, the better you will feel, the better you will focus, and the better you will perform.

When it has been possible to gain access to competition venues, many athletes I have worked with found it helpful to go there when no one else was around to get the feel of the place, to feel good in that place, to walk through or think through their game plan or race plan, or to trace the steps that they wanted to follow on their competition days. Some of these athletes walked from their warm-up area into the performance arena just as they would in the competition. Others got into their starting position or imagined themselves performing the way that they wanted to perform while being right there in the place where they would do it. Anything that helps you feel more ready, more relaxed, more confident, more focused, and more in control can enhance the quality of your performance on the big day.

3. On-Site Performance Phase

The task that lies before you at your big event is the same task that you have performed many times before. The most important part of performing to your capacity within this context is to respect the patterns that have worked best for you in the past—during the lead-up time, on-site at your venue, just before you compete, and during your performance. Follow your normal precompetition routine and do your normal warm-up. Then focus fully on executing your performance—step by step, shift by shift, section by section. Follow your focus plan to stay on track. Use your refocusing plan to get back on track if you start to drift away. Decide to follow your plan. Then follow that plan.

Expect to feel different when you enter your Olympic context and know that you can perform to your capacity within it. Know that after you begin performing, playing, or competing, everything that is irrelevant will fade away. Everything will again be familiar. It will be just you and your totally connected focus, you and your performance.

Remember to follow the same patterns that freed you to perform your best in previous events. Rest well. Carry a positive perspective. Draw on the relaxed intensity required to bring out your best. Focus on what is within your control. Connect totally with your performance. Nothing else matters. Just focus on doing your job and executing your performance, which you have done many times before. Plan your own path. Follow your precompetition routine. Focus on staying connected. Take it step by step. Give everything that you possibly can that day. You are not asking yourself to do anything unreasonable—only to perform as you are capable of performing.

Many athletes and performers I have worked with who performed to their capacity in their Olympic context found that responding to the following two questions in their final preparation phase helped strengthen their confidence and direct their focus:

1. Why I can. List the reasons why you can achieve your goals in this event.
2. How I will. Outline how you will achieve your goals in this event. What do you have to focus on to achieve your goals?

4. Postperformance Phase

If you prepare the way that I have suggested, when your big event is over and you return home, you will know that you prepared as well as you possibly could, given the constraints and complexities of your life. You will know that you gave everything you could, and you will have no regrets. If you gave everything that you could on that day at this point in your life, you have won a personal victory.

You achieved one of your lifetime dreams just by representing your neighborhood, your city, your state or province, your county, your region, your school, your club, your country, your family, and yourself at your competition. Regardless of where you placed in the contest, you need to keep things in perspective. You know that you tried your best within a challenging context, regardless of your performance outcome. You have grown as a person and a performer through your efforts in this pursuit, although you may not yet fully realize it.

Just competing among the best in what you are doing is a great accomplishment. Few people reach the high level of skill that you have attained, in any field or endeavor. The people who know you are proud of you for what you have done and for how you represented your family, your community, your school, your region, or your country. Think about the wonderful experiences, opportunities, and accomplishments that you have gained from committing yourself to this pursuit. Think about the friends you have made and the many lessons you have learned on your journey. You will carry these memories with you for the rest of your life. Take some well-deserved time to rest and embrace simple joys before moving forward to one of the many other exciting challenges that lie ahead.

Implications for the Future

Much of what frees you to remain positive and focused in the big challenges that you have faced or are facing right now is relevant to your future, when you will be performing, living, and facing life's other big challenges. The challenges that lie ahead may be even bigger or more important—such as competing in more prominent performance events; being more consistent with your best performances; overcoming injury or sickness; maintaining health; giving birth; dealing with setbacks, loss, failure; rebounding from the death of a loved one; or being your best when it counts most in relationships, parenting, teaching, coaching, your studies, your profession, business, or any other performance domain.

Olympic contexts, in and out of your sport or performance domain, are highly charged, emotional events, because at that moment you feel as if your life, mission, reputation, value, relationships, or worth is on the line. And in some cases the outcome really does matter. Before you enter these kinds of contexts, plan your path, and when you are immersed within the challenge, draw on your best focus. With a focus plan to remain positive and deal effectively with distractions, you will conserve your energy, carry a more confident perspective, enhance your performance, and contribute more to your team's performance. The outcome of thorough planning, detailed mental preparation, and full focus in any important performance context is success.

We all face challenges in life in which the demands are high, outcomes are important, and our ability to remain positive, composed, and focused is put to the test. When entering these challenges, pause for a moment to think about what you want to accomplish, how you want to focus to do it, and why it is worth doing well. Remember that small, positive shifts in focus make a huge difference when working through obstacles, performing in stressful situations, or living within challenging, emotionally charged contexts. Anything that makes you feel better, happier, more relaxed, more confident, or more focused on what you control, inside or outside this context, can enhance your focus, joy, and performance. Moving along this path is a choice that you make for yourself. Arriving at the place where you want to be is a step-by-step process. Making your best focus consistent gives you your best chance of mastering this quest.

CHAPTER 17

Actions

You now have at your disposal some of the best-known strategies to enhance your focusing and guide your personal pursuit of excellence. When you apply relevant strategies that you have read about in the previous 16 chapters, your options for personal growth

> *Man cannot discover new oceans unless he has the courage to lose sight of the shore.*
>
> *André Gide*

will become clearer and your chances of reaching your personal goals will increase significantly. Of course, to achieve positive change, you must act on relevant knowledge and experience. Without action, nothing changes.

Experiencing and choosing to refine strategies will help you understand what works best for you and help you discover how to direct and sustain your best focus so that you can achieve your goals. This approach usually means practicing a strategy long enough and often enough for its positive effects to surface in a consistent, natural way. Even when no signs of improvement are immediately evident, you can be laying the foundation for future use or personal growth. The three main topics presented in this chapter describe actions that you can choose to take that will allow you to live and perform closer to your potential:

1. *Docide*. Act on your decisions.
2. Persist. Focus through the obstacles
3. Retain your purpose. Remember why you are pursuing your goals and dreams

Docide

From what you have already read in this book, or parts of this book, it has probably become clear to you that the doing side of deciding is what has the greatest positive effect on our performance and our lives. The doing or action part of deciding is so powerful and so important that I decided to give it a name. The name I chose is *docide*. Three critical steps are present in docides. First, decide what you want to improve, change, or act on. Second, decide to do the things that you think will help you make that change or improvement. Third, actually do what you decide to do. Doing the good things that you decide to do is what brings meaning, positive change, and joy to all lives.

Some great examples of the power of dociding have already been presented in this book. Beckie Scott, in the last race of her World Cup career, docided to focus beyond the extreme fatigue and exhaustion that she was feeling and focus all her energy on the step in front of her to win her final World Cup race. Thomas Grandi, after 12 years of competing on the World Cup circuit, docided to focus fully on putting two back-to-back races together for his first World Cup victory, and then docided to do the same thing in his next race for consecutive World Cup wins. Chris Hadfield docided to become an astronaut by taking every step required to become one, even though at the time it was considered an impossible dream because there was no astronaut program in his home country of Canada and there were no opportunities for non-U.S. citizens to do the training in the United States.

A final example of dociding is the story of my father's docision that saved his life. When my father was 82 years old, I took one of my graduate students from China and her family to visit my father at his farm in Maryland. She was an expert in qigong, one of the ancient martial arts. Shortly after her arrival, she led us through some basic qigong exercises, which combined deep abdominal breathing (breathing through the diaphragm) and slow synchronized arm movements. This way of breathing allows a person to get more air into the bottom part of the lungs. Many classical singers, musicians, and athletes use the technique. We stood out there by the cornfield, feeling the warmth and freshness of the morning air, and did these breathing exercises for about half an hour.

Six months later, I got a call from my mother telling me that my dad had been in a bad car accident and was in the intensive care unit at the hospital. He had collapsed lungs and a broken sternum. I jumped on the first plane that I could get on, flew to the nearest airport in Washington, DC, rented a car, and drove to the hospital. By the time I reached his room, he was coherent and I was able to speak with him. He told me what happened.

He was driving down a two-lane country road to pick up some supplies. As he came over a hill and started down the other side, a car in the wrong lane was speeding straight at him. The vehicles collided head on. The impact drove the steering wheel and dashboard into my father's chest. At that point he could not breathe, no matter how hard he tried. His first thought was that he was going to die because the pressure of the steering wheel on his chest prevented him from getting any air into his lungs.

In the heat of that moment, when his life was hanging in the balance, he remembered the breathing exercises that we had done together next to the cornfield—qigong. He instantly focused on trying to breathe with his lower abdomen, which was not being crushed by the steering wheel. He focused on breathing in slowly and feeling his stomach rise and extend. He was able to get some air into the lower part of his lungs, which kept him alive until the emergency medical team arrived on the scene and was able to extract him from the car and rush him to the hospital.

His deciding to do the abdominal breathing saved his life and gave him another 10 years to live, learn, and grow. He worked vigorously on his rehabilitation and paid special attention to strengthening and expanding his breathing capacity through breathing exercises. During his recovery he had every part of his wheel of excellence working for him—focus, commitment, belief, mental readiness, positive images, distraction control, and ongoing learning. And it worked its wonders.

This example shows the power of deciding to act on your decisions when it really counts—the power of putting the *do* into your decisions. My father probably would have died within minutes right there in that car if he had not decided to take that one abdominal breath, and then the next, and the next. We can extract a positive lesson from that chapter of his life: One breath, one action, one positive step can change the course of your life. In my father's case taking one positive step literally gave him the gift of another 10 years to do the things that he loved to do, to reconnect with family, to meet grandchildren he would never have met, and to embrace the simple joys in his life.

I know that you either have or will have stories about the power of your own connected focus and decisions. When you feel so inclined, send one of them to me. I know that I will learn from it, and perhaps I will be able to share it with others who can grow from it.

Decide to pursue your dreams.

Decide to make the improvements that you are seeking.

Decide to become the best person you can be.

Decide to live the gift of your life to the fullest every day.

Persist

A big part of the challenge of pursuing excellence is to be persistent in pursuing your goals and in accepting yourself as a worthy, competent human being throughout the journey. When you apply specific self-growth strategies to your personal situation, expect improvement, but don't expect instant miracles. Sometimes positive changes occur instantly, but often it takes some time. For example, if you've been highly stressed in competitive situations for years, don't be disappointed and give up on a strategy if you are not totally calm by tomorrow. Although I have witnessed dramatic, literally overnight, improvements, personal growth is more often a progression. Take it step by step, day by day, moment by moment, and be persistent.

You will have ups and downs in training and in guiding your focusing skills, just as you do in physical training. Sometimes you will feel mentally strong, totally focused, and totally in control; other times you may temporarily slide back into less constructive ways of thinking or focusing and thereby upset yourself or underestimate your potential. But as soon as you get your focus back to where it should be, you will roll back into control. With persistence you will become fully focused in ways that are best for you more frequently and will gain greater control over yourself and your performance.

I deliberately use the term *persistence* rather than the word *effort*. With some approaches, persistence involves noneffort rather than effort. Did you ever try to go to sleep and end up tossing and turning for what seemed like hours? You keep telling yourself, *I have to get to sleep; try to go to sleep.* Then as soon as you stop trying hard, you slip effortlessly into a deep, restful sleep. In some cases, noneffort, or less conscious effort, yields results that forced effort continually chases away. You can achieve some things more readily by "trying easier," by taking your time, or by moving toward your goal in a more relaxed or unhurried way.

Persistence means giving something enough time to work. Don't be too quick to say, "I tried that and it didn't work." How long did you try it? How often did you practice it? How fully did you focus on it? Did you gradually introduce the strategy, first in a relaxed setting and then under more stressful circumstances? Did you provide yourself with enough opportunities for the feeling, or focus, to surface naturally without forcing it or rushing for instant results?

A focusing strategy may fail because of a lack of connection or full focus when implementing it or because more persistence is required in its application. For example, practicing a refocusing strategy a couple of times and concluding that it doesn't work is like training a new skill or performance program a couple

▶ Years of persistence have led Maria Sharapova's to the heights of tennis. Remember to keep going through the ups and downs of your journey.

of times or for one minute and then claiming that it doesn't work. One minute of training may not work, but extensive, high-quality focused training does work. Failure to achieve immediate success with a focusing strategy does not mean that it will never work. Imagine if you had approached the refinement of physical skills in that way! How skilled would you be today?

Some strategies, of course, will not be compatible with you, and you should not waste time on them. But if you select a strategy that feels right for you, even a little bit right, give it a chance to work for you. Remember these points when trying a new approach for personal growth or improved focus control:

- Go with what seems workable for you.
- Don't overload yourself with strategies; start with one or two simple strategies.
- Try the approach in less stressful situations until you sort things out.
- Create a reminder to help bring on the desired response or focus (for example, *focus, power, flow, control, relax*).
- Practice using your reminder as a way of getting into your best focus.
- Before the day or event begins, think about how you would like to feel that day or focus in that event; remind yourself of the perspective and focus that you want to carry.
- Try to let positive feelings and a fully connected focus surface naturally.
- Prepare a backup refocusing strategy in case the feeling or focus doesn't surface or you lose that best focus at some point.
- Give your chosen focus strategy or reminders a chance to work.
- Expect improvement, but not overnight miracles.
- Be willing to lose a little in the short run to gain a lot in the long run.
- Remember that experimentation, persistent refinement, and keeping joy in the pursuit are necessary for progress and perfection.

When you are trying new strategies or different ways of focusing or refocusing, guard against thinking too much about what you are thinking about. A female fencer made this comment:

> In the first two bouts of the tournament I was thinking so much about what I was thinking that I didn't fence. It took losses in those two bouts for me to realize what was happening. I was expecting everything to just happen, and it didn't. Once I started to focus on fencing my opponent, things slowed down. I began to relax, and I won the next two bouts. The latter two wins were against much stronger fencers than the first two losses.

During the event, focus on the doing. A cat pursuing a mouse is not thinking about what she should be thinking about. She is focused on the doing.

The purpose of your focusing strategy is to get into that fully focused, fully connected mind-set.

The best time to evaluate (or think about what you focused on during the performance) is after the event, unless an immediate change in focus is required within the game, race, performance, or match. In this case, do a brief evaluation and refocus quickly in the heat of the moment or at a break in the action. If thinking begins to interfere with your best, fully connected focus during the event, change channels by focusing on something more constructive and concrete that will get you back on the fully connected track.

The process of learning to be consistent in connecting fully, refining your focus, and channeling your emotions in positive directions is a bit like learning to walk on a beam, fence, or wire. You may wobble or even fall a number of times before you become fully stable, balanced, and in control. You need the same kind of persistence to walk, run, and excel with your mental skills as you do with your physical skills.

Setting daily focus goals, writing down your focus reminders, and rejoicing in positive steps along the way can help you become better and more consistent. But for any strategy to work well, you must want to improve your focus, your performance, or your life. Everything begins with your commitment to make that positive change or to improve. No one can force you to want to grow or improve; this decision must come from within you. After you have made that decision and decided to act on it, persistence does not guarantee that you will achieve your ultimate goal; it does guarantee, however, that you will continue to learn, improve, and grow along the way. Embracing a journey that you choose gives your life substance and meaning, even when you do not arrive at a specific distant destination.

Retain Your Purpose

What is your purpose for doing what you are doing and for pursuing the goals you are pursuing? What do you want to accomplish in your performance domain or to experience in your life?

If you continue to move forward in a purposeful direction that you have chosen , you will add joy and meaning to your life, but this task requires that you retain a sense of purpose. If you want to get to where you want to go, you need solid personal reasons for wanting to get there. Your ability to retain a personal sense of purpose in pursuing your mission is a key factor that keeps you going through the obstacles and tough times.

Some athletes and performers retain a sense of purpose in their mission because they love parts of their experience and parts of the pursuit. It feels good to be fully connected to something and to become really good at something. It feels good to be accepted, valued, or respected. It feels good to wake up knowing that you have something that you want to do or a meaningful challenge to pursue. It feels good to be part of a mission or team, to accept challenges in positive ways, and to push beyond what you have previously done. It feels good to be strong and fit and to have a familiar pattern or routine that you follow in your day.

Sometimes embracing the simplest joys of your experiences or pursuit is enough to sustain your purpose. Sometimes engaging yourself in your pursuit makes you feel more fully alive and takes you to places you have not gone before. And sometimes you need a reminder to appreciate the good things you have, the good things you have done, and the good things you can do to retain your sense of purpose.

The time you are living, the moment you are experiencing, and the opportunity you have in front of you this day, this second, only exist right now and will never exist for you in the same way again. Embrace this gift of life, this gift of time, this opportunity, and this gift of the moment. Choose your own way to sustain your personal sense of purpose so that you come as close as possible to living the life that you would love to live. This will give you the best chance of doing the things you really want to do and experiencing your life fully, given the time that you have to live.

Chris Hadfield provides an excellent example of retention of purpose. As a nine-year-old Canadian farm boy, Chris watched the first man walk on the moon on a live television broadcast. From that moment on, he wanted to be an astronaut. That vision drove every major decision that he made for the rest of his life. At the time becoming an astronaut was an impossible dream; Canada didn't even have an astronaut program. Still, he persisted while many other youngsters let their dreams fade away. I asked Chris how he was able to persist through the many challenges and seemingly insurmountable obstacles that he faced along the way. His response was simple—retention of purpose.

> If you want to achieve a very challenging goal, you have to have a reason for doing it, you have to really want to do it, you have to persist through a series of obstacles, and you have to keep in mind why you are doing it and why it is important in your life. This retention of purpose or passion is what keeps you going toward your goal. There will be seemingly insurmountable setbacks if you set yourself any sort of difficult goal. You'll get to a stage where the whole horizon is black and you don't see any way through. That happened to me several times—I mean I chose as a kid to be an astronaut when I grew up. It was a black horizon from the beginning; there was no way; it was impossible at the time. But things always change, given time. There are always new possibilities.

> The important part in achieving, or even coming close to what you dream of doing, is retention of purpose. Every day you're going to have a choice to go a little bit closer to where you want to get, every single day. And then there will be some break points in your life where you really fundamentally choose whether you're going to head that

direction or not. And if you don't make that choice, if you don't change direction, you will end up where you're headed. Guaranteed. So you need to fundamentally choose which direction you want to go, start heading that way, and maybe you'll get where you want to go.

The purpose that I chose for myself, the goal I wanted to achieve as an adult, I internalized deliberately at nine years old. I was by no means a robot headed that way, but I always had choices and I thought, *Well, someday, maybe, I'll get to be an astronaut, and if I am, I really should know about this; I better study this; I should do this.* I was lucky enough that when I got to the point in my life where I was qualified, the opportunity arose, and I was in a position to take advantage of it. I think that basic retention of purpose through a whole life not only gets you to your goal but also makes life more interesting and fulfilling because you're headed in some direction that you like. And your life loses its random and therefore unfulfilling nature. I really enjoy it.

PART IV

Realizing
Excellence

CHAPTER 18

Composure

Preparing to perform with confidence and composure in your performance domain is like preparing to paddle a wilderness river. You must embrace the challenge, plan an appropriate course, take stock of the difficulties, and find a way through the obstacles. When you choose a particular course, do so for good reasons, and have a plan to get back on course if the current pulls you to one side. Know what your focus will be before you start. If you can avoid an obstacle or take advantage of an opening by changing course in midstream, be focused and adaptable enough to do so. If one approach does not work, try another. Have a recovery plan in case you spin out of control or capsize, so that all is not lost. Having a backup plan on a wild river or during a challenging pursuit will allow you to maintain composure and prevent a plunge over a falls.

Composure becomes possible when you embrace the positives, focus in the present, and know that you can get through the obstacles.

To avoid potential problems in your performance pursuit, consider these reminders:

1. Embrace the challenge that you are about to face as being worthy of you and your focus.

2. Plan a course that you believe can take you to your goals.

3. Run your course and focus plan through your mind so that you are clear about what you want to do and how you want to do it.

4. Think about potential obstacles, look them over, and become familiar with them.

5. Plan a strategy to overcome each obstacle and plan a backup strategy in case an unexpected problem or unforeseen obstacle arises.

6. Begin your performance by focusing fully on the first few moves. Remain focused, alert, and ready, with mind and body working together, flowing in the same direction, throughout your performance.

7. When an obstacle surfaces, see the obstacle, but don't let your mind remain with it; focus on finding a way through it, over it, or around it. Focus on the next step, the opening, the opportunity.

8. Continue to focus forward, taking advantage of your strengths, the strengths of others, the opportunities within the obstacles, and the flow of things within you and around you.

If you begin to focus on implementing solutions before problems get out of hand, you will experience less stress, a more connected focus, and better results. If you wait until a situation is out of control, or until you or someone else is in a panic mode, implementing an effective solution becomes much more difficult. You have a much better chance of regaining control quickly and staying in control if you catch things early, as they are surfacing, and remind yourself to stay cool, breathe, relax, focus on what you control, focus on the next step, and decide to find a way through it.

When you know that you will be entering a situation that has challenged you or created stress in the past, prepare yourself mentally and physically to be your best in that context. Plan your path, plan your best focus, and do something that relaxes you before you walk into that setting so that you begin in a calmer state. Even if your stress does begin to rise as the challenge approaches—and it probably will—you will be calmer and more focused because you started in a calmer state. You are ready to direct your focus to do what works best for you.

Creating a Focus Plan

Performing your best when it counts most requires that you focus on doing what is ultimately best for you and your mission. Maintaining your best focus is easier if you bring a positive perspective into the situation, focus fully within your performance, and have a prepracticed plan for overcoming obstacles. Know what you want to do and how you are going to focus to do it—before you do it. Decide that you are going to carry a positive mind-set and bring your best focus into the event. Know what you are going to do if something pulls you out of your best focus so that you can get back on track quickly.

To be as prepared and composed as possible and to experience as few setbacks as possible, top performers develop effective on-site focus plans and refocusing plans. An on-site focus plan usually includes an athlete's preferred preperformance focus and his or her best performance focus. In some cases, athletes also outline the sequence of key steps that they will go through from the time that they arrive at the performance site to the time that they finish their performance. Your refocusing plan should list potential problems or distractions that could arise and your plan to avoid, minimize, or focus through each of them.

Performers in all disciplines can gain from personalized, on-site focus plans. Every world champion, Olympic champion, and top performer with whom I have worked has developed an effective way of preparing mentally for competitions or major performances. They have learned how to maintain focused composure by focusing consistently in ways that are effective for them. They know what their best focus is. They know how to enter that focus. They know how to maintain their best focus when it counts. You probably have the beginnings of a good focus plan that only needs refinement to take you where you want to go.

Think through and practice your focus plan so that it works for you when you need it. Answer the following questions to help develop or refine your best focus plan:

1. How do I want to focus? (What focus is going to give me my best chance of performing to my potential?)

2. What should I do to get into my best focus? (What am I going to say to myself or do to ensure that I enter my best focus?)

3. Why should I do it? (Why should I bother getting myself into my best focus?)

4. What should I do if it doesn't work? (What am I going to do if I can't get into that focus on the first attempt or can't maintain that focus?)

5. How did it go? How effective was I at implementing and maintaining my best focus? When was my focus best during this performance? Why was it best at that time? How can I improve it? How can I act to make those improvements?

To determine how you want to focus and how to get into that focus, think about what you would like to do when you arrive at the performance site so that you will feel the way you want to feel, physically and mentally. List your preferred preparation activities in the sequence in which you would like them to occur. You may want to use the following on-site focus plan (figure 18.1) as a guide. Some performers prefer, and gain from, detailed descriptions of activities, focus reminders, and actions. Others prefer more of a sketch, image, feeling, or simple focus reminder to guide them into their best focus. To recall the perspective or focus that you want to carry, think about a previous best performance, then remind yourself to simply connect fully with the performance in front of you. Let events unfold naturally by fully connecting with your performance.

What you choose to focus on is your choice. You can direct it or redirect it any way you want. Plan and practice focusing on what will help you bring out your best. Ideally, your best on-site focus will become automatic so that you will need only a simple reminder to "focus" or to "flip the switch" to activate your best focus in important events.

After you have outlined your preferred on-site preparation activities and your best focus reminders, think about why they are important to you. What can each of these activities or reminders contribute to your best feelings, best focus, and best performance? Knowing why they are important for you and

Figure 18.1   Sample On-Site Focus Plan

Event: Track Sprint

What is my best focus? Focus on the doing—one step at a time.

What should I do?	Why should I do it?	What should I do if it does not work?
General warm-up: long, slow stretching	To feel loose, relaxed, and calm	More stretching, relax, use reminder—*I can run well no matter how warm-up feels*
Event preparation: keep warm, active; stretch periodically until event time	To stay loose	Extra sweatsuit, run loose, relax
Replicate part of race at full speed, short duration but intense enough to sweat	To feel confident in speed	Visualize best previous race; feel it; then simulate first 20 meters
Simulate start with preceding heat with cue words	To feel ready for explosive start	Simulate in imagery if not possible physically—think explosiveness in imagery
See myself, feel myself run the way I want to run	As a last-minute reminder before letting my body do it	Remind myself how I want to feel and run
Approach blocks: breathe; relax; be ready, alert, strong	To feel 100 percent ready	Remind myself of past best, of untapped potential—*I need to feel butterflies; I'm going to run well*
In blocks: ready position, breathe out, relax	To feel that everything is under control	Let my shoulders relax, focus on breathing
Set position, think blast off, blast off	To fly off the blocks as fast as lightning	Explode, uncoil, spring like a cat

1. How did it go? What went best? What can I improve?

_____

2. What improvements or refinements can I make in my focus plan for next time?

_____

your performance will motivate you to act on them consistently in important performance situations.

Suppose that a preparation activity or focusing strategy did not work the way that you wanted it to. What are you going to do? First, draw the lessons from the experience and improve by acting on them. Think about what worked well and why it worked well. Think about what didn't work and why it didn't work. Determine whether it worked for any part of your performance. Think of a refocusing strategy or reminder that you can use within your performance context that can bring your focus back to where it will do you the most good. An effective refocusing reminder can be a simple word, thought, or image. Find one that works for you and practice using it before, within, or after an event. Keep refining it until it works for you or until you find something else that works to get your focus where you want it to be.

Backup refocusing strategies can also be helpful. You normally bring them into play only if your original best focus strategy or refocusing strategy is not doing the job. For the most part, backups remain in reserve, but you should be ready to call on them if you need them. Your improved focus plan consists of the following four action steps that can help you prepare to perform your best and maintain focus and composure throughout your performance:

> **Step 1.** Get yourself focused in a way that works best for you and allows you to maintain that fully connected focus for the duration of your performance. Your goal is to respect your best focus from start to finish.

> **Step 2.** Use a refocusing strategy, if needed, to shift your focus back into your most positive or best fully connected focus. You use step 2 only if you are having difficulty getting into a positive and connected focus or if it momentarily slips away.

> **Step 3.** Go to your backup strategy if your first refocusing strategy is not working for you.

> **Step 4.** Carefully evaluate your focus after every performance to make continual improvements in the quality and consistency of your best focus. Think about how it worked for you or against you in the performance and how you can improve it. Every time you perform you can draw out lessons and act on them to improve your best focus.

When your performance or event is over, assess the overall effectiveness of your focus plan. How did it go? How was your focus during the preperformance phase? Was it where you wanted it to be? How was your focus during your performance? What parts went well? When was your focus at its best? What was going on then? What were you aware of or focused on when your focus was best? When did your focus drift away from where you wanted it to be? What was going on then? Where do you need additional work to improve the consistency of your focus and your performance?

Many athletes who experience their best performances in high-intensity events engage in positive preplanned activities or routines right up to the moment that they perform. Just before the start, they zone in on or recall their best performance focus and then connect completely with their task from the start signal to the end of their event. If you think that you might benefit from seeing the detailed focus plans of great performers in various pursuits, see my free online book *Psyched: Inner Views of Winning*, my free online *Journal of Excellence*, and my audio CD *Performing in the Zone* (refer to page 303 for more information).

Turning Fear Into Focus

Many athletes and other performers who enter situations in which they are being watched and evaluated or in which the risks of serious injury are high have confided in me that they often feel extremely nervous and sometimes afraid before those performances, and that it "isn't a good feeling." Shifting focus totally into the performance or connecting fully with the doing is often the fastest way to release the fear or turn fear into focus. An absolute connection or full engagement with the step in front of you clears your mind of all other thoughts and relaxes your body enough to have a great performance. Pure focused connection works wonders here.

©Corbis

▶ Outstanding athletes like Derek Jeter are effective at maintaining their composure even when under pressure. Plan a strategy to help you maintain focus.

If you are feeling stressed or worried before your performances, consider some of the following options:

➤ Before you enter the performance arena or begin to perform, block out the outside world and any fears or worries that you might have about outcomes because those worries are not going to help your performance. Leave them in the car, bury them somewhere in the sand, dirt, or snow, or flush them down the toilet.

➤ If you are feeling fearful or if the outcome seems vitally important, slow your breathing and immerse yourself in preparing to do the good things that you are going to do.

➤ Think only about what you are going to do. Then click into the Zen zone, where only connection counts.

➤ Nothing else in the world matters during this time.

➤ Just connect fully with what you are going to do.

➤ It's just you and your connection, you and your performance.

➤ Shift your focus to pure connection and pure trust.

➤ Pure focus frees you from forcing, frees you from tension, and frees you from worry.

➤ Focus by connecting, not forcing. Let your worries go.

➤ Free your focus and your body to do what they are capable of doing.

➤ Take control by giving up the need to control.

➤ Focus fully on the connection, on the doing.

➤ Let your intuition lead you naturally.

➤ Be calm, focused, and in the moment. Let your performance run freely.

If doubts surface about your ability to do what you want to do or perform the way that you want to perform, consider the following reminders:

I totally belong here.

I commit to making it a good one.

I control my feelings and the attitude that I bring into this performance.

I choose my focus. I choose my focus.

I choose to focus fully right off the bat, from start to finish.

I decide to make it great.

I decide to embrace the challenge through the ups and downs.

I decide to draw the positive lessons from each experience.

I am lucky to be here doing what I love to do.

So it's cool.

Full focus.

Simple joys.

Nothing else matters.

Developing a Refocusing Plan

At the World Student Games, track athletes were corralled in a cramped holding area for about 30 minutes before being lined up and marched directly from the entrance tunnel to the starting blocks. Their last possible contact with their coaches or teammates was more than 30 minutes before the event. At the Moscow Spartakiade, divers were crowded into an extremely small and impersonal waiting area between dives, which provided little sense of personal space. As divers on the 10-meter platform prepared for their dives, large flags, strategically placed at eye level, began to move at the other end of the pool. At major competitions, athletes often face numerous distractions in the course of one day.

Every performer can gain from having an effective refocusing plan for potential distractions. To develop your refocusing plan, start by listing the things that usually bother you at competitions, followed by other things that could bother you. Let's say that you are preparing for an important event that comes along only once or twice in a lifetime. You want to be as prepared as possible to cope with both expected and unexpected circumstances that you may face at this event. Therefore, you should find out as much as you can about what these events have been like for other performers or athletes in the past; you can learn from former competitors, athletes, coaches, sport psychologists, videos, DVDs, and articles in magazines, in newspapers, and on the Web. Based on your own experiences as well as the experiences of others, you can make an intelligent guess about what the event will be like for you and how you need to prepare for it.

Think about distractions or hassles that have affected you in the past, as well as particular things that are likely to happen at the upcoming event. Include distractions that could arise in the week or two leading up to the event. Speculate about what might occur when traveling; at your lodgings and training site; at the competition site; on the day of the event; within the performance; between halves, periods, or performances; and after the competition. Develop a refocusing plan for circumstances that might pose problems. Your aim is to avoid as many bothersome distractions as possible and to cope effectively with those that you cannot or do not wish to avoid. You may prefer that no storms blow your way, but should they come, you need to know how to avoid them, focus through them, and be prepared to overcome them.

You can divide your refocusing plan into major if-then components:

If this happens, then I do this.

If this doesn't work, then I do that.

Plan your refocusing strategies in detail. Write down reminders that will help you do what you want to do. Use your reminders in practices and simulated conditions. Become familiar enough with them so that you can call on them naturally in challenging situations.

If you have practiced staying cool, relaxing your pace, changing channels, channeling your focus, accepting uncertainties, and embracing challenges, you are less likely to become upset over various kinds of distractions, changes in schedules, long waits, outside pressures, unfamiliar conditions, regimented procedures, or demanding expectations.

Unexpected circumstances often occur at major events. Although you cannot anticipate every possible adversity, you can prepare an effective on-site refocusing response to use in the face of almost any unexpected happening. If you feel yourself starting to react negatively to something, use these thoughts or feelings to signal a shift in focus. Saying *shift focus* or *change channels* several times in a row will generally break you away from the distracting thoughts long enough to refocus on something more positive or constructive.

The whole refocusing sequence might unfold as follows: *I don't like these feelings, and I don't have to stay with them. Shift focus, shift focus, shift focus. This doesn't have to bother me! It's no big deal. I can still do what I want to do. Relax. Focus!*

At this point, focus fully on doing something that is within your immediate control—performing the skill that you are currently doing, preparing to do the skill that you are about to do, or doing something else that is absorbing and constructive. If the distraction occurs just before your performance, shift focus to your final preparations for executing your performance—the feel of it, the form of it, the flow of it, or the game plan that you want to follow. Take a deep breath, relax as you exhale, imagine what you want to do, and then focus on doing it with full focus.

Focus your energy on things you can control rather than things you cannot control. We cannot control other people's thoughts or actions, the caliber of competition, or the past. We can, however, control our preparation, our focus, and our performance. We can make every effort to focus in ways that will free us to do our personal best. No one can ask for more than that; no one can do more than that. Nothing beyond your sincere attempt to focus your best and perform your best matters. Other competitors are who they are, and you are who you are—a separate entity. If you begin to compare yourself with others, use that realization as a reminder to focus on your own preparation, your own strategy, your own focus, your own performance.

Your on-site focus plan and refocusing plan free you to enter your performance arena with composure and confidence. You have an effective plan to make things go right and a refocusing plan in case something goes wrong. You are ready and focused. That's when good things happen!

CHAPTER 19

Balance

Overload. When it happens you begin to feel yourself being pulled in too many directions at once. Your focus drifts from one thing to another, your tension rises, and your gut knots up as you think about how you can meet everyone's

> The greatest gift you can give yourself is harmony within yourself.

demands, including your own. You lose your sense of inner harmony and let things bother you that normally you would let go. You become less focused, less tolerant, and more irritable toward other people, especially those you love, not because they are the ones making the demands but because they just happen to be around. I don't like feeling overloaded, and I don't like treating people in negative or hurtful ways, even temporarily. I bet you don't either.

When too many people want a piece of you or place demands on you at the same time, remind yourself that you can only do what you can do. You are not Superwoman or Superman—and even superheroes only focus on executing one task well at a time. Given the complexities of your life and the fact that there is only one you on this planet, do the best you can and let the rest go. Pick the things that you think are most important right now and focus on doing them well. Worrying about anything beyond what you are doing right now will only slow you down. Then nothing gets done, or nothing gets done well.

Coping with Overload

Let's say that right now you are already feeling pulled in too many directions and are feeling stressed. You might find yourself thinking, *I don't like being in that overload state even temporarily. I don't like feeling pressured or rushed. I think that it is ridiculous to get caught up in this feeling.* You might decide, as I have chosen to decide, *I am not going to let that happen again.*

For the moment, avoid additional demands. Find a quiet place to escape where you don't have to answer to anyone. When you remove yourself mentally or physically from what created the feelings of overload and allow yourself to relax and reflect on what you were feeling, you can usually put things back in perspective. Short time-outs to relax and reflect can put you back in control of your life. Allow yourself a little time to embrace some simple joys and regain a more balanced or positive perspective. When you feel in a better frame of mind, simply try to meet your current demands as best you can, taking one little step at a time.

To take that first critical shift back into control, say to yourself, *Breathe, relax, focus.* Then focus on one thing that you can do immediately, right now! Focus on that step. Do that one thing. When you complete that step, focus on the next step. Then take a break so that you can return to the next step with more energy, focus, and purpose.

Even if you can't complete something right now or are late for a deadline, don't beat yourself up over it or blow it out of proportion. This time you can't do it, or it will be late. Not meeting this deadline or not doing this task is not going to kill you or them. Relax. Breathe. Slow down. Learn something from the experience about how to control your schedule. Plan your time and path to prevent this circumstance from happening again. Punishing yourself more than you already have won't help. Take a break. Go for a walk or run. Do something that you really enjoy. Embrace a few moments of silence. Draw out the lessons and move on.

Listen to your feelings, listen to your body, and listen to yourself. Slow down and relax. You know when things are getting out of balance. Physical signs, emotional signs, and changes in feelings can tell you that you are overloaded. You just have to tune in to them. You may start to feel tense, grumpy, negative, or irritated by things that normally do not bother you. You may begin to feel physically drained, easily distracted, upset, not focused, or unmotivated. Your body, mind, and emotions are telling you to slow down, but you are not listening.

If you begin to listen to your personal signs and relax your pace before the overload becomes too heavy, you can save yourself a lot of grief. You don't need to rush everywhere and through everything. Take it easy. Move in a confident, unhurried fashion. Focus on connecting fully with your experiences. When you sit down to talk with someone, be there, relax, focus, listen, and then relax again for a few moments before responding. Slooooow down when you walk, eat, drive, or cycle from one place to another. Walk relaxed. Run relaxed. If the phone rings, relax for a few rings before responding, or if you want to avoid additional demands, don't answer it at all. Relax in the shower, in front of a fire, in the sauna, in your favorite place. Eat relaxed and drink more slowly. After eating, take a little time to do nothing but enjoy some quiet time alone or with your loved ones. Relax a bit every day. Do something that you love to do—listen to music, get yourself into an uplifting mental space or relaxing environment, relax the muscles in your body, stretch out on the grass or beach, or do whatever makes you feel good. Plan to relax more fully before and within stressful settings. If necessary, take a five-minute time-out from the stress-related situation to relax, to be alone, or to refocus.

If people you love may be feeling neglected because of your overload, talk with them about your feelings. Reassure them that you love them. Let them know that what is making you irritable is your overload and that you are working on getting it under control. They will appreciate knowing that they are not the cause of your short temper, irritable responses, anger, or unhappiness. Just talking with them may reduce your load and help you put things in perspective. The long-range challenge is to prevent overload, embrace the different loves of your life, and live your life more joyfully. You can begin to live your life with more balance right now.

Decide to live this day free or freer from worry or stress.

Decide to live it free from anger.

Decide to live it free from overload.

Decide to do something today that you really enjoy.

Do something you love to do with someone you love or like.

Live your day with quality focus and complete connection.

Pick one day and decide to live it fully. Then do it again the next day.

If you simply respect your own needs for personal space, personal accomplishment, exercise, good nutrition, rest, meaningful interaction, and simple joys, you will do yourself and everyone around you a great favor.

Preventing Overload

As you become more skilled as an athlete, coach, or performer in any field, people and circumstances will place more demands on you. The better you get, the greater the demands will be. Top performers face all kinds of demands. Everyone wants a piece of them, and if these performers give in to every demand, they will have nothing left for themselves or their loved ones.

Regardless of whether you gain a high profile in your sport or profession, you will encounter periods when the demands of life seem to overwhelm your capacity to meet them. This situation is common among developing athletes, teenagers, university students, parents with young children, teachers, coaches, business executives, and people and performers in most fields.

To prevent overload, you must first think about priorities and what balance means to you. What are your priorities at this point in life? What are your priorities in your studies, work, or performance domain? What are your priorities outside your school, work, or performance domain? How many additional commitments can you take on and still embrace these priorities with quality, focus, and complete connection?

► To be successful, Serena Williams must balance the demands on her time off the court. To prevent overload, carefully assess the demands on your time.

Assessing Demands

If you find yourself in a situation in which demands on your time exceed the hours available to fulfill them, you have to take control of your life. No one else can live your life for you. Decide how much you can realistically handle and how much you want to take on. Maybe you feel that you can reasonably handle two additional demands this month (for example, outside requests, social events, interviews) but nothing extra next month before your most important events. At some point in your career you may find that you cannot answer all your e-mail, letters, and calls, so you must either get someone to help you carry that load or answer only the most important ones. You must set priorities and follow them. Otherwise you may surrender some of your positive energy, energy that is essential to the pursuit of your goals, to people who demand a lot but don't give much in return, or to people with good intentions who don't realize how challenging it is for you to meet your current commitments to your work or training, performances, rest time, and loved ones.

Before saying yes to anything that makes additional demands on your limited time, think about what the gain will be and what the cost will be in time and energy. You can be sure that any given task will take longer than you have been told. A 10- to 15-minute interview often ends up taking at least an hour or two out of your life—talking on the phone, making arrangements, thinking about what to say, getting there, waiting until everyone is set up and ready to go, getting home, and so on. In agreeing to a request, indicate exactly how much time and commitment you are willing, and not willing, to give. Set your conditions and call the shots before you accept.

If you are not sure whether you want to do it, my advice is simple: Don't! Remember the word *no*. Saying no can be difficult at times, but doing so is often the only way to maintain quality in your performance and preserve some balance in your life. Usually, being respectful and honest in turning down additional requests reduces your load and level of stress. You can simply say, "I would love to do it, but I have so many commitments already that I simply can't fit it in." Your life is not likely to suffer, or be any less fulfilling, for turning down a request. On the contrary, your life will probably be better because you will have a little more time for yourself, your loved ones, and the things you love to do.

If you are not sure whether taking on an additional commitment will help you live your life more fully, at least delay committing yourself. Give yourself a few days to assess the relevancy of the request to see how it fits with your overall schedule and priorities.

If you are a busy person and want to say yes to opportunities, choose things that are personally uplifting (for example, time for you, time with family or friends, or time doing things that you really enjoy or find uplifting, exciting, or relaxing). Balanced excellence is not a question of working any less diligently while you are training, studying, working, preparing, or performing; it is a question of lightening your load and relaxing more fully outside of training, performing, or working hours. Accept only the things you really want to do and respectfully let the others go. Choose to do things that give you positive energy, make you feel good, or make a positive and meaningful contribution to you, others, or a cause that you believe in.

Occasionally, you may still find yourself feeling momentarily overwhelmed by too many demands. Most of the time, though, you can predict how much you can handle comfortably and adjust your pace or your perspective before getting into trouble. This may mean saying no to certain people, situations, or requests, but it means saying yes to your life. Sometimes we have to remind ourselves to direct the course of our own lives rather than let others direct our lives for us. Ongoing stress inhibits the immune system and contributes to illnesses and diseases that cut our lives short. And stress is one of the biggest barriers to living a joyful life. You have one life to live. Make good choices. Choose to live fully and wisely.

Managing Commitments

Challenging or creative work often occurs in waves. This day or week may be extremely heavy, which is fine as long as tomorrow or next week is lighter. When possible, spread out your workload over a reasonable period and leave spaces for simple joys between sessions. Plan meetings, presentations, workshops, social commitments, major work commitments, travel, and other scheduled activities so that they are not back to back, with one still incomplete while others are starting or with no time between one and the next. Accepting a series of back-to-back commitments for a time that seems far in the future can come back to haunt you when that time becomes the present.

Worrying about deadlines or about being late or not ready for something takes time, energy, and focus away from your tasks and creates stress. Be realistic in making additional commitments—that is, overestimate rather than under-estimate the amount of time, energy, and work involved in getting something done with quality. Start preparing earlier to meet deadlines by setting short-term goals. Leave early for appointments, classes, meetings, or practices so that you arrive early without having to rush. Accept the fact that at a certain time you will have to stop working on one mission to complete another.

For long-term excellence without burnout, relax your schedule enough to fit in some quiet time for yourself between whatever demands you are facing every day. Set priorities so that you can say yes to those things that you really want to do. Choose to do more things that lift you and fewer things that drain you. Schedule regular dates or meetings with yourself to do simple things that relax you, lift you, reenergize you, or make you feel more focused and fully alive. If you feel your stress level rising, remind yourself to breathe in slowly and breathe out slowly. You can take a one-breath relaxation break almost anywhere and anytime. To put things back in perspective, relax for a few minutes—no distractions, no calls, no e-mails, no thoughts—just you and your breathing.

Scheduling Time for You

A critical part of preventing overload and maintaining physical, mental, and emotional health is scheduling time to do some healthy things that you love to do outside your work or performance domain. Run, walk, play, find a quiet time, spend time in a quiet place, garden, or do anything that gives you a feeling of harmony or connection. Make time for reflection or for doing something that lifts you, makes you feel joyful, or makes you feel more alive. These kinds of personally uplifting experiences can help you enter any context feeling more in harmony, more balanced, more resilient, and less likely to overreact to whatever challenges you may face.

Balanced excellence becomes possible when you have less stress and more joy in your life. You can add joy and balance to your life by taking positive actions inside and outside your performance domain:

1. Reduce your stress, connect your focus, and find simple joys in your work, school, or performance domain.

2. Relax more and find more simple joys outside your work or performance domain.

Set some personal guidelines to ensure that you schedule enough time for quality rest, quality preparation, quality performance, and enjoyment in living. Then follow those guidelines! You can do a lot more quality work within a shorter time if you are well rested, fully focused, and in a positive state of mind. Set a personal goal to maintain a sense of harmony in your life. If your priorities or pace leads to disharmony, make adjustments. Learn to relax in the face of stress and find joyful ways to recover from the stresses that you face.

Decide to act in ways that add joy, balance, and harmony to your life. A life that includes those elements will be better for you, your relationships, and your long-term health. Your focus will be clearer and more connected, and you will be on the path to ongoing personal excellence.

CHAPTER 20

Consistency

Consistent high-level performance depends on consistent high-quality focus. After you discover what focus works best to bring out your best performance, the challenge of consistency lies in respecting your best focus on a consistent basis. This is true regardless of

> *The quest for consistency is won when you consistently respect the focus that works best for you.*

what your best performance is at this point in your sport, life, or career. When your performance falters or falls short of your potential, you are most likely failing to respect a focus that works best to bring out your potential. You do not lose your physical or technical skills from one minute to the next, from one day to the next, or from one week to the next. What you lose, what you are missing when you do not perform your best, is the focus that frees you to perform to your capacity.

You win the quest for consistency by finding and sustaining a positive, connected focus that works for you. Over the course of your life or career, you will refine and improve the focus that brings out your best performance. There will always be a way of focusing that brings out your best and a way of focusing that prevents you from performing your best. Your quest in pursuing excellence is to discover, respect, and fine-tune your best focus.

People who consistently perform close to their potential have learned to do three things effectively: direct and connect their focus, channel their emotions in positive directions, and bounce back from setbacks quickly and efficiently. Consistent high-level performers have refined their ability to focus completely on what they are engaged in. If the need arises, they can quickly shift focus from negative to positive, from off target to on target, particularly in response to big challenges, self-doubts, anxiety, errors, or setbacks. If you learn to do this, your chances of getting the most out of your preparation and the best out of yourself when it counts most will increase dramatically. If you don't learn to do this, you will likely become an obstacle on your path to consistency and excellence. You can perform your best consistently by developing the focusing skills required to perform your best consistently. This begins long before the day of your biggest contest through many hours of focused preparation, performances, and experiences.

Reacting to Setbacks

Many people react to setbacks by becoming upset with themselves or others or by losing it emotionally. If they fall behind or confront an obstacle, they lose focus, cease to perform well, back off, or give up. The earlier you learn to react to obstacles, setbacks, and challenges in a positive and focused way, the better off you'll be. Your focus can lead you through things that you never thought you could get through and take you places that you never dreamed you could go.

A setback within a game or performance (for example, making a mistake) can drag you down, but it can also serve as a positive reminder to focus fully on the next step, to redirect your energy in a more productive way, or to analyze errors at an appropriate time (which is usually not in the middle of a performance). After games or performances, mentally replay key moves or turning points, and try to find lessons that will help you focus better for the next outing. Carefully review what went well and what you can improve. You may be disappointed or frustrated with certain parts of your performance, but you can pass through it quickly by extracting and acting on constructive lessons that can help you be better in the future. As one of the world's best athletes said, "As a less experienced player I reacted more emotionally; I was angry at myself. Now I concentrate more on being in the game, and later I analyze errors or losses at an appropriate time, replay key shots and turning points, draw out important lessons, and act on them."

One player experienced real problems with emotional outbursts during games. "If I lost a rally, I hated my opponent. . . . I would get so angry that I could lose eight points in a row because of that. I had problems controlling my temper to the point of shouting and breaking rackets." He made a strong effort to get his temper and focus under control. When he played with controlled focus, he played as well as anyone. One strategy that he used when he became angry was to try to take advantage of his anger by constructively directing his burst of energy into the next rally, to read and react, to hustle more, to move faster, and to smash harder. He shifted his focus away from anger (at himself or his opponent) and reconnected it to playing the game with renewed vigor. Focusing your mind forward on the attack, even after making an error, is obviously preferable to focusing backward on what you can no longer control.

The problem with becoming angry or upset is that the emotion usually interferes with your best performance focus. If you are mentally chastising yourself because of the last shot, move, or event, you cannot at the same time be focusing fully on the present skill or preparing for your next move. You can't dwell on how you blew the last shift, gate, or routine and at the same

©Tim Tadder/Corbis

▶ Phil Mickelson doesn't let setbacks interfere with his focus. Control your focus and commit to continual improvement so disappointments don't hold you back.

time perform well in the current moment. The only way to free your body to perform in the present is to clear your mind of negative thoughts about the past or future and focus fully on the remaining tasks that you can control.

Someone who flies off the handle or dwells on the negatives might say, "Oh, but it doesn't matter that much if I do it during practices or my daily life." Ah, but it does. If you become practiced at negative thinking or losing emotional control, chances are good that the habit will carry over into performances or competitions. Moreover, negativity or destructive emotional outbursts takes the joy out of sport and life. The path to personal excellence includes enough obstacles; adding negative thinking, anger, or self-putdowns offers no advantage. Staying positive, relaxed, and focused is important for regaining the flow of a performance, particularly after an error, argument, or setback.

To speed up the learning process, think about how you would prefer to respond in challenging situations, set personal goals for improving the quality and consistency of your focus, and work toward achieving those goals. The next time that something goes wrong in a game, performance, routine, or relationship, use that setback as a signal to focus on doing what you know will enhance the rest of your performance or interaction. For example, during a gymnastics routine, skating program, or team game, let any thoughts about an error slip away by focusing fully on the next move. In a sport that offers a brief break from the need for intense focus, such as a racket sport or golf, quickly analyze the reason for the error and move on. For example, while walking back to receive the serve or walking forward to address the ball, take a deep, relaxing breath and focus fully on what you want to do next.

A top tennis player learned this lesson through experience. As a rookie he quickly discovered that as soon as he became upset, he couldn't play well. After learning this about himself, he grew into a veteran by taking a different approach:

> I practiced reacting the way I wanted to react, which changed my feeling going into the game. I could go in with more confidence. . . . I tried to think about what caused a mistake and corrected it. I thought about what made me lose and analyzed it. I was disappointed, but I tried to learn from it.

This athlete's early recognition of the critical importance of focus control, along with his commitment to make continual improvement, allowed him to become one of the best players in the world.

Learning Self-Control

The lessons from the journeys of many athletes show that the most important influence on performance is your control over your focus going into it and your focus while engaged in it. A warm-up is separate from your performance. The first event, first shift, first move, first inning, or first period is separate from the second, and the second is separate from the third. A less-than-perfect showing in one event, skill, move, or shift does not mean that you are destined to have a poor showing in the next. What sets you up for a poor practice or performance is usually negative thinking or a focus that is not fully connected on the right things. If you remain positive and fully focused, you are capable of performing at least as well as you ever have before, regardless of what you just did or thought.

When you think about your real capabilities, about why you can do what you want to do, and about how you will focus to make it happen, at some point something will click inside your mind and you will say to yourself, *Hey, that's right—nothing that happened before this moment has to affect this. If I focus fully on what I am doing right now and on nothing else, I can really do this.* This simple insight or acceptance of your capacity may seem like a small step, but its effect can be gigantic because you are taking control of your focus and your performance.

You still may catch yourself focusing on the negatives from time to time (for example, *I messed that up, so I'll probably mess this up too*). But if you have already thought about how unproductive that kind of thinking is and take control by focusing on something positive or constructive, you can often turn things around right on the spot. For example, you might say to yourself, *Stop. Refocus on the positive. I can do as well here as I've ever done. Now let's get focused and do it*. Focus on the first step and nothing else. Focus forward, focus ahead, connect fully, and go. Let your positive thoughts and images lead you and remind you of what you can really do. Then focus fully on doing it.

Pat's Journey

Pat Messner, former world champion in water skiing and a professional musician, reflected on how she went about gaining greater personal control in practice and in competition:

> I began competing when I was 10 years old. At that time, I felt that having days when nothing goes right and everything goes wrong, days when I felt I was the worst competitor on earth, and days when I would be mad at anything, was all part of the competitive life. I was wrong, and it wasn't an easy thing to find out. It happened because of an experience I had in the Western Hemisphere championship in Mexico. It was in March, and that was during our off-season. During the practice session, I couldn't do anything right. I felt like I had never skied as badly. This practice session made me believe that there was no way I was going to place, let alone win! I decided I might as well relax and enjoy myself.

> Before the actual event, I went through my usual stretching and warm-up. The only difference was that I wasn't thinking about what was to come. I just sat down on the grass, listened to some music, and waited for my turn. This was very unusual for me, because I'm usually very nervous. I just didn't seem to care. I listened to the music and relaxed. Believe it or not, I've never had a better tournament. I skied better than I ever had before. Not only that, but I became Western Hemisphere champion. What did all this prove? It proved to me that if I could stay relaxed and calm and focused at all my tournaments, maybe I'd always ski better.

> Since that time I have learned many things that may be as helpful to you as they were to me. I've tried a number of different methods of relaxation. The method I found best is a simple thing anyone can do anytime, anyplace. Sit down or lie down and listen to some relaxing music. I can take my music right down to the dock and listen till it's time for me to ski. I let my mind do what it likes. I don't take responsibility for my thoughts. I just let them pass by. If you don't like music, then try reading a book. I also found this to be very helpful.

Another important thing for me is running through my event mentally just as if it were real. I try to feel as if I am actually doing the run. If you find it hard to "feel" yourself or you can't picture yourself, watch a video of yourself or someone you admire. Sometimes it helps to give yourself audio cues as you go. I also try to simulate as many tournament conditions as possible in practice so that if unusual conditions should occur, I won't be as affected by them.

Sometimes it seems that the better you are, the easier it is to get upset by little things. I found that if I moved my focus away from what was making me angry and thought about something else, I'd feel better. Sometimes I set a goal for myself, like the next two out of three times I get a chance to get mad, I won't. Most days it worked pretty well. On other days, the more I tried not to get mad or upset, the madder I got. It's days like that when I'm probably better off having a day of rest rather than practicing. Continuing to practice when I'm upset accomplishes absolutely nothing.

To try to improve her focus control during practices, Pat followed the mission to excellence process outlined in chapter 5 of this book. Her goal was to make the best of as many practice sessions as possible in preparation for the world championships. Here are three self-control strategies that she chose to implement:

➤ **Relax**. Try to relax yourself physically. Calm yourself. Take deep breaths and feel your body get loose as you exhale. Pat and her coach tried a little experiment. "Each time I frowned he'd tell me, and I'd try to correct the situation by relaxing. I found that when I did, my whole body felt more relaxed and I could do the trick easier."

➤ **Focus on correction**. Focus your attention on how to correct mistakes instead of getting mad at yourself. If you make any errors, repeat the move mentally and correct the errors in your mind before trying it again. When practice is going well, write down what you think might be some of the reasons for your success. Refer to this list to improve future situations.

➤ **Encourage yourself**. Avoid statements such as *You dummy; you can't do anything right; you will never make it to the championships; give up*. Remind yourself of the facts. It's not that you can't do anything right; you're simply doing one little thing wrong. Praise yourself for all the things you are doing right.

Pat experimented with each of these strategies, sometimes stopping practice for five minutes to attempt to change her focus. She said, "If you do not change the way you feel, the rest of the practice will be a waste of time." This acknowledgment gave her a good reason to refocus. She found all these strategies worked well most of the time, but she still got upset every now and then, no matter what she tried. Under those circumstances, Pat sometimes found it helpful for her coach to remind her of what she had accomplished or to point out that she was being silly. "My behavior either got corrected, or he convinced me to take the day off." She found it helpful to have a coach "who makes me realize that I'm only human."

If, after multiple attempts, Pat could not rectify a problem, she could leave practice knowing that she had given it a good shot. Her positive focusing skills improved greatly over time. She also realized that almost everyone has a bad day, or even a bad week, at some time. Bad days usually happen when you need a break mentally or physically. Getting upset about it doesn't help. Refocus. Relax. Take the rest of the day off. Learn from it. Come in fresh tomorrow.

Sandy's Journey

Sandy, a talented young female gymnast, had just made the team to compete in Europe. Immediately afterward, she had two weeks of consistently bad workouts. She and her coach had been arguing regularly, and then for the last couple of days her coach had not spoken to her at all. Two weeks remained before Sandy would depart for her first international competition.

The coach called to ask whether I could help. Sandy and I stretched ourselves out on a blue mat in the corner of the gym and had a nice little talk. She spoke about the poor workouts and arguments, and expressed sincere concern about not being ready for her big meet in Europe. She told me that workouts usually started out OK but that she became upset when the coach said something negative, such as "That's terrible," "You don't listen," or "You don't try." At that point the workout would begin to slide, which led to more negative comments by the coach or no interaction at all, bad feelings, some tears, and a lousy workout overall.

"Sandy," I said, "we know that the coach isn't perfect, but then not many of us are. She says some very negative things, and I've talked to her about giving more positive comments. She's improving a little, but it's a difficult thing for her to do. An important point for you to keep in mind is that this is her way of trying to help you. She does care, and she does want you to improve—to be ready for this meet—and you want that too. At this point I think it is easier for you to control your reaction to her than it is to hope that she will change. You can, in fact, control your own moods if you really want to."

Sandy said that she really wanted to improve the gloomy practice mood and agreed to try the self-control approach.

"What do you think about before a bad mood begins?" I asked.

"I think, *The coach hates me; she thinks I'm no good; she's mean to me; I'm never going to do this right.*"

"What do you feel when a bad mood begins? Are there physical sensations that you are aware of? Are there certain emotions that begin to surface? Do you know when it's starting to happen?"

Sandy had specific thoughts and personal signals of an impending mood change, although she had never thought about them before. She discussed some of them, and I gave her this advice: "OK. When you start to experience these thoughts or feelings—these personal signals—take a deep breath. Say to yourself, *Relax.* Then say to yourself, *Turn this thing around. I want to have a good workout. She's here to help. I am not going to waste the night feeling lousy. I can control this.* Then immediately focus on the trick that you're trying to do or the routine that you're trying to improve. Run it through your mind. Then do it.

"Your challenge for the next week is to look for any signals of a bad mood coming on and then turn it around before it gets to the destructive stage. Don't let it ruin your workout, and don't let it drive you to tears. You may not be successful in turning around every bad mood right away, but if you can do it even half the time, that's a big improvement. That's success. Even doing it once is better than what is happening now. Your ultimate goal is to be able to turn potentially bad situations into good ones all the time. You have the capacity to do this, and you are the only one who can do it because you are the person who controls your thoughts and your focus."

We devised a little mood chart with various "mood faces" to help Sandy assess her feelings and record her progress through the next two weeks. At the start of each practice she recorded her prepractice mood on the mood chart. For each event, she also recorded her mood at the start of the event, mood changes within the event, and her mood at the end of the event. If her mood changed within the event, she indicated what had happened by marking the face that it had changed to. If her mood changed more than once during the event, she drew an arrow from one face to the next to indicate the changes that had taken place. At the end of practice Sandy recorded her postpractice mood.

You can adapt this chart to suit your needs, in sport or in another part of your life. A personal comments section should be part of the chart, primarily to help you (athlete or coach) discover what influences your mood. If your mood begins to decline and you are able to stop the slide or improve your disposition, then jot down what you did, focused on, or said to yourself to turn things around. This notation will help you discover what works best for you and what does not work. You will then be in a better position to use things that work (key words, images, positive thoughts, focus reminders, or actions) whenever you need them.

Let's look at what happened to Sandy's mood control during the first week:

Day 1. We discussed Sandy's concerns and the use of the mood chart approach.

Day 2. She started practice feeling happy and ended feeling so-so. Her pattern the previous week had been to start practice feeling happy and end feeling sad.

Day 3. She started practice feeling so-so and ended feeling very happy. She demonstrated to herself that she could lift her mood.

Day 4. She started practice feeling sad, mostly because she was feeling sick. She was able to work through this and end feeling happy after a productive workout.

Day 5. She started feeling happy and ended feeling very happy. This was wonderful for all of us because it showed that Sandy was starting to get things under control.

At the end of the week Sandy and I went over her mood charts. Both of us were pleased with her progress. Sandy's mood charts showed even more improvement the following week, and she left for Europe feeling excited and more in control. She then had one of her best-ever performances in her first international competition. As her self-awareness and her focusing strategies for mood control continued to improve, the necessity for conscious attempts to control and chart her moods declined. She learned to maintain her best focus more of the time and to solve many problems before they arose. If her mood did occasionally start to slide, she knew from experience what she could focus on to control it (almost always).

Karin's Journey

Karin, a teenage gymnast, was inconsistent in both practice and meets. One day she could do everything well, and the next day she could blow everything. Karin told me that she knew whether it would be a good day or bad day before she got into the gym. If she had had a long day or felt at all sluggish, she would take those thoughts and that mood into the workout with her. Karin's pattern of being up one day and down the next was not restricted to training sessions. In her last competition she fell on every routine, although she had done the same routines in practice. Why? She explained, "I knew I would have a bad day because I had a bad warm-up."

"Karin," I began, "unless you are seriously overtrained or ill, no matter how you feel on the way into the gym, you can turn things around to have a productive workout. Haven't you ever felt sluggish before practice and still had a good workout?" She had. "How is that possible? It is possible because you have the same body and the same skills that you had yesterday, when you had a good day. On your sluggish day, if your life depended on it, you could not only mount the beam, but you could jump over it and still have enough reserve energy to do everything you want to do.

"The next time you 'know you're going to have a bad day,' surprise yourself. Leave your negative thoughts in your locker. When you step through the gym door, decide that you are going to have a great day. When you see that apparatus, challenge yourself to feel strong, feel energetic, feel radiant. Remind yourself why you are here. If you are here, you might as well make the best of it. Why waste two or three hours? Focus fully for at least one event so that you leave having had a good workout on something. If you can do it once, even in one event, you know you can do it again. When you do energize yourself on a sluggish day, or turn a negative feeling into a positive focus, try to be aware of how you did it so that you can do it again and again. You may not always have a super workout, but most days can be good days, and you can make those not-so-good days better than they might otherwise have been."

Karin worked on bringing a more positive perspective and more complete focus into her practices and competitions. As a result she made significant strides in the consistency of her best performances. It wasn't that she couldn't do the moves or routines. She was simply letting her negative focus get in the way of her good performances.

Controlling Moods

Mood control means focusing on the positives and not upsetting yourself needlessly over things that don't really matter, unfamiliar circumstances, or events that you cannot control. When athletes compete in places or countries culturally different from their own, the best performers are those who do not allow the food, the accommodations, or the system to have a negative effect on their performances. They view those differences as relatively unimportant (which they are) and rely on the thoroughness of their overall mental and physical preparation.

Thinking the right way before you even get out of bed in the morning, particularly on an important day (and they are all important), is a great way to start out on a positive track. Try focusing on thoughts like the following while you are still lying in bed: *Today is going to be a great day. I'm going to do some things that lift me* (think about what they are). *I'm going to accomplish what I set out to do. I feel strong. I'm loaded with energy. I'm focused. I'm ready, and I am going to really live this day.*

Positive, action-oriented thoughts can help put you in the right frame of mind, no matter how you are feeling when you first open your eyes to the daylight. Choose to do something that makes you feel the way you want to feel or love to feel—connected, joyful, and productive. Mood control depends on focus control, and it is within your grasp. Controlling your mood is largely a matter of looking for the good—in yourself, in your situation, in the world—and seeking out the opportunities in the obstacles, the gentleness in the storm.

If you tend to focus on the negatives, remember that you can learn to shift your focus to the positives. One of the benefits of focusing on the positives is that doing so leads to positive emotions, which in turn have a positive effect on you, your performance, and your relationships. Focusing on the negatives leads to negative emotions, which have a negative effect on you, your performance, and your relationships. Uncontrolled negative emotions can fuel the flames of your own destruction. The sooner you learn to shift away from negative thoughts to positive ones, the sooner you will take control of your performance and your life. Top performers experience setbacks, fatigue, fear, stress, and self-doubts, just like everyone else. But they have developed effective focusing skills for letting go of their negative thoughts and refocusing on positive ones. As soon as you start to focus on doing the little things that free you to feel your best, be your best, and focus your best, you put yourself back in control of your mood, your life, and your performance.

You are one tiny focus shift away from gaining or regaining a positive perspective. One simple positive thought or positive action can do it. By making that focus shift sooner rather than later, you will save yourself and others unnecessary anguish. At some point you will probably make that positive shift in focus anyway, so why not plan to make it now and save everyone a lot of energy?

Positive perspectives are vital because they inspire us, energize us, and bring meaning and joy to our pursuits. They generate positive emotions that free us to do the good things that we want to do, alone and together. Negative perspectives do the opposite. They drain emotional energy that we could otherwise channel in positive directions. So dwelling on the negatives has no value. If you can simply change the thought, perspective, focus, or interpretation that led you to the negative emotion, you can usually move to a more positive reality. You gain control over negative emotions by taking control of your thoughts and focus. You have a choice here. Positive changes in your focus begin with you. If you find yourself slipping into a negative focus and you would prefer to remain more positive, consider the following actions:

Prepare Yourself to Be More Positive

➤ Get more rest. Slipping into a negative focus is more likely to occur when you are tired or fatigued, so find a way to get enough rest or relaxation, either for short times during the day or at night.

➤ Find ways to reduce the stress or overload in your life. The more stress you have in your life, the more susceptible you are to negative shifts in mood.

➤ Do at least one thing each day that is just for you—something that you really enjoy. This alone can lift your spirits and enhance your focus.

➤ Keep track of the good things that happen to you each day. Write down the simple joys that lift your life each day, in and out of your performance domain. The more positives you can find and appreciate, the less likely you are to be overcome by negatives.

➤ Embrace your successes (small and large) and tune in to your positive emotions when they do occur. Soak in them for a while. Revisit them often. They can keep you focused on the positives.

➤ Remain open to the positive emotions of the people around you. Celebrate their simple joys and successes with them. They can provide you with positive energy, inspiration, and perspective.

➤ Sometime each day, ask yourself, *Am I focusing on the positives or the negatives?*

Protect Yourself From the Negatives

- ➤ Stop dwelling on the negatives. Shift your focus to start dwelling on the positives.

- ➤ Stop revisiting things that went wrong in the past, whether in a performance or a relationship. Shift your focus to what went right or to positive things that you will focus on from this day forth.

- ➤ If you find your focus slipping back to negative memories or daily negative experiences, tell yourself to stop! Then focus on changing channels to something more positive or more uplifting.

- ➤ Instead of focusing on the negatives in positives, start focusing on the positives in negatives.

- ➤ If a negative thought or image pops into your mind, let it go, release it, erase it, let it float away.

- ➤ If you can't let a negative thought go, shift your focus to something positive—a memory that reflects a more positive reality or an experience that clearly demonstrates your capacity to perform well or confirms that you are special and loved.

- ➤ If the negative thought returns, shift back to a positive memory, a positive vision of the future, or a positive action that you can engage in right now. By shifting back to positives every time a negative thought creeps in, you will eventually gain positive control.

Plan for Positive Action

- ➤ You have two options to create positive change—change your focus or change your environment. If you change only your environment and maintain the same focus, nothing will likely change. If you change your perspective and focus, everything will change.

- ➤ Develop a personal plan for remaining positive more often and for getting back on a positive track more quickly, with as little self-inflicted pain as possible.

- ➤ Set a specific time limit for remaining negative or moping around. Then shift to a positive focus and move on.

- ➤ If you are not feeling the way that you want to feel or focusing the way that you want to focus, step back and take a break. Do something that you really like to do. Find your own space. Clear your mind. Clear your path. Then focus on the things that you want to do.

- ➤ Pause long enough to breathe, relax, and reenergize. Let your mind and body relax. Free your focus to center on positive thoughts, positive images, and positive parts of your life, experiences, performances, and future.

- ➤ Practice focusing on the positives and shifting your focus from negative to positive whenever the opportunity arises.

- ➤ Plan a positive path. Act on your plan. Follow your own best path.

CHAPTER 21

Resilience

I remember my first experience at the U.S. Eastern Intercollegiate Gymnastics Championships particularly well. It was my second year at Syracuse University, and I had worked especially hard during the summer and the regular season to regain lost ground from an injury to my arm that had sidelined me during my first year of university competition. I was about 19 years old at the time, and I wanted to prove something to myself and those around me. I also wanted to feel worthy of my scholarship. So I concentrated my effort on the trampoline. This was the first event I could get back to after my injury because my arm was not absolutely essential to work out on the trampoline.

> Your task is to make the journey from immediate loss to eventual gain as rapidly, smoothly and comfortably as possible
>
> Colgrove, Bloomfield, and McWilliams, 1993, 22

During the season I consistently outscored my competitors in that event and thought that I had a good shot at winning the intercollegiate title. Actually, I thought I would win it, and so did my coaches and most of my teammates. I had prepared well and was ready—so I thought. I remember hearing my name called, jumping up on the tramp, bouncing high into the air, throwing one trick, and landing on the springs. That was the end of my routine, the end of my hopes, the end of my dreams.

What a way to end the season! I was really upset. All I wanted to do was get out of there. I didn't want to talk to anyone, I didn't want to go out to eat with the team, and I wasn't looking forward to responding to the standard questions like "Did you win?" or "What happened?" when I returned to campus. I was down for about two weeks. What did I accomplish by coming down on myself, by denying myself enjoyment, by punishing myself? I had failed to meet an important goal that I thought had been a realistic one. I had carried out one of the worst performances of my career when it was most important for me to do my best. But I hadn't tried to do poorly.

This loss turned out to be a golden opportunity to learn something that is difficult to learn under any other circumstances. I was disappointed, but it wasn't the end of the world. It didn't mean that I was a worthless person. It had nothing to do with my ability or my overall value as a human being. It had everything to do with my focus that day. I was able to put things in perspective by looking for positive lessons in an unfortunate experience. I asked myself, *What did I learn about myself? What did I learn about my focus? What did I learn about those around me? What did I learn about performing my best in big events? What did I learn that could help me in the future?* Only then did losing become a positive learning experience. Largely because of that learning I was able to go back the following year and win that intercollegiate title and other titles as well. From that time on, the perspective and focus that I took into sport and life allowed me to gain something from the experience itself, regardless of numerical outcomes or the achievement of preset goals.

Overcoming Loss

Significant losses in sport and other performance domains have a way of colliding with self-esteem. The vibrations can result in self-doubt, self-damnation, worry, and even guilt. Although these thoughts can become overwhelming, there is no reason that they have to be. Remember that this loss is not you; it is just something that you are currently experiencing. You have many qualities within you, some of which are still untapped, and your loss does not define you to significant people in your life. You can deal with the experience of loss and grow from it. The hurtful feelings will fade—they always do. Although you have lost, you have gained something from the experience, and you are a stronger, wiser person—perhaps even a better person or performer—for it.

To lose is to be human, and we are all human. Every thinking, feeling, living person experiences loss. No one escapes it. Even the greatest performers fail, but they have developed strategies to learn and benefit from these experiences. They certainly don't like falling short of a goal, so they try to put their loss in perspective and do a careful evaluation to prevent similar occurrences in the future. They may conclude that their particular approach or game plan didn't work this time, or that they didn't focus fully on the task, or that the cards weren't falling in their favor that day. They don't tear themselves apart for long in response to loss. They simply prepare better or in a different way for the next opportunity, which may or may not be in a sporting context. For example, Michael Jordan has stated, "I never think about the mistakes I made in a game for more than 10 minutes." Tiger Woods said, "I like to look back at matches I've played. I like to look at what I did right." We can learn much from these athletes about looking for good things in less-than-best performances and about not dwelling on mistakes.

We tend to be most susceptible to feeling down when we expect to do well and do poorly instead, when we expect to win and lose instead, when we expect love or acceptance and experience rejection. In some cases, our expectations may have been unrealistic. Sometimes we have not prepared or focused as well as we could have, a condition that we can correct. Sometimes we have done everything in our power to make good things happen, but for reasons beyond our control events do not go as we had hoped or planned. We must recognize the difference between circumstances that are within our control and those that are beyond it. Dwelling on the negatives or trying to control things that are beyond our control is futile. No matter how much energy you invest in trying to control the past, you cannot make it happen. Instead, use your limited energy constructively by directing it toward positive ends and future possibilities.

Loss can make you feel miserable, inadequate, or helpless. But it can also challenge you to draw on your strengths; persist through the obstacles; get to know yourself better; examine your focus and your priorities; put things in perspective; and reflect on where you are going, why you are going there, and how you will get there. A time of loss can widen your perspective and redirect your course in positive ways in sport, in performance, and in life. As unpleasant or hurtful as loss may be, it can result in greater appreciation for what you have or had. A loss may motivate you to learn how to prepare for, avoid, or cope with situations that may arise in the future. If you can draw anything good out of your loss or put what remains in perspective, loss has a positive side.

Life is a constant process of growth, transition, and adaptation. The better you become at finding the positives, living the simple joys, and focusing through the obstacles, the happier, healthier, and more fulfilled you will be. If you can view difficulties or setbacks as a challenge, a test of your inner strength, and an opportunity for personal growth, then you can turn those experiences into advantages. Finding the lessons in loss has an interesting, sometimes magical way of putting you back in control.

Learn to put a loss in perspective—whether it is a small loss that feels big or a big one such as losing a loved one. Grow from the experience and rejoice in the good things that you did, had, and still have. Find a positive reason to move on. You can

© Icon SMI/Icon/SMI/Corbis

▶ NFL coach Tony Dungy sets an example as someone who has found a positive way through great loss.

honor the people you lost by remembering the good things that they have given you—the positive memories, the things that continue to live within you even after they are gone—and by embracing your own life. Live fully. Don't just go through the motions. The lessons that you take from loss can help you learn to live and perform better.

Allison Forsyth's Story

In the final training run for women's downhill skiing at the 2006 Olympics, several talented ski racers had bad falls, including the great American skier Lindsey Kildow, who was second overall in World Cup downhill standings, the highly successful French skier Carole Montier, and one of Canada's leading ski racers, Allison Forsyth. The most serious injury was the torn knee ligaments sustained by Allison Forsyth. As it turned out, her ski clipped a little hole in the snow. She went down hard and was rushed off the hill in a helicopter to the main hospital in Torino. The day before the Olympics began, she flew home for ACL surgery on her left knee. But she agreed to do a short media interview before she left the Olympic village. Parts of that interview follow:

> I had a lot of family and friends who were going to come here to support me. But the bottom line is that I know that they were not coming here to see someone ski race; they were coming here to support the person they love. My mom has been very ill lately, and she really wanted to make this trip to see me ski race. I called her this morning, and she'd already heard the news. She's getting on a plane tomorrow to come to Calgary and take care of me, and I can say for the first time in a long time, I'm really looking forward to having my mom take care of me for a while.

> For sure, emotionally it's hard right now. I had all my friends and family with their plane tickets booked and arriving in a couple days to watch me. But I know everyone at home loves me and cares for me and loves me as a person and not as a ski racer, and they'll be there for me no matter what. I just want to thank everyone for supporting me as a racer and as a person. I'll be back, and I look forward to having your support.

> Right after my crash I decided that I didn't want to end my racing career that way. It was a "see you in 2010" moment. I'm from British Columbia—Nanaimo! You better believe I'll be there in the 2010 Olympics. We have an amazing team here, we have an amazing staff, and they are all here to help me and to help us achieve our goals. Right now my goal is pretty simple—to get healthy again and to get back in winning form. I just feel so confident that I have such an amazing support staff, team wise and family wise, behind me to make sure I can do that.

What the public and press did not know was what was going on behind the scenes. Allison agreed to share some of our interactions about what happened to her just before the Olympics and what happened after she flew home.

About two weeks before the Olympic Games, my mom called me to let me know that her cancer was back. Being the always stoic mom, she acted as if it was no big deal and admitted that she hesitated to tell me so close to the Olympics. Of course, I was concerned because with the stage 4 breast cancer that my mom had, any relapse could be fatal. My first step was to call my sister to find out everything that my mom didn't tell me. She confirmed that the cancer was back but eased my mind a little in telling me that all the tests that my mom was to have done and whatever treatment was necessary was not to going to happen until after the Olympics. My mom was coming to the Olympics in Torino to watch me compete. She said it was something she was going to do even if it was the last thing she ever did. But before that happened, I crashed and tore my left knee in the second training run of the Olympic downhill.

So I arrived home on the 14th of February. I was really excited to see my family but could not help but notice that it took my mom an awfully long time to climb up the short six stairs to my living room. She didn't look good, and it started to sink in just what could be in store for us. The week progressed, and my mom and I simultaneously deteriorated. I went in for surgery carrying my crutches and came out using them. My mom went from walking up the stairs a little slowly on the first day to being barely able to walk at all by the fifth day. I lay in my bed, and my mom lay in hers in my guest room across the hall. We would try to talk and joke with each other through the walls. From the moment I came out of surgery, I was healing, but my mom wasn't. The rapid decline in her motor skills and physical functioning made it clear to everyone there that the cancer was rapidly attacking her system.

So we cried, we laughed, and we cried some more. We spent some very special quality time together. I will never forget what happened next. We had just had a great dinner with some close friends of mine, and they were helping my mom to the car. By this point, she was pretty much immobile. As I hobbled along behind, my friend Chris turned to me and whispered, "You know, today is the day of your giant slalom event in Torino. Today your mom was supposed to truck through the snow to sit in the stands and watch you. It never would have happened." My mom would never have been able to make it to that race that day, and she probably would have died over there in Italy. Instead, as I watched the rest of the Olympics on TV with my leg up, my mom was rushed to be put directly on a miracle drug that has given her, to date, eight more months of life. It has been eight months since the loss of my Olympic dreams. But I happily gave those up, and I would do it again in a heartbeat because what happened to me at the Olympics has given me another eight months with my mom—time I would not trade for any gold medal in the world.

It's interesting how life presents us with challenges and basically taunts us into deciding what we are going to do with those challenges. Are we going to accept them and persevere, or are we going to let them crush us? This injury has been a challenge that I have chosen to persevere through. I have learned so much about myself, my life, and the people in it. I am committed to keep going until the Olympics in 2010 because I know now that I am on a path that I have chosen, but fate is guiding me. My destiny is still out there. I took one for the team—by that I mean my family—but I have been given back everything and more because of it. I have been given back my mom, even if just for a short time.

I will never forget the moment when I realized how much my mother loved me. It was two days after my surgery, and my mom was lying in her bed across the hall from where I was lying in mine. She was in severe pain, as was I. She was not able to walk, nor was I. Everyone was upstairs doing things, and my mom just said casually through the walls, "Alli, is there anything I can do for you? Do you need anything?" I just kind of smiled to myself and started to cry, casually responding, "No, Mom, I'm fine." And I know I will be fine because my mom has already given me everything I need. (Note: Allison was at her mother's side when she passed away in April of 2007 and shared the story you have just read at her mom's memorial service.)

Bruce Malmberg's Story

Bruce is a high-performance international archer—long-time member of the national team, seven-time national champion, national-record holder, and multiple winner of the Atlantic City Archery Classic. Bruce and I worked together for many years on focusing and becoming super relaxed to the point that he could shoot between heart beats, perfecting shots through imagery, following a specific preshot routine that worked consistently, and drawing on every experience as an opportunity to learn something about himself. At a point when he was at the top of his game, his life was instantly turned around by a career-threatening setback. Bruce shared his resilient personal journey through adversity.

I had arrived home after a training session and had sat down to have some lunch when I heard screaming in the backyard. Our cat was being attacked by a vicious pit bull terrier. As I went to the patio door to see what was happening, my wife opened the door and ran inside, closing the screen door behind her. Suddenly the dog came crashing through the screen and into our house. The dog charged at my wife, who was holding our cat. I jumped between them and pushed the dog to the floor. The dog broke free and came at us again. This time I grabbed the dog and threw it toward the door, where I thought I could get it out of the house. The dog jumped up and charged again, attacking another one of our cats. It had our cat clenched in its jaws and ran out the backdoor. I ran through the door and tackled the dog on the lawn, at which point it turned and attacked me. I can still remember feeling the pain of the pit bull's teeth biting through my hand and its crushing grip. This was followed by a flurry of punching, biting, and wrestling to keep the 80-pound (36-kilogram) pit bull off me and my vital organs.

I yelled at one of my neighbors who was watching to call 911. She just stood there, and I yelled, "Go call now." That five minutes of unexpected terror on the lawn seemed like an eternity. Everything seemed to move in slow motion, yet it was happening too fast to recall. When it was over, our cat was dead, and both the dog and I were bleeding from everywhere. The pit bull did not stop his relentless attack until my wife ran out of our house with a kitchen knife and stabbed him.

The last thing I remember was handing our lifeless cat to my wife and saying, "Get him to the vet." The next thing I knew I was lying in the yard with the paramedics working on me to stop the bleeding and one of them telling me that I was badly hurt. One hundred and eight stitches and three days in the hospital later, my shooting career was over and my life had turned 180 degrees. The deep bites and gashes in my hands, arms, chest, and legs had been heavily bandaged, and I had no use of my hands. I had a great deal of tendon damage in both arms, and for a national archery team champion, that spelled *finished*.

I spent two weeks in a daze and had not even thought about shooting until a good friend of mine asked, "How's this going to affect your shooting?" Wham, what a reality check. The trauma of the event and the ongoing barrage of reporters calling the house had me so focused on the event that I never really thought about the consequences of what had happened. I guess I had assumed that I would always be able to do what I love to do—shoot my bow.

After a week of depression, I literally thought, *If Terry were here he would kick my butt right now*. I made a decision that day that no matter how long it took, I was going to regain the use of my hands.

The first thing I did was to set small achievable goals for myself. The next thing I did was to keep track of them. It was not going to help me to set goals if I did not keep track of them. The physiotherapist said that it would probably take 12 to 18 months to regain full use of my hands, maybe longer. It was then mid-August, and I wanted to make it to indoor provincials and nationals in March.

As I began to shoot again, I actually set a goal to not kill anyone when I went to the shooting range for the first time. I achieved that goal! The entire first month was the most frustrating of all. My hands and arms were healing and the pain was considerable. Before the attack, I used a hand-held release to shoot the bow, but that was not possible now. One of my sponsors sent me a release mechanism that I could strap to my arm to release the arrow. I modified it to meet my own needs, and it worked very well. I asked another sponsor to send me a lighter version of equipment, and in a short time I was shooting again.

I continued to set and work on achieving my short-term goal. If I was not achieving my short-term goals, I was not trying hard enough. The biggest thing that spurred me on was that a number of my competitors had written me off. They even joked about not having to worry about me any more. Talk about incentive! After seven months of diligent rehab and training, I shot and won the provincial indoor championships and placed second by 1 point in the national championships. I refused to let the dog attack stop me from doing what I loved.

Now, four years later, I am again using my hands to shoot. Sometimes there is pain, but I think of how far I have come in four years. I think of the four provincial titles, four national titles, and the two Athlete of the Year awards I have won since that dog attack. It shows me that something good can come out of everything. It shows me that what Terry taught me is true—that anything is possible if your mind and your heart are in the right place. In all the time that I was working to get back to top form, I never lost sight of what I saw myself as, and I am now that. I just keep achieving and resetting every day. I am happy in my sport and my life.

Making a Transition

At some points in your life, when things are going well, you might feel a bit like a hero. At other points, when things aren't going well, you may feel more like a zero. This shift in feelings may occur from one second to the next, from one day to the next, or from one week to the next, but the shift is usually most pronounced during major challenges, transitions, or times of uncertainty.

A medalist at the Olympic Games had been convinced that excelling in her sport was the only important thing in her life. Her coach told her that all those people out there (outside the training regimen) "weren't doing anything important." As she said, "Then I stopped competing and became one of them." It took her a long time to regain perspective and confidence in herself as a person.

If you believe that you are important only because of your performance in one area of your life, what remains when you are no longer performing as well or not performing at all in that domain? An all-consuming marriage to sport or work to the exclusion of everything leads to imbalance. The breakup of this kind of marriage may be difficult, especially if you leave thinking that you're finished, that you're no longer good enough to be there, or that without the activity you're nothing.

Growing apart from your sport or performance domain doesn't have to produce those feelings, but it often does. All dedicated performers have a commitment to fulfill a dream of excellence. Preparation, training, and performance regimens become the major focus in life for most high-performance athletes, particularly during the years of greatest passion and improvement. But distinguishing between "the most important thing" and "the only thing" is important. Both allow you to pursue excellence, but only one allows you to do so without abandoning the rest of your life.

You can pursue high levels of excellence while still embracing other parts of your life by maintaining a sense of balance and harmony. Balance is finding passion, beauty, and meaning in the different loves of your life and living those loves every day or at every opportunity. Finding balance does not mean setting aside equal time, but making the best of the time that you have and connecting fully with each experience. To maintain or restore the balance in your life, respect the different loves of your life, embrace the simple joys, be more playful, enjoy moments of relaxed connection with others, create special times for yourself, and know that you are worthy, valued, and loved apart from your performance.

One of your first challenges in attaining balanced excellence is to establish priorities for each day, week, month, year, or phase of your life. Then you must focus fully on the priority in which you are engaged, while you are engaged in it. Shifting your focus completely from one priority or experience to the next as you move through your day, week, or life is a great asset in all transitions. Each pursuit that you choose to embrace or make a priority can become one of the wonderful adventures from which you will learn and grow.

Leaving Competitive Sport

Virtually all competitive athletes are destined to experience declines in physical performance and profile in their chosen sport over time. A certain level of uncertainty usually accompanies transition out of high-performance sport, which may result in stress, fear, or at least some concern about what lies ahead.

The same occurs with other transitions—leaving high school or college and hoping to move into the workplace, or moving out of an established home, workplace, or relationship. Ultimately, the challenge is to embrace the many new opportunities, possibilities for personal growth, and unexpected new adventures that transitions provide.

Dramatic changes can occur for high-performance athletes in transition. They lose the predictable structure of the day, the clarity of daily goals, the clear direction in which they are headed in both the short term and the long term, and everyday contact with teammates and friends, some of whom are like family members. Many athletes initially feel lost upon retirement from high-performance sport, and even not-so-high-performance sport. In sport you know the daily routine, the weekly routine, the monthly routine, the yearly routine. The pattern is predictable and doesn't change much. When you step out of that environment, you have no set routine. No one tells you what to do, when to do it, and how to do it. Nobody plans your day, your workout, your performance schedule, your travel, your hotel, your meals, your life. You have to begin to plan your own day and your own path. This new circumstance offers many advantages when you begin to see it as an opportunity, embrace each day, and open yourself to the unlimited possibilities of your life.

The initial time of uncertainty between leaving an established routine and creating a new one that has meaning for you is the first challenging part of transition. Finding something to pursue with passion, an activity in which you can find a sense of meaning or make a positive difference, is often the most difficult ongoing challenge of transition. You could choose to pursue many things—for yourself, for your loved ones, for others. All noble or uplifting paths are worthy in some way, but choosing your path is not always easy.

One of the great advantages that you have in transition is being able to apply what you learned and used to excel in your sport (or other chosen performance domain) to the new choices you make and the new directions you take. When one set of physical or technical skills that you have or had diminishes, you are not less of a person. You simply channel some of your focusing strengths, which always remain with you, into other meaningful pursuits. What you have learned from your journey thus far in life can help you immensely to contribute and grow for the rest of your life. The ultimate challenge in your life is to continue to live, learn, and grow in positive ways by drawing on your most positive and best-connected focus. The focusing skills that you learned through sport will help you excel in other pursuits and find ongoing meaning, balance, and joy in your life. At times this goal may seem elusive, but through time, focus, and persistence, you can make it reality.

For some athletes the retirement experience is difficult. Others have a relatively easy transition. One athlete said, "I thought it was easy. I had other hobbies, a career, and a personal life that could easily be expanded and improved." People who have relatively fluid transition experiences seem to have one or more of the following things going for them:

➤ They have been respecting other parts of their life during their competitive years.

➤ They have meaningful options to consider upon retirement.

➤ They have the complete support of at least one important person upon retirement or immediately afterward (a parent, coach, close friend, or loved one).

Following are some suggestions from athletes who have been through transitions. Before making the decision to retire, they suggest that you take the following steps:

➤ Find a coach who respects you as a whole person rather than just as a performer. A more personal coaching approach can help you leave your sport feeling more worthwhile after many years of dedicated training.

➤ View your personal development through education, work, family, or friends as an integral part of your overall training program.

➤ Take time to relax and enjoy something outside your sport or performance domain.

➤ Think about what you want from your sport or performance domain and from your life. Get to know yourself well enough to decide what is best for you.

➤ Change your routine in the off-season. Go to school, take some courses, spend some time in nature, or do something else that you enjoy.

➤ Make time for meaningful experiences other than training and performing. Schedule other activities into your overall program (for example, time for you, time with others, time for simple joys, time for seeing something other than competition and training venues, time for educational activities).

➤ Focus some of your energy on new areas of interest while still actively competing so that if something interests you, the option is there for continuation or expansion after retirement.

➤ Think of transitions as opportunities to enter a new phase of your life, to learn something new, to grow, to develop, to contribute in other areas, and to embrace life.

The same athletes suggested taking the following steps after making the retirement decision:

➤ After you have made your transition decision, let your family and friends know that you would appreciate having their support. Let them know if there are specific ways that they can help you.

➤ Consider exploring interesting pursuits, training, adventures, or opportunities in areas in which you already have strengths or an interest.

➤ Stay actively involved in sports, fitness, exercise, and other outdoor activities for the sheer joy of participating in them and for health-related benefits. Consider participating in self-paced activities or get involved in veterans' events. Adjust your goals accordingly.

➤ If possible, arrange to share experiences with others who are going through a similar transition. Exchange thoughts and feelings about your experiences, progress, setbacks, and adaptation to a different lifestyle.

➤ If the transition situation is getting you down, you might want to discuss your concerns with someone close to you or see a counselor for personal, educational, career, business, or leisure planning. Counselors are available on virtually all university campuses and in most towns and cities.

Finding a New Path

My transition out of competitive sport began with coaching and going back to school. At that time I began doing my master's degree in counseling at the College of William and Mary in Williamsburg, Virginia, and was coaching the university gymnastics team and diving team at the same time to pay for my education. I was also still working out with the gymnastics team and doing an occasional performance. I distinctly remember an incident that made me reflect hard on the issue of transition. A group of gymnasts, acrobats, and circus performers from Europe who were on tour in the United States asked me if I would be willing to perform with them when they were in Williamsburg. I said that I would be happy to do it.

On the day after the performance, I had a meeting with my master's degree supervisor. When I walked into his office, he stood up, shook my hand, and congratulated me. He had been at the performance the previous night and said that he was amazed at what he saw me do. The only other place he had ever seen me was sitting in a classroom or in his office. He went on to say, "If you could ever be as good at counseling people or helping people in this field as you are as a gymnastics performer, that would be truly incredible." I was about 24 years old at the time and never envisioned myself being that good at anything else—probably because I never put that much time or focus into anything else.

After I finished my degree, I directed my path to something that I thought I would love to do. I applied my focus and passion to become as good as I could be in my profession as a teacher, coach, and consultant in applied sport and performance psychology. I am much better at what I do right now than I ever was an athlete. Perhaps more important for me is that I am making a greater contribution to others through what I am doing than I ever did as an athlete. The lesson is that although you may not think that you can do anything as well as what you are doing right now, I am telling you that you can! Everyone's dream is, and should be, different. Choose to do whatever you want to do and focus on making your dreams a reality.

If you have gained from an experience, if it has contributed to your personal growth, if it has helped you in any way or given you a sense of meaning (even temporarily), then it has been of some real value. Draw on the positive lessons from your previous experience and get on with developing other competencies and embracing the rest of your life. Open your own doors. Recognize that as one phase of your life is ending, another phase is just beginning. Consider directing some of your hard-earned knowledge to the benefit of others—for example, by helping, teaching, or coaching others; by working or playing with a group of children, youth, or developing performers; by giving clinics or workshops; or by writing about your experiences. Consider committing part of your time or life to worthy causes like battling problems such as obesity, poverty, or poor health. There are many areas in which you may be able to make a meaningful contribution or make a real difference in people's lives. Your profile or experience as an athlete or performer may give you an advantage in opening doors to initiate meaningful missions.

If you do not want to pursue or follow one of the thousands of career options that currently exist, create your own path or make your own opportunities. Think about the skills that you have and the areas that you would like to pursue. Then choose to do whatever it takes to move in that direction. The applied work that I am now immersed in as a high-performance focus coach and as a person committed to teaching children positive living skills did not exist when I retired from competitive sport or when I graduated from the university. I was passionate about those areas, and I found a way to weave them into my life and my work.

Your knowledge, your potential to contribute to others, and your understanding of yourself and the needs of others will continue to grow throughout your life, long after your physical or technical performance skills begin to decline. It is never too late to try something new, to enter a new line of work, to contribute in a different domain, to accomplish new goals, or to do something for the sheer joy of the experience. For example, an 82-year-old woman recently received her undergraduate degree from the university where I teach. For a variety of reasons she was not able to act on this dream earlier in her life, and when she finally walked across the stage with diploma in hand, she was both smiling and crying.

Contrast this situation with someone who is so afraid of looking less than perfect that he simply avoids anything in which he is not already proficient. This viewpoint closes doors and eliminates many opportunities. If you have spent most of your time specializing in one or two activities, you may not be proficient in others. Yet you can enjoy other pursuits immensely, be challenged by them, and improve rapidly after you take the first step and realize that it doesn't matter what others might think or expect. Just being you, pursuing what you want to do, is fine.

Don't let anything get in the way of your growth, your positive passions, and your enjoyment. Remember that you don't have to be proficient at everything or at all times to contribute or enjoy what you are doing. If you are not exceptionally proficient at some activities, your friends, family members, or colleagues might even like you more. You are human just as they are. You aren't great in everything.

Hans Selye, renowned pioneer in stress research, wrote the following words in the introduction to his book *The Stress of Life* (1978). "Most of our tensions and frustrations stem from compulsive needs to act the role of someone we are not. . . . 'Resolve to be thyself; and know that he who finds himself, loses his misery.'"

Living the Transition

I know from experience that transitions can be challenging for some people. Even those who have had a positive sport experience, are well balanced, and are great human beings can struggle with transition. The following story highlights the frustration that a highly successful athlete can experience in the process of finding a new and meaningful direction. University and professional athletes who have competed in sport for most of their lives and are living through transition have expressed similar feelings.

Athlete: I am finding it hard to express adequately what is going on at any given moment these days. I decided to put off trying to describe it until I think things have stabilized and I can say, "I feel this . . . or I feel that . . . ." The clarity—for better or worse—doesn't seem to be coming though.

Terry: Sometimes it is difficult to have clarity within transition because things are not yet clear. They are in the process of surfacing and becoming. The wind may blow in many different directions before you set a firm course that takes you where you want to go.

Athlete: To sum it up in a nutshell I'm having a bit of a tough go these days—and have been having it for quite some time now. The weight of the stress that I feel sometimes in trying to move down a different path or find a new direction, without actually knowing what that is, or even what it might be, could be, or may be, is crushing at times. It is a complex challenge to know and be fully aware that "inner peace" and confidence and happiness and contentment with life have to come from within, and are completely within my control, and yet sometimes have the sensation that those states are totally out of my reach. I don't really know how else to describe this state of being right now.

Terry: Part of the challenge and journey through transition that will ease the crushing sensation of not knowing what your new path is or will be—is to slow down, don't rush it. Don't feel obliged to find that new path or accomplish all things right now. Your new path or direction will emerge as you lighten up on the need to know or do it right now. Just enjoy the simple things outside, inside, alone, with others, and free yourself to do some of the simplest things you love to do. Some good feelings are within reach right now, because you can live them each day. Other meaningful possibilities are not yet within your vision or reach, but they will be. If you try to force them to surface or put pressure on yourself to reach unclear goals right away, that may make them more elusive. Try easier. Slow down. Breathe. Relax. Be where you are for a little while. There is no rush to the finish line. There is no urgency to know or reach those unknown goals immediately. Do the simple things that lift you every day and trust that the bigger directions will surface. They will come to you when you are ready and feel ready. Remain open to possibilities and seize them when they feel right. Let go of feeling obliged to grasp for them or accomplish them today.

Athlete: There are, of course, many great things in my life still and so many things to be thankful for that I also feel quite stupid at times for being down and feeling like I'm not living life to the fullest. How can I be so young, healthy, and accomplished and feel so inadequate and useless?

Terry: We all go through times like this, and it is fine. It is part of living through uncertainty and transitions. It is part of personal growth and self-discovery—growing through the feelings. Sometimes feeling down or feeling that we are not living our lives to the fullest provides the inspiration and insights that eventually guide our future decisions and better realities.

You are probably feeling the way you are feeling right now because you don't feel you are where you want to be—yet! Remember the yet! Finding what you want and doing what you want are just being delayed at this moment. It will come.

Athlete: I hope it doesn't sound as if I'm not functioning right now. In fact, I am. I have been doing quite well with the public speaking engagements, and I've taken on a couple of other things that I am really looking forward to doing (some of which we have already discussed).

So, I haven't quite retreated to a place of utter despair . . . and I definitely know that staying active physically has a direct impact on my mood and outlook, which was an important discovery.

Terry: This will be true for your whole life, so no matter what else happens hang on to your physical activity and to your special time with nature.

Athlete: I just find that it is harder to stay out of the funk than in it and that this transitory postretirement period has taken much longer than I expected. It is not the training, competing, travel, or even the team that has left a hole so much as knowing there was a purpose to getting up in the morning and that at the end of the day, another step forward (however small or large) had been taken. I had a job and focus and direction and everything came after that. Now, I feel productive if I leave the house and get a couple of trivial things done on the same day—not quite what I had in mind for my life you know. . . . I mean, there were days when I was competing that I couldn't wait to be done and be released from that lifestyle so that I could get on with things and start up one of the thousand ideas or projects that I had in mind.

Terry: The bottom line probably lies in finding something you feel is worthy and that is worthy of your efforts. What were some of those ideas or projects that you had in mind when you were competing? If you can pick one or two of the interesting things that you might like to do and explore the possibility of pursuing them, then maybe your days will feel more complete or more meaningful. Remember, it is also sometimes nice not to *have to* do anything. Just *choose to* go for a run, spend some time in nature, play, and do one or two things that make you feel good or productive or helpful or useful in some way. Each activity, idea, or project you choose to do or act on takes on meaning in its own right.

If you are experiencing some of the feelings that the athlete spoke about, remember that having those feelings is OK, and that you will be OK even if you are feeling some of those things. You are experiencing what many others experience. Somehow, they draw on their strengths and find a way through the fog to greater clarity in their lives. Sometimes you have to accept that it takes time to find another meaningful path or another absorbing focus. There is no need to make everything happen immediately—right now! Positive new directions often take time to emerge or reveal themselves. An unhurried approach is often the way of meaningful transitions and the way of finding worthy new directions in life. Clarity, direction, and focus often come when you stop trying to force things and instead allow possibilities to unfold and grow in their own way. Every path you embark on leads to other paths and other opportunities. The process is all about taking little steps—some of those little steps will lead you to clearer insights, better possibilities, and new realities.

Each project you embrace that gives you joy or a sense of meaning or purpose will help you move forward. Ultimately, the best place to be is finding a sense of meaningful contribution and feeling a sense of balance in your life. Give what you can give and feel good about it. Embrace the simple joys along the path. This is the best place to be.

You have a great opportunity in front of you to become a better, less stressed, and more balanced person by applying some of the mental skills that you have learned and perfected and by living some of the strategies presented in this book. You can direct the focus and positive perspectives that you used to excel in your sport or performance domain to become a better performer in anything that you choose to pursue. You can use the same skills to become a better person, to embrace each experience, and to live the simple joys in your life.

I wish you the best in this transition and the many other transitions that will follow over the course of your life. I know that you have the capacity to negotiate this transition successfully and to continue to become a stronger and wiser person. Embrace the different steps of your transition and try to find something positive in the uncertainty. Make the best of it. See the transition as a new opportunity, a worthy challenge, a new venue for knowing yourself better, and a wonderful opportunity for personal growth.

CHAPTER 22

Coaching Relationships

Understanding the process of what frees people to excel is critically important in our world, whether we are pursuing excellence in sport, coaching, teaching, parenting, learning, leading others, living, or performing to our potential in any worthy human endeavor. Facilitating excellence is largely a cooperative venture. Cooperation, respect, and collaboration play a huge part in nurturing successful relationships and in enhancing performance in all areas of life. Coaches, teammates, and even competitors can play a meaningful role in helping you become your best.

> We can all gain from competent coaches and leaders who believe in us, help us grow our confidence, and inspire us to reach our goals.

Whether you are a coach or an athlete, two key forces drive you to achieve excellence and make meaningful contributions:

1. Finding and pursuing something you love or find meaningful, and
2. Feeling accepted, valued, and respected through being engaged in a meaningful pursuit.

Does love for what you are doing or gaining a sense of self-respect from the contributions you are making have anything to do with sustaining your ongoing pursuit of excellence? Great coaches, teachers, and parents play a critical role in making excellence possible. We all know that children thrive on feeling loved, accepted, valued, and respected. Coaches, athletes, teachers, and parents also benefit from such feelings. People of all ages blossom and become their best in a supportive, respectful environment.

A critical part of the job of coaches, teachers, parents, and support staff is to ensure that the athletes feel accepted, valued, and respected, at least within our presence. We all win in sport and life, and help others to win, by giving love and respect and gaining it in return.

Characteristics of Great Coaches

Almost all athletes have had a number of coaches during their lives, and many athletes become coaches in some capacity. Some may coach themselves or coach teammates in an informal way. Some coach children or become team coaches. Who are the coaches who had the greatest positive influence on you and your performance? What did they do that separated them from other coaches? The truly great coaches I have worked with helped athletes continue to love what they were doing and encouraged them to pursue their dreams. They believed in their athletes, helped them believe that they could overcome tough challenges, and made the journey enjoyable. This kind of coaching facilitates personal growth and makes excellence a realistic possibility.

Great coaches (and effective performance enhancement consultants) are committed to doing what is best for their athletes or performers. They are secure enough within themselves to respect and listen to the people with whom they work. They value input and act on good suggestions from the coaching staff, the support staff, and the athletes or performers. They respectfully listen, even when they do not totally understand or agree with another point of view. They respect the experience, qualities, and potential of others. They believe in their athletes to the point that those athletes can feel that belief in their gut. Great coaches care about their athletes as people and performers, and challenge them to push their limits so that they become the best that they can be. They support their athletes every step of the way, especially through the big challenges, difficult times, injuries, and setbacks.

At the high-performance level, almost all coaches are competent with respect to technical and tactical skills. What

©Ellen Ozier/Reuters/Corbis

► Coach Mike Krzyzewski epitomizes the qualities of an outstanding coach.

separates great coaches from the rest are people skills. Outstanding coaches are masters at communicating and building respectful, trusting relationships.

Truly great coaches significantly influence the lives of athletes and performers and help them grow as performers and people. They have mastered the art of coaching people largely because they made a commitment to fine-tune their capacity to listen, respect, challenge, support, and believe. In the preparation or lead-up phase to important competitions or events, listening, respecting, and challenging athletes or performers in positive ways is critically important. In the on-site performance phase, great coaches demonstrate their belief in their performers, support them in simple ways, and occasionally remind them of where their focus needs to be. These factors are central to facilitating excellence. Believing in people and their capacity to perform is important in all phases of development and within all contexts. Belief is the mother of reality, and it needs lots of nourishing through the difficulties of every meaningful journey.

Great coaches give athletes good reasons to believe in themselves, their team, and their capacity. They seize opportunities to enhance confidence and avoid speaking or acting in ways that undermine confidence. They challenge performers to push their limits, but they do it in positive and respectful ways rather than negative or disrespectful ways. This approach is empowering. All outstanding coaches have some of these great human qualities and constantly look for ways to become more effective at meaningful communication. The best-case scenario for any team is when all athletes or performers, coaches, and support staff work together to bring out the best qualities in everyone.

Excellent coaches and team leaders understand that when athletes, team members, or professionals in any performance context feel valued, supported, and respected, they give more of themselves, give more to others, and perform at a higher level on a more consistent basis. Outstanding coaches, directors, and team leaders recognize the immense value of respectful collaboration. They respect and engage in ongoing collaboration with those with whom they work or play. They recognize the value in respectfully challenging all team members to become the best that they can be and to be key players in shaping their own destiny.

In high-performance contexts or major events, coaches and support staff, like the athletes they work with, face higher levels of stress, more demands, higher expectations, and more distractions than they are accustomed to. They have less personal control over their environment than they normally do. To be their best when it counts most, coaches and support staff can also benefit from having positive focus plans, effective refocusing plans, and distraction control plans. Positive action plans can help coaches remain calm, confident, and focused in times of increased stress. Action plans remind coaches to continue to project belief into the people with whom they work, through the good times and the troubled times.

Positive Communication With the Coach

As an athlete, you have to remember that coaches are people. Most of them are trying to do their best, and they aren't mind readers. If you want things to improve, you must take some responsibility to communicate with your coach. I know that some coaches are not ready or willing to listen at times. But at other times they are, particularly if you can find a quiet time to talk outside practice or the performance arena. Consider meeting individually with your coach during a relaxed time to talk constructively about what you think will help you or the team improve. Tell him or her what makes you work best or perform most efficiently, what kind of communication you prefer, what upsets you, and what hinders your workout or performance. You might be able to help each other in ways that will improve both your effectiveness and the overall team performance.

If you don't feel comfortable meeting with your coach or if doing so seems threatening, then focus on improving your on-site communication. Whenever the coach does something that you find helpful (before, during, or after practices or performances), let him or her know about it right away. For example, when the coach's comments are helpful or constructive, offer a thank-you. Tell your coach that the feedback helped you. If your coach has contributed to a good workout or performance and is giving the kind of feedback that you like, communicate this before leaving or as soon as possible. Help the coach understand how to help you.

One way to show your coach that you want to improve is to ask for additional help or for further clarification on his or her feedback (for example, "Coach, I'd really like to improve this; what specifically should I focus on doing?"). Asking for clarification will help you get the feedback that you need for technical or tactical improvement. The other way to demonstrate your commitment is to practice and perform with fully focused intensity. The more you show your commitment to improve through your actions, the more likely it is that the coach will help you.

When you recognize that you can help improve the communication between you and your coach, you can take several distinct but interrelated actions to improve your performance:

1. Think about what works best for you to bring out your best performance.

2. Work on improving your positive communication skills with your coach.

3. Take full responsibility for focusing on doing what works best for your best performance and your team's best performance.

4. Work on improving your capacity to direct and control your focus, emotions, and actions.

5. Draw from the positive perspectives and positive focus of your best teammates (or line mates) and those who are closest to you if you need additional support, inspiration, or advice.

6. If all else fails, remember that the best place to find a helping hand is often at the end of your own arm. You control you, and you control your focus. Decide to make your focus work for you, not against you.

Maintaining Respect

The challenge of every coach is to bring out the best in each of his or her athletes. One of the challenges for athletes and performers is to find a way to get the best from their coaches and support staff, and the best from themselves. Rarely do all athletes or team members love their coach or team leader. And very few coaches love all the athletes or team members on their teams. So the challenge becomes one of getting the best out of each other regardless of whether there is a natural bond or perfect fit between coach and athlete, or between leader and team member. Everyone has something of value to offer, so focus on getting the best out of what each person has to contribute.

Problems within a coaching context rarely result from the coach's lack of technical knowledge. The cause is usually a communication or respect issue. Athletes or team members feel an absence of listening, understanding, respect, positive challenge, belief, caring, or support. When these kinds of feelings surface within any kind of performance team and the coach does not address them, declines in motivation, confidence, and performance are not far behind.

Performance is enhanced most readily when coaches and athletes work together to create a positive environment and share the responsibility for successfully pursuing the mission and improving ongoing communication. If you want to get the best out of yourself and your situation, commit fully to the mission and solve the problems along the way in a mature, collaborative, responsible, and respectful manner. The reminders in figure 22.1 can help you and your coaches create a positive environment that fosters excellence.

We are all human beings first. Most of us appreciate support or recognition for the good things that we are doing, and we like to receive constructive comments about ways to become even better or more consistent. If the suggestions for improvement come from genuine care, love, or respect, they are always better received. Although coaches often focus on results because their jobs depend on results, they too are people. You can create stronger bonds with your coaches when you treat them as thinking, feeling human beings with lives outside their performance domains. All of us are people first, and ideally we will become better people because of our involvement with our teams.

Respectful communication is a two-way venture. Both you and the person with whom you are interacting are responsible for making it work. Granted, communicating openly and constructively is not always easy, especially in conflict situations or where power struggles are occurring. A helpful approach

Figure 22.1   Athlete and Coach Excellence Reminders

Believe

1. Share your vision.
2. Project your belief.
3. Believe in your mission and your team.
4. Help team members to believe in themselves.
5. Identify positive roles and goals with team members.
6. Become the most positive coach or athlete you can be.

Challenge

1. Challenge your team.
2. Challenge everyone to be what they can be.
3. Challenge team members to focus on what brings out their best and the team's best.
4. Challenge team members to draw out and act on the lessons from each performance.
5. Challenge yourself to be what you can be—as a coach or athlete.
6. Commit yourself to ongoing learning and improvement.

Support

1. Value people and their contributions.
2. Listen to people and their different perspectives.
3. Be positive and respectful in your interactions.
4. Act in positive ways every day.
5. Give honest and constructive feedback.
6. Continue to support and show respect for others.

Remember

1. Remember to focus on what brings out your best.
2. Remember to act in positive ways, especially through the tough times.
3. Remember to act on lessons learned and suggestions for improvement now.
4. Remember your commitment to ongoing learning and ongoing improvement.
5. Remember that everyone on this team wants to win.
6. Remember that everyone needs time to rest and regenerate.

Appreciate

1. Appreciate the small steps and simple joys.
2. Appreciate the opportunities you have in front of you.

3. Acknowledge good effort.

4. Rejoice in simple successes.

5. Keep the love in the pursuit.

6. Help all the athletes and coaches keep the love in the pursuit.

Focus

1. Bring your best focus to every pursuit.

2. Focus fully on the step in front of you.

3. Wherever you are, be totally where you are.

4. Take care of your own needs.

5. Seek balance in excellence.

6. Connect totally to bring out your best and the best in others.

in some situations is to share your thoughts in writing, perhaps through a handwritten letter or card or a diplomatically written e-mail that you review carefully before you send. You may want to share a page or chapter of a book that outlines the benefits of a certain approach and follow up with a face-to-face discussion about it. Communication is sometimes a delicate process, but in almost all cases the effort is worthwhile.

Communicating Your Preferences

To optimize your chances of performing well in important events, consider communicating your on-site preferences to your coach. Good coaches are interested in helping athletes perform to their capacity, so they will usually accept and act on this information. Talk with your coach about what you would like him or her to do, or not do, at the performance site. Be specific in your instructions (for example, "I'd prefer to be left alone," "Remind me that I can do it," "Talk calmly," "No last-minute changes," or "Give me corrective feedback only during time-outs").

Often, athletes will not share information that influences performance outcomes when they feel it is too risky to communicate honestly with their coach. This reluctance to share information applies to both training or preparation sessions and performances or competitions. Take, for example, the fact that every player I interviewed on one professional football team felt that the coach's pregame pep talk, as well as the last-minute changes that he made in the game plan, either were a hindrance or did nothing to contribute to the players' mental preparation for the game. The athletes said, "I'm not motivated by it. I know my job. I'm ready, and I don't need him to make me ready. Rah-rah stuff is of no benefit." As one of the more accomplished players stated, "The standard pregame speech that so many of us have heard before is simply not doing the team or individual players any good. However, it may be a method of tension release for the head coach. Having been in the locker room on many occasions, I think it is. If this is so, he should find another way of doing it, away from the players."

Performers in a variety of disciplines report that their best focus or their confidence may be shaken if the coach makes too many changes or places additional demands on them just before a game or performance. The moment before a game or performance is not the time for the coach to add new moves or strategies, change well-established routines that work, make detailed comments about improving technique, give complicated instructions, or even require athletes to sit and listen. Last-second changes before important competitions tend to be more detrimental than helpful in almost every sport, unless athletes have been extremely well prepared or trained to adapt to them. For certain athletes, last-second instructions can spell disaster. One thing that players don't need are lingering thoughts such as *Maybe I'm not as well prepared as I thought. . . . Maybe the coach doesn't have confidence in me. . . . Maybe the coach doesn't have confidence in the game plan that we practiced all week. . . . Maybe I (or we) won't be able to perform that well.* My advice to you is to stay positive, respect your best focus, and stick with what works.

As game time approaches, the coach's job of preparing athletes for the contest is over. He or she must shift gears so as not to interfere with the athletes' last-minute mental preparation. Some athletes appreciate a word of encouragement, a simple reminder, or a reassuring comment, but beyond that most prefer to be left alone during their final focus preparation for the event. If athletes could be totally honest with their coaches, most would say, "Leave me alone so I can concentrate," "Watch from a distance so as not to distract me," or "I'll come to you if I need you." At high levels in sport, athletes know what they want to do and they have a focus plan to do it. At all levels in sport, the time just before the event is the athletes' time to focus on their performance and the coaches' time to free them to do it.

If you, as a player, have an assistant coach whose temperament or style of communication fits best with your precompetition needs, request that he or she interact with you on-site in place of the head coach. I suggested this strategy to some high-level coaches whose team was preparing for an important tournament. The head coach was high strung, whereas the assistant coach was calm and low key. Before the sudden-death elimination match, the two most hyper players on the team interacted only with the calm and reassuring assistant coach. They both played the best games of their lives and were instrumental in determining the final outcome, which was in their favor.

Sylvie Bernier also used this best-fit approach when winning her gold medal in diving at the Olympic Games. At Sylvie's request, her personal coach, who was at his best during regular training, sat in the stands during the final on-site Olympic practices and competition, while another member of the coaching staff who was calmer, more supportive, and less inclined to give last-minute technical input interacted with her on deck. Her personal coach agreed to this arrangement because he knew that Sylvie would be calmer and more fully focused on executing each dive, and she was.

Common Coaching Errors

Every coach, every athlete, every performer, every person makes errors. We would all be better and improve a lot faster if we paid attention to those errors, learned from each of them, and acted in more positive or constructive ways because of them. Too often coaches, athletes, leaders, and team members keep making the same errors over and over, day after day, month after month, year after year. The errors become a habit, or way of being. This habit then becomes a major obstacle to the attainment of our noble goals. Every performance error, every bad choice, every loss of focus, and every flawed interaction is an opportunity to get better. You should rejoice in the error because it is your direct path to improvement. The error provides the real value of the experience, and you can turn it into positive action.

If you do not learn from and improve as a result of an error, you are wasting an opportunity. If you do not act on that error to improve yourself or your performance, the result is the same as if you did not have the experience. You stay the same. Experience is of value only if you learn from it and get better because of it. Regardless of whether your performance was good or bad, you (and members of your team) can learn from it and get better from it only if you act on it.

If coaches or athletes make an error at a performance site, they should have a plan to focus through or beyond the error, to get back on track, to shift focus back to something more positive that is within their immediate control. After the performance, coaches and athletes should draw lessons from these errors so they are not repeated. Coaches must ensure that they do not become distracted from their game plan or become a distraction for athletes, and athletes must ensure that they have an effective plan to stay focused on executing their game plan, regardless of what happens.

Athletes can improve the consistency of their performance by preparing themselves for all potential distractions. Some coaches have a tendency to become uptight or wired in the final preparation phase before an important competition. At a time when you might gain most from a coach who boosts your confidence and gets you focused on executing your task you might be faced with the opposite. A common coaching error is trying to get athletes pumped up before an important competition. For example, instead of saying, "Let's just focus on following the game plan—one step, one move, one rush, one battle at time," a coach may say, "This is a crucial game. Everything is riding on this. All of our work was for this; don't blow it." If you take this to heart or do not have a solid refocusing plan, you could become overactivated or distracted from your best performance focus. As an athlete or performer you should always come back to your best focus and what works to bring out your best and the team's best, regardless of what the people around you are saying or doing.

Another common coaching error leading into major events is overtraining, overloading, or overworking athletes. As an athlete, during the final training phase leading into a major competition, you might feel as though you are being overloaded or forced to cram for an exam. Guard against overtraining or overworking by resting more away from the training site and by talking with your coach about reducing the load or increasing the recovery time so you will be strong and healthy going into the event.

Overload in the final preparation phase, excessive technical input, demands for last-minute changes in familiar performance patterns, and an overall increase in stress are major reasons why many athletes and coaches perform below their potential during important events. When you have done a program or performance a hundred times without a major problem and then screw up in the biggest game or competition of the year, everyone wonders why. The reason is directly related to overload, heightened demands, increased stress, and the need to perform under a different set of circumstances. At times like this, you do not gain from additional demands or stress from management, media, your coach, or anyone else. To get back in control and on a positive track, you simply need to respect the focus and preparation patterns that work best for you. Nothing more and nothing less.

Another common coaching error at all performance levels is failing to build the confidence of all team members. Confidence can be a fragile thing, especially if expectations are high and some things have not been going well. Coaches can help athletes perform their best by helping them focus on good reasons to believe in themselves and their chances. Coaches should be the first and biggest believers because athletes and performers often feed off the coach's beliefs.

Coaches may be quick to tell athletes or performers when something is wrong yet may not offer specific advice about what to focus on to make things right. Pointing out how things that can be improved is valuable, and equally important is pointing out things that the athlete or performer did well and acknowledging the progress and positive contributions that they have made. Likewise, athletes or performers may fail to express appreciation for the good things that their coach does. Both athletes and coaches benefit from positive feedback, support, and encouragement. Without the positives the road can be long and lonely. We all like to be acknowledged for the good things that we do, and most of us are open to specific suggestions about how we might become better. Start by pointing out good things and then target an area for improvement.

Positive feedback motivates us, makes us feel good about ourselves and our efforts, and enhances self-confidence. Statements like "You should have been better" or "You should be more confident" rarely instill additional confidence. But when coaches and teammates remind us of the good things that we have done and demonstrate their belief in us, our confidence rises. Cutting people down or dwelling on the negatives usually undermines self-confidence, whereas a focus on the positives does just the opposite. Even the best athletes, who are generally confident in their abilities, gain from positive feedback, support, and knowing that someone they respect really believes in them.

One of the major coaching criticisms relayed to me by experienced athletes is that some of their coaches fail to listen and act on their input and suggestions. Great coaches often act on athletes' wisdom when it is clearly communicated to them because they respect their athletes' experience and want a good performance result. The same holds true for most great athletes. Others dig in their heels and resist. The resisters are often not taking advantage of the collaborative human resources available to them. Even if you meet resistance, you can take the good things that a coach or athlete has to offer. And you can keep working on improving your communication; people do change, and miracles sometimes happen.

Your last option, if you are simply totally incompatible with a coach, is to consider a coaching change that may bring the joy back to your pursuit and improve the quality of your performance. If you decide to go this route, talk with other athletes about their relationships with prospective coaches, visit a couple of workouts run by coaches with whom you think you might be compatible, talk with the ones you like, and then make a decision.

CHAPTER 23

Team Spirit

Nobody gains from living in a sea of hate or conflict. A bit of conflict now and then, within a team, is manageable, but ongoing tension or conflict can break the spirit of even the best team or family. A great team carries a spirit or sense of mission that can lift every team member. A team that is posi-

> *In the end, it is upon the quality and commitment of individuals that all group movements depend.*
>
> Robertson Davies

tive and free from ongoing conflict brings out the best in everyone and inspires everyone to give more for the team and to the team mission.

Negativity and conflict have a toxic effect on individual and team spirit—within sport teams, work teams, study teams, families, and relationships. Every comment that you make and every action that you take has the potential to affect the spirit of those on your team, whether you are a team member, coach, staff member, or administrator. Positive actions drive good things; negative actions drive bad things. Being positive with teammates and family members and challenging each other in positive ways brings out the best in everyone. Being negative does the opposite. All team members should recognize this truth.

The first team goal should be to do no harm to your own performance or your teammates' performance. Achieving this goal means carrying a positive perspective into your own performances and projecting a positive spirit onto teammates. If you are not mentally ready to focus on the positives, then at least refrain from being negative. You do not have to love or like everyone on your team, but you must do your job the best you can and free your teammates to do their jobs the best they can without interference. Do not become an obstacle that interferes with the achievement of team goals. To achieve great things within a team context, you have to put the team mission above everything else.

Fostering Team Harmony

One of the most satisfying experiences in sport is being a member of a team that gets along well and works as a cohesive, collaborative unit. When you live, work, and play together in harmony, the chances of enjoying the journey and achieving mutually beneficial goals increases significantly. By committing yourself to act in simple ways that make teammates feel valued, appreciated, respected, and supported, you go a long way toward improving team spirit, harmony, and performance. Team spirit grows when all team members feel that they have a meaningful role to play, when all team members are challenged to be what they can be, and when they all have some fun in the process of getting where they want to go. Help each other, believe in each other, and genuinely encourage each other to become whatever you have the potential to be, individually and as a team. Work and play together to create a positive atmosphere, a feeling of acceptance, and a sense of unity. Direct your collective focus toward accomplishing your collective mission. Then you will have better practices and work sessions and consistently higher-quality performances.

Harmony grows when you look for the good qualities in teammates and they look for yours, when you take the time to listen to others and they listen to you, when you respect their feelings and contributions and they respect yours, when you accept their differences and they accept yours, when you choose to help them and they help you. Harmony and improved team performance is rooted in mutual trust and respect.

When you know that someone needs you, cares about you, appreciates you, respects you, believes in you, and accepts you, with all your imperfections, trust and harmony are nurtured. When you help others and they help you, you begin to appreciate each other. When you get past the surface and begin to understand the problems, feelings, challenges, or perspectives of others in a more intimate way, you feel closer or more connected to them. Opening the door to real feelings, as difficult as this may be for some people to do, creates a more intimate or real connection.

When Olympic and professional team sport psychology consultant Cal Botterill studied the link between moods and performance in highly skilled athletes, he discovered that team harmony was a key factor in performance. Each athlete's mood had a direct effect on his or her performance, and athletes on the road often cited positive interaction with their coaches, roommates, and teammates as having a positive influence on their moods and performance.

Some of the Olympic and professional teams that I have worked with have had their fair share of disharmony and interpersonal conflicts. Some team members felt ignored or left out, some athletes believed that the coach did not respect them, people refused to room with others, and team members withdrew emotionally or physically from the group. In one case, a physical shoving match occurred on-site before an international competition. Rarely do teammates or coaches intentionally try to create conflict or resentment, or set out to hurt their teammates' feelings or performance. No one gains from that process. Both parties go through unpleasant turmoil and experience stress and distractions that ultimately hinder team focus and team performance. The root of many interpersonal conflicts within teams is lack of commitment to an overriding team mission, lack of awareness of other people's feelings, or misinterpretation of the actions or intentions of a teammate, colleague, or coach.

Merely being together at work, practices, games, competitions, or in social settings like team parties does not necessarily increase mutual liking or harmony among team members. For harmony to develop, individuals must commit to a common mission or goal, and be linked in some interdependent way so that they rely on one another and help one another in the pursuit of their goal.

Harmony or compatibility sometimes flows naturally among members of a team. When this ideal circumstance is not present, it is important to discuss the commitment required from everyone involved to put the bigger mission above the conflict or disharmony so that everyone works hard and supports one another to achieve a worthy, higher-level goal. When all team members make a decision to be supportive, remain flexible, be their best, find good qualities in teammates, and work together to accomplish mutually beneficial goals, collectively they put their team on the path to harmony and excellence.

Open communication is an important step in preventing and solving potential problems among team members. Respecting another person's needs, feelings, or perspectives is difficult when you do not understand what they are. It is never too early or too late to move along a more positive path, turn a negative into a positive, or transform a wrong into a right. The best time to begin is right now.

Staying Positive

Building positive team spirit is itself a worthy goal because of the way that it makes you and other people feel and because it leads to improved performance for all team members. Whenever people are linked together in pursuit of challenging, mutually beneficial goals, several action points become essential for individual and group success.

➤ Find the good qualities in each team member.

➤ Recognize the good things that each can do or contribute.

➤ Commit to remaining positive through adversity; remember that all challenges, great and small, demand that you overcome adversity or obstacles.

➤ Embrace the challenge of getting along and making things work.

➤ Focus on doing your job the best that you can.

➤ Help teammates accomplish their individual goals and the overall team goals.

➤ Put the mission above the conflict or obstacle.

➤ Remember that when you carry a positive perspective, you can tolerate or work with almost anyone in any context for short-duration missions.

Teammates are in a great position to help one another learn, provide positive challenges or positive rivalry, help each other believe in themselves and the mission, constructively analyze one another's performances, provide a lift or word of encouragement when needed, and share actions and perspectives on how to focus in ways that benefit all team members. You can feed off the great things that your teammates or training partners do in practice and in performances, and you can improve because of their intensity, execution, determination, and skill level. Teammates are also in a great position to identify what actions or inactions are interfering with individual and team goals. If you believe that someone on the team or in the organization is doing something that is negatively affecting the team's performance, consider talking with that person—directly or through a team representative (the team captain, coach, assistant coach, manager, or a trusted staff member). If there is even a small chance that your intervention will be helpful, it's worth a try. Respectfully share your appreciation for the good things that are happening and your thoughts on what could lead to better team performance.

Team members, staff members, and others associated with the team should become aware of which of their actions may help, or hurt, your performance and the team's performance. If coaches or teammates do not know that they are doing something that is interfering with team focus or team goals, there is little chance that they will change their behavior. If they are aware of what helps you prepare best for your tough challenges or performances, they will be in a position to help you set the stage for your best performances, or at least not inadvertently interfere.

Positive, meaningful communication among teammates and between coaches and athletes is extremely important for attaining best possible performances, nurturing team spirit, and maintaining personal well-being. How many times did this kind of positive communication happen today? Can you make it happen more often tomorrow? What actions can you take to enhance team spirit, team harmony, and team performance?

Athletes offered the following suggestions for promoting positive interaction among teammates:

➤ Get to know your teammates well.

➤ Talk with your teammates.

➤ Listen to your teammates.

- ➤ Avoid using put-downs.
- ➤ Decide that you will get along.
- ➤ Take responsibility for yourself and do what you can to improve the situation.
- ➤ Encourage each other.
- ➤ Accept individual differences.
- ➤ Include everyone.
- ➤ Show others that you care.
- ➤ Be a positive example.
- ➤ Believe in your teammates.

Respected athletes and performers in every domain are in prime position to lead by example and thereby create the positive atmosphere that encourages others to give their best and build the best team possible. A team is only a team if team members act like a team. Otherwise, it is just a bunch of individuals doing their own thing for themselves. The following sets of rules and reminders can help you build strength, spirit, and unity on your team.

Follow Best Team Focus Rules

Focus on why we can accomplish our goals (not why we can't).

Focus on opportunities (not obstacles).

Focus on solutions (not problems).

Focus on supporting others (not putting down others).

Focus on the positives (not the negatives).

Focus on moving forward step by step.

Focus on turning lessons learned into improved performance.

Strive for Personal Excellence

Become the most positive person you can be, with yourself and others.

Decide to be your best—as an athlete, teammate, and person.

Focus on doing what brings out your best.

Focus on the step in front of you.

Find the positives during the tough times.

Commit to ongoing learning and ongoing improvement.

Lead by example.

Challenge and Support Your Teammates

Challenge your teammates to be what they can be—as athletes, teammates, and human beings.

Challenge your teammates to focus on what brings out their best and the team's best.

Challenge each other to act on lessons learned from each game or performance.

Show your teammates that you value their contributions.

Acknowledge good focus and great effort.

Remember that every one of your teammates wants to win.

Help each other find a way to win.

Keep the Joy in the Game

Find ways to keep the love in your pursuit.

Appreciate the simple joys and opportunities that you have each day.

Rejoice in small steps and simple successes.

Help your teammates keep the love in the pursuit.

Keep things in perspective.

Take time to rest and regenerate.

Take care of your own needs.

Live Your Core Values: Respect and Support

Respect your own potential.

Respect your teammate's potential.

Respect your best focus.

Learn something from every experience.

Support your teammates.

Respect everyone's contribution.

Work together to bring out the best in everyone.

Taking Advantage of Differences

There are vast individual differences among members of all teams—different experiences, different perspectives, different responses to stress, different ways of focusing or coping with distractions, different strengths. These differences can work to your advantage and strengthen your team if you are willing to learn from each other, work together, and share your strengths. No coach or performer knows everything. But when teams of people put their heads together, they can know almost everything that is important for team success. Your team will become much stronger if you follow these steps:

1. Decide as individuals and as a group that you are going to excel, or be the best you can possibly be.

2. Help one another excel by sharing your thoughts on how you gained some of your strengths and how you mentally prepare yourself to per-

form your best. Share your visions or questions about how to improve the consistency of best performances.

3. Encourage each other when someone makes a small or large improvement or gives a great effort.

On most teams, athletes mentally prepare pretty much on their own and keep many of their best thoughts and insights to themselves. Teams and individual athletes who make up teams could gain significantly if they shared insights about their individual strengths and talked about mental strategies that allow them to bring their best focus into the performance and sustain that focus for the duration. Let me give you some examples: One player can remain incredibly focused in pressure situations, another is superb at preparing to take advantage of opponents' weaknesses, a third can stay highly motivated in practices and bring a high level of intensity to every shift and every game, and a fourth can maintain positive focus after a setback or when coming back from behind. You can all gain something of value if you discuss how various team members approach these and other important challenges in your sport (for example, how do you get yourself to focus for a full game, every shift, every rush, every race, even when you are completely exhausted? How do you react to errors or criticism constructively?).

No one is where he or she wants to be in all areas at all times. We all have room for improvement—technically, physically, tactically, mentally, and emotionally. Additionally, a coach cannot give individualized feedback to all athletes at every practice or game, particularly in sports that involve many athletes or have several events or drills going on at once. Teammates, however, can watch, correct, advise, and encourage each other. If a teammate wants to improve in some area, you or someone who excels in that area can offer help in a constructive and nonthreatening way. You might say, for example, "It may not work for you, but I find this works for me." Linemates or playing units can discuss collective strengths and target specific areas to improve. Fellow athletes can often see and understand better than anyone what other team members are doing, not doing, or what might help them get better. Together you can review opponents' strengths and weaknesses and make tactical suggestions that may be of value to individual players. Regular discussions that are open and constructively oriented among team members before and after games or performances can do wonders for team morale, focus, harmony, and overall performance.

Support one another for taking steps in the right direction. In performance situations, physical skills are enhanced when you are focused and your emotions are working for you, not against you. Everyone's task becomes clearer and more attainable when teammates and coaches are working together for each other, or at least not against each other.

Resolving Conflicts

Imagine that you are going on a space voyage to another planet. You must live, work, and train within a space about the size of an average office. You must remain with your team in this space for several years. You have no chance of leaving until the mission ends. Living and working in harmony would be critical to your survival, the survival of your teammates, and the overall mission. Who would you want with you on this mission? What would you do to avoid conflict or maintain some sense of harmony on a mission like this?

Crew members for long-duration space missions have to be well selected for compatibility and adaptability; otherwise, communication might break down and destroy the essential human links that would allow them to succeed. Sport teams rarely choose their members based on their natural compatibility or their ability to work well with others. On our earthly teams, having a natural fit among all team members is improbable, so making the best of what we have and adapting in positive ways to situations becomes critical to completing our mission successfully. Everyone has to be willing to adapt a little to gain a lot.

We do have several advantages over our long-distance voyagers. We do not have to leave behind our family, friends, and everything familiar or comforting for years at a time. We have the advantage of being able to step away from our teammates, enjoy a beautiful natural world, and rejoice in many other simple pleasures. These breaks make our task easier and allow us to return to our daily mission with renewed energy and greater tolerance for those with whom we are linked. We can get away, enjoy some personal space, and come back fresh to make the best of the opportunities that we have. Every day is a new opportunity.

When a communication problem arises, one person is often more responsible for creating it. But both usually end up being upset by it and need to share the responsibility to implement a workable solution. Coaches and teammates should consider three ways to reduce conflict and improve team harmony:

1. Work on improving your communication skills. Set a goal to become a better listener and work on expressing feelings respectfully and constructively.

2. Work on improving your skills at respectfully helping others and respectfully receiving help. Set a goal to give assistance more readily and to receive suggestions more openly and enthusiastically.

3. Work on improving your focus control. Set a goal to focus on acting in ways that let you and your teammates achieve your best results, and work on refocusing to stay positive or constructive when things don't go your way.

One of the many instances in which I've been asked to help resolve conflicts within a team involved a team of young athletes who train every weekday.

Coach X called me with some urgent concerns about interpersonal conflicts on the team. The atmosphere was filled with tension, practices were degenerating, and spirits were low. Conflicts existed between the coach and certain athletes as well as among some team members. The problem had escalated to the point where practices were being ruined and many people left practice feeling emotionally upset. The coach was fed up. The athletes were fed up. Coach X described the situation as desperate.

I agreed to go in to try to help resolve the situation. I began by asking the coach and each athlete to write their responses to the following questions, hoping that their answers would provide some insights into the situation and some possibilities for resolving the conflicts.

➤ What is the main reason that you come to practice?

➤ If you could change anything you wanted about practice, what would you change?

➤ Is there anything the coach or other athletes could do to make you feel or work better in practice? What about at competitions?

➤ What would make practice a more uplifting and more productive place to be?

➤ When the coach is at his best, what does he do?

➤ When the coach is at his worst, what does he do?

➤ What are two things in your life that you like to do best?

➤ What are your overall goals in your sport?

After reviewing the responses to the questions, I spoke to the group to share their overall views. Everyone, athletes and coach, said that his or her involvement in this sport was one of the things in life that he or she liked best. They all wanted to improve their skills and have positive and productive practices. They felt great when they learned a new move or perfected an old one, and so did the coach. The overall goals of the coach and athletes were similar, but sometimes they got in each other's way, and as a result none of them achieved their goals. At those times, nobody enjoyed being there and nobody learned much.

I told them that the quickest way they could all have more uplifting and productive practices was to work together and help one another. Based on their responses to my questions, I created some positive workout suggestions to pinpoint exactly what each of them could do to make practices more like they all wanted them to be. I wrote these workout suggestions on index cards (cue cards) and gave them to the athletes and the coach as reminders that they could use for subsequent practices (see figure 23.1, *a* and *b*). Their goal was to do as many of the actions listed on one card as possible in one practice (or performance) session and to do the remaining ones at the next practice.

I used several different reminder cards because I did not want to have too many reminders on each card, but I wanted to include all the main reminders that came out of their written responses to my questions. I wanted to respect their input and suggestions but not overload them with reminders during any one practice (or performance). You could make up similar cards with your positive reminders to make your practices or performances the best they can be. If you choose to use cards, write down the reminders that you think might work best for you. Then try them to see what works best. Select the best working reminders to keep with you in case you need them in practice or performance situations.

To find out how these attempts to improve team harmony affected interactions, we observed Coach X's team before and after the intervention. The rate of positive verbal interaction (for example, praise, compliments, and encouragement) doubled. More important, negative criticism (for example, yelling and put-downs) ended almost completely. The coach commented, "Everything is working out much better now. Everyone seems to be more happy and relaxed. All the athletes seem to be really working and trying hard."

Figure 23.1a   Coach Reminders

Coach Reminders—Card I

1. Absolutely no yelling—no matter what happens, stay cool.
2. Smile—show that you are in a good mood. Let athletes know that you are happy to be there.
3. Point out what athletes do well and then correct constructively.
4. After giving correction, briefly explain why.
5. Say something positive not related to the sport.
6. Be encouraging and reassuring with words and actions.

Coach Reminders—Card II

1. Give positive feedback every chance you get.
2. Lighten up a little—loosen up.
3. Give specific instruction and encouragement.
4. Tell the athletes what they did well tonight.
5. Say goodnight and leave the gym happy.

Coach Reminders—Card III

1. Show that you care and want each athlete to be there.
2. Say hello to everyone sometime today.
3. Give everyone some positive individual feedback sometime today.
4. Listen closely when athletes give input or express a feeling.
5. Respect and act on the athletes' input.
6. Feel good about your own progress.

The moral of this story is that everyone on a team, even in individual sports, is linked together like a family. What you do and how you respond to others affects how others feel and how they respond to you. To ensure that this kind of family remains happy and productive, each of us has to do our part. We may need to put forth a little extra effort in the beginning, but it's worth it in the end. When we encourage each other, help each other, listen to each other, and interact with each other in positive and constructive ways, everybody will be more positive, work harder, and learn more. We will enjoy being in that kind of setting, and when we eventually leave that team we will be not only better performers but also better people.

Besides maintaining open lines of communication, teams can participate in other activities that help create a positive environment. An activity that I have found to be successful with teams of experienced athletes, coaches, classmates, workmates, or families involves simply sharing the good qualities that we see in our teammates. The way to do this is as follows: First, write each

---

Figure 23.1b   Athlete Reminders

Athlete Reminders—Card I

1. Smile and say hello to everybody.
2. Stop, look (establish eye contact), and listen when the coach is correcting you. Make a real effort to correct the skill.
3. Be ready to go—stand tall.
4. Come to practice with all the personal equipment you might need.
5. Help a teammate today.
6. If your coach or another athlete has been helpful, tell him or her that you appreciate it.
7. Set a good example by approaching skills and drills with full focus and good intensity.

Athlete Reminders—Card II

1. Think positive thoughts today; make someone else feel good too.
2. Ask the coach what you should do to make something better and then really try.
3. Remind yourself that your coach is trying to help you reach your goals.
4. Give 100 percent focus and effort today.
5. Watch a teammate and compliment him or her on something that he or she does well.
6. If anyone is getting discouraged, try to cheer him or her up.
7. Tell the coach that he or she really helps bring out your best when he or she respects and encourages you.
8. Remember upcoming events and important dates.

team member's name (including the coaches and support staff) at the top of a separate piece of paper. Then pass these sheets around the room from person to person and ask everyone on the team to write down one thing that they admire, appreciate, respect, or enjoy about that person. This activity can also be done orally, but writing things down adds a special dimension. Everyone leaves the room with a collection of uplifting comments from their team-mates, which they can post somewhere or refer to when they need a little lift. People often share positive comments about their teammates in this context that they never would otherwise. Reading over the comments definitely feels good. By creating a positive foundation, teams create an environment in which they are able to work together and deal with conflict more successfully when it does occur.

Inspiring Others

When one person on a team takes a step up, others on the team are usually inspired to do likewise. Everyone on the team can gain from the inspiration provided by one person, even in individual sports. This is the true power of leading by example. When a few more people take a step up, their action inspires even more teammates to step up. When a whole team takes a step up, magic happens. This is the true power of team.

When Canadian Beckie Scott took a step up and started winning World Cup and Olympic races in cross-country skiing, her teammates began to follow her example, even though no one from Canada had ever done it before. Her teammate Sara Renner started to reach the World Cup podium and won an Olympic silver medal in 2006. Their younger teammate Chandra Crawford, only 22 years old at the time, won an Olympic gold medal in 2006. Chandra commented, "It has been so awesome having Beckie and Sara and having their leadership and success to learn from. I was so inspired by them." She went on to say, "On those days where I got my butt kicked, I learned so much and knew I could do something about it next time."

The biggest positive change that occurs when one athlete on your team takes a step up is the belief that you can do it too. It is no longer an impossible dream. You train with these people every day, and you stay with them in training (at least sometimes). You begin to think, *If they can do it, I can too*. That belief can work magic. You learn what it takes to perform at that level, and you commit to doing what it takes.

When Thomas Grandi took a step up in alpine skiing by becoming the first male athlete from his country to win a World Cup in a technical event in alpine skiing, others on his team also took a step up. They could race with him and sometimes even beat him in training, so they thought, *Why not do it in a race?* I have witnessed this phenomenon with athletes in many sports and in many countries, and I am still amazed at how fast this transition to the top ranks can happen. One teammate's accomplishment creates a whole new positive spirit of believing, which in turn leads to a positive new reality for others associated with the team. This is the true power of leading by example. You feed off the intensity, success, and example set by a teammate that you know is like you in many ways—human.

If you like and admire the athlete who provided the inspiration for taking a step up, it is an advantage for the future of the team, but you do not have to like a person to be inspired by his or her performance. Even if you do not like or admire some characteristics of this person, you can be inspired by certain things that the person does, and that person can be inspired by certain things that you do, on or off the performance field.

I have also witnessed this stepping-up phenomenon during championship team events when everyone on the

▶ Athletes like LeBron James can inspire their teammates to accomplish more.

team decides to play or perform with full focus and full intensity every second out there. When a team is on a focused mission, every single one of them, they end up beating teams that they are not supposed to beat because of the spirit and focus that they bring to their game or performance. They carry this relentless spirit and focus into every shift, every play, and every stroke. They never let up; they never give up. They just keep coming at you, creating their own opportunities and giving everything they have from start to finish. Every single member of a team can make the choice to raise the level of his or her individual contribution. When every player chooses to do this, the effect on overall team performance is extremely powerful.

CHAPTER 24

Positive Self-Direction

I have never worked with an athlete or performer who went into a performance arena and tried to screw up, nor have I ever met a person who intentionally went out to mess up his or her life. But people do screw up or fall short of their ideals, most often when they do not focus fully

> *To live your life in your own way, to reach for the goals you have set for yourself, to become the person that you want to be—that is success.*

on the positive possibilities. When you choose to make positive self-directed choices and focus fully on acting on those good choices in real situations, you will usually go in the direction you want to go.

Positive self-direction centers on making positive choices that will take you where you want to go in the manner in which you would like to get there. This kind of self-direction becomes possible when you choose to drive your own life by making positive focused choices and to carry out positive focused actions. To move along this path, choose the direction in which you want to go in certain parts of your life and decide to act on those choices. This process is similar to being on a flowing river and choosing your best course instead of letting the river make all the choices for you. If you let the river lead you, or give yourself up to the river, you risk being swept off course, crashing into rocks or plunging over the falls.

Choosing positive self-direction puts you in control of your own course, your own life, and your own destiny, as much as is humanly possible. You control things that are within your control and make good choices about negotiating the challenges and obstacles that may not be within your control. Positive self-direction gives you your best chance of getting your focus to work for you to chart the course and live the life that you would like to live.

Positive self-direction involves not only choosing your own best course but also traveling in a manner that you would prefer to travel. How would you prefer to be as a person and performer on your present journey—through the good times, the challenges, and the tough times?

Choosing Self-Direction

Here are some simple questions to ask yourself that can help you make positive self-directed choices to improve the quality of your performance and joyfulness of your life. You can target these questions to any important part of your life. Write your response to the questions that are most important to you.

- ➤ What is good or great in your performance right now?
- ➤ What is missing in your performance right now?
- ➤ What is good or great on your team right now?
- ➤ What is missing on your team right now?
- ➤ What is good or great in your organization or work right now?
- ➤ What is missing in your organization or work right now?
- ➤ What is good or great in your relationships right now?
- ➤ What is missing in your relationships right now?
- ➤ What is good or great in your life right now?
- ➤ What is missing in your life right now?

If everything is good and nothing is missing, then you are on a wonderful path. Keep doing what you are doing. If something is missing that could take you closer to your goals or dreams, think about what you can do about it and then make a self-directed choice to do something about it!

Choose to do the things that you want to do.

Choose to live the life that you want to live.

Choose to be the person you want to be.

Choose to live your life to the fullest.

The path to personal excellence is full of ups and downs, progression and regression, great steps forward and plateaus. As long as you maintain control over your choices, you guide the direction of your life. Good choices free you to do the things that you want to do and allow you to achieve the goals that are important to you.

The pursuit of personal excellence is challenging and fulfilling. Relish its intensity, cherish its beautiful moments, and accept its lessons and risks. Many lives lack this sense of passionate absorption and personal meaning—the charged-up feeling, the flow of adrenaline, the body telling the mind, *I'm ready, let's go*. Embrace this opportunity. Experience it and let it work for you.

When we gain control of our inner world of focus, competing or performing need not be the fearful experience that it has been for some people. It can be a unique opportunity to embrace the excitement, to raise your level of performance, to experience things more fully, to be stimulated by others, to test your focus, and to extend your limits. Meaningful challenges and self-directed choices lead you to your personal and professional goals. They stimulate you to contribute and perform as you never have before. They bring out your best. And even if they don't, they provide lessons for living your life more fully. When you keep your sport, performance, and life experiences in perspective, you always emerge better from the experience.

When you begin to view big games, important performances, or challenging life experiences in a positive light, you can enjoy them more and look forward to them. The better you have prepared, the less fearful and more confident you will likely feel going into the event or experience. But when you are at the performance site or in the experience, you have done everything that you can do. You cannot control what you did not do. You cannot control what is beyond your control. You might as well focus fully in the moment and enjoy the experience, thereby freeing your body and mind to work for you. Most of us need freedom from thoughts like *have to* or *should have* to connect fully with the experience and deliver our best, most flowing performances.

If you find yourself questioning the value of your pursuit or your life, you may be failing to appreciate the good things that you do have. When you focus on the negative, you push away the positive. Nonetheless, the good is there, although you momentarily turn your back on it. Why not choose to open your heart to the joy of the pursuit, to the value within yourself, to the worth in others, to the possibilities of fully engaging yourself in this moment, however long or short it may be? Why not choose to embrace your life and let the sun shine through during the challenging times as well as during the joyful times? How else can you live life to the fullest?

The essence of positive self-direction is that you decide the course of your own actions and your own life. You decide whether to embrace an opportunity or not to embrace it, you decide to do something or not

©Tannen Maury/epa/Corbis

▶ On the journey to personal excellence, Peyton Manning and other great athletes learn to enjoy challenges and important performances.

to do something, and no one else can do that for you. I challenge you, and encourage you, to *docide* to embrace the things that are important to you, to embrace your life right now, to live and perform with no regrets. To move in this positive self-directed way, docide to do the following:

➤ Pursue the good things that you love to do and in which you find personal meaning.

➤ Respect the personal choices that bring out your best.

➤ Put yourself in situations where you feel valued, respected, accepted, or loved.

➤ Make positive self-directed choices that are in your best interest and the best interest of the people you love.

➤ Trust your intuition about what is truly best for you when making important decisions in your life.

➤ Help those with whom you live, work, or play feel loved, valued, and respected, at least within your presence.

➤ Win the game of life by bringing your best focus and the best you to your pursuits.

➤ Fully embrace each step of your journey.

Following Your Best Path

When pursuing our performance and life goals, we must be careful not to fall into the fatal trap that R.M. Pirsig described in *Zen and the Art of Motorcycle Maintenance* (Pirsig, 1984, 206). The following excerpt recounts an incident that occurred on the author's cross-country motorcycle trip with his teenage son. They stopped in the mountains to do some hiking on steep mountain trails that had switchbacks (trails that go back and forth across the mountain because the slope is too steep to go straight up). His son saw the switchbacks above him as he was hiking and continually complained because he was here and not there, and even when he got "there," he complained because he always wanted to be somewhere else.

> He's here but he's not here. He rejects the here, is unhappy with it, wants to be further up the trail but when he gets there will be just as unhappy because he will be "here." What he's looking for, what he wants, is all around him but he doesn't want that because it is all around him. Every step's an effort, both physically and spiritually, because he imagines his goal to be external and distant.

Wherever a pursuit involves only a distant destination and no joy in the step-by-step progress toward it, a harsh reality is not far ahead. The real trip is in embracing or loving the journey, not necessarily in the arrival at a specific place. Unless you immerse yourself in the simple joys of your current experiences and really embrace them, dreams tend to remain dreams; worse yet, they explode or fizzle away. This is all the more reason to become fully absorbed in the experience at hand, as well as others.

In a book titled *Love*, Leo Buscaglia (1996) writes about the importance of embracing a fully connected focus in different parts of your life. When you choose to be fully focused in any context of your life, your life immediately becomes a better place to be.

> Live now. When you are eating, eat. When you are loving, love. When you are talking to someone, talk. When you look at a flower, look. Catch the beauty of the moment. (p. 22)
>
> There is only the moment. The now. Only what you are experiencing at this second is real. This does not mean live for the moment. It means live the moment—a completely different idea. (p. 73)
>
> Change is inevitable. Feelings change, attitudes change, desires change, love changes. We cannot stop change, we cannot hold it back. (p. 92)

Changes, transitions, or new paths toward love, respect, and self-growth are always good. We can choose which paths we go down, what some of those changes are, how we negotiate those changes, and whether we focus on the positives or negatives, the opportunities or the obstacles, within those changes.

Castaneda's Don Juan speaks of the direction and choice of change in *The Teachings of Don Juan: A Yaqui Way of Knowledge* (Castaneda 1985, 107):

> You must always keep in mind that a path is only a path. If you feel you must now follow it, you need not stay with it under any circumstances. Any path is only a path. There is no affront to yourself or others in dropping it if that is what your heart tells you to do. But your decision to keep on the path or leave it must be free of fear and ambition. I warn you: Look at every path closely and deliberately. Try it as many times as you think necessary. Then ask yourself and yourself alone one question: Does this path have a heart? All paths are the same. They lead nowhere. They are paths going through the brush or into the brush or under the brush. Does this path have a heart is the only question. If it does then the path is good . . . if it doesn't then it is of no use. Both paths lead nowhere, but one has a heart and the other doesn't. One makes for a joyful journey; as long as you follow it you will be one with it. The other will make you curse your life. One makes you strong, the other weakens you.

Choosing a path with heart is great advice for all of us. When we follow a path with heart, we are choosing a path that feels right for us, that resonates with our inner being, that intuitively feels like the right choice. Our intuition or gut feelings are usually right for us, and even if they are not always the best choice, we can always choose to change our path. My experience is that when I embark on a path, it always leads to many other paths and many other opportunities that I never anticipated when I started down that first path. Where I started my career path is certainly not where I ended up, because so many other exciting options opened up along the way. New paths always present themselves in life. As long as you remain open to the possibilities that feel right for you, you will find paths with heart.

The depth of my understanding about what is required to excel has changed over the years. When I first started working in the performance enhancement field, I thought that the path to excellence was to work, work, work; to shut out the rest of my life; and to live only for the dream. I was wrong! You do have to work extremely hard, but you don't have to shut out the rest of your life and you don't have to live only for the future. You can achieve the highest levels of personal excellence through a high-quality focus and still have a balanced, happy life in the here and now. The path to personal and professional excellence is the self-directed focused path with heart.

A renowned filmmaker, artist, and friend was a living example of embracing a balanced life with heart. When he worked, he became fully absorbed in his work, but he always left room for play. In fact, nothing—and I mean nothing—got in the way of his play. His pure connection in his playtime enriched his life as much as any achievement or honor bestowed on him did. It gave him something to look forward to with enthusiasm every day, and it let him return to his work with a fresh perspective and positive energy

He set high goals and pursued them vigorously, but on a day-to-day basis he never failed to appreciate the time that he lived with his family, friends, and nature. He appreciated each experience so much that his enthusiasm and positive energy radiated to all those around him. I reflected on the way that he had come to keep playfulness at the center of a life that otherwise revolved around perfection and the pursuit of excellence. A near-fatal heart attack, which almost grabbed his life early in his career, helped teach him this lesson. He was thankful for another day of living, then another, and another. So many days to live and experience and enjoy. The lesson is to live every day of your life fully while you can. A gift of life!

WORKS CONSULTED

Armstrong, L.1998. *It's not about the bike*. New York: Broadway Books.

Arntz, W., B. Chasse, and M. Vicente. 2005. *What the bleep do we know?* Deerfield Beach, FL: Health Communications (www.whatthebleep.com).

Botterill, C., and T. Patrick. 2003. *Perspective: The key to life*. Winnipeg, Manitoba: Lifeskills (available from mcnallyrobinson.com).

Buscaglia, L. 1996. *Love*. Greenwich, CT: Fawcett.

Castaneda, C. 1985. *The teachings of Don Juan: A Yaqui way of knowledge*. New York: Simon & Schuster.

Coelho, Paulo. 1993. *The Alchemist*. New York: Harper-Collins.

Colgrove, M., H. Bloomfield, and P. McWilliams. 1993. *How to survive the loss of a love*. New York: Bantam.

Ellis, A., and R.A. Harper. 1976. *A new guide to rational living*. North Hollywood, CA: Wilshire.

Frankl, V.E. 1998. *Man's search for meaning*. New York: Simon & Schuster.

Genge, R. 1976. Concentration. *Coaching Association of Canada Bulletin*, 12, 1–8.

Halliwell, W., T. Orlick, K. Ravizza, and B. Rotella. 1999, 2003. *Consultant's guide to excellence: For sport and performance enhancement*. www.zoneofexcellence.com

Hamill, S. 2005.*Tao Te Ching–Lao Tzu*. Boston: Shambhala.

Li-Wei, A., M. Qi-Wei, T. Orlick, and L. Zitzelsberger. 1992. The effect of mental imagery training on performance enhancement with 7- to 10-year-old children. *The Sport Psychologist, 6*, 230–241.

Mitchelle, S. 1988. *Tao Te Ching–Lao Tzu*. New York: Harper-Collins.

Orlick, T. 1986. *Coaches guide to psyching for sport: Mental training for athletes*. Champaign, IL: Human Kinetics.

Orlick, T. 1986. *Psyching for sport: Mental training for athletes*. Champaign, IL: Human Kinetics.

Orlick, T. 1995. *Nice on my feelings: Nurturing the best in children and parents*. Carp, ON: Creative Bound.

Orlick, T. 1998. *Embracing your potential: Steps to self-discovery, balance, and success in sports, work, and life*. Champaign, IL: Human Kinetics.

Orlick. T. 2004. *Feeling great: Teaching children to excel at living*. Carp, ON: Creative Bound.

Orlick, T. 2006. *Cooperative games and sports: Joyful activities for everyone*. Champaign, Il: Human Kinetics.

Orlick, T. 2008. *Positive living skills: For children and teens*. Carp, ON: Creative Bound.

Orlick, T. 2008. *Teaching children positive living skills: Teachers and parents guide*. www.zoneofexcellence.com

Orlick, T., and J. Partington. 1986. *Psyched: Inner views of winning*. Available free at www.zoneofexcellence.com

Orlick, T., and J. Partington. 1988. Mental links to excellence. *The Sport Psychologist, 2*, 105–130. Available free at www.zoneofexcellence.com

Pirsig, R.M. 1984. *Zen and the art of motorcycle maintenance*. New York: Quill.

Ravizza, K., and T. Hanson. 1995. *Heads-up baseball: Playing the game one pitch at a time*. Redondo Beach, CA: Kinesis (PO Box 7000-717, Redondo Beach, CA 90277).

Rotella, B., with B. Cullen. 1995. *Golf is not a game of perfect*. New York: Simon & Schuster.

Russell, B., and T. Branch. 1979. *Second wind*. New York: Ballantine.

Selye, H. 1978. *The stress of life*. New York: McGraw-Hill.

Suzuki, D.T. 1993. *Zen and Japanese culture*. New York: Pantheon.

Suzuki, D.T. 1999. Introduction to *Zen in the art of archery*, by E. Herrigel. New York: Vintage.

ADDITIONAL RESOURCES

Audio CDs by Terry Orlick

All available from www.zoneofexcellence.com.

Audio CDs for Athletes and Performers
CD #1 Focusing for Excellence—*Relaxation and Stress Control Activities*
CD #2 Focusing for Excellence—*Exercises for Strengthening Focus and Performance*
CD #3 Focusing for Excellence—*Practicing in the Zone*
CD #4 Focusing for Excellence—*Performing in the Zone*

Audio CDs for Children
CD #1 Spaghetti Toes—*Positive Living Skills for Children*
CD #2 Changing Channels—*Positive Living Skills for Children*

Audio CDs for Tweens, Teens, and Adults
CD #3 *Focusing Through Distractions*
CD #4 *Relaxation and Joyful Living*

Books by Terry Orlick

Every Kid Can Win, with Cal Botterill, 1975.

The Cooperative Games Book, 1978.

Cooperative Games and Sports, 2006.

Positive Living Skills: For Children and Teens, 2008.

Teaching Children Positive Living Skills: Teachers and Parents Guide, 2008.

Winning Through Cooperation, 1978.

The Second Cooperative Sports and Games Book, 1982.

Mental Training for Coaches and Athletes, edited with John Partington and John Salmela, 1982.

Sport in Perspective, edited with John Partington and John Salmela, 1982.

New Paths to Sport Learning, edited with John Salmela and John Partington, 1982.

Psyching for Sport: Mental Training for Athletes, 1986.

Coaches Guide to Psyching for Sport, 1986.

Psyched: Inner Views of Winning, with John Partington, 1986.

Athletes in Transition, with Penny Werthner, 1987.

Sharing Views on the Process of Effective Sportpsych Consulting, with John Partington, 1988.

New Beginnings: Transition From High Performance Sport, with Penny Werthner, 1992.

Nice on My Feelings: Nurturing the Best in Children and Parents, 1995.

In Pursuit of Excellence, audio book, 1997.

Feeling Great: Teaching Children to Excel at Living, 1998, 2001, 2004.

Embracing Your Potential: Steps to Self-Discovery, Balance, and Success in Sports, Work and Life, 1998.

Consultant's Guide to Excellence in Sport and Performance, with Wayne Halliwell, Ken Ravizza, and Bob Rotella, 1999, 2003.

In Pursuit of Excellence, 1980, 1990, 2000, 2008.

DVDs

Touching the Void. 2003. www.mgm.com/dvd. A powerful real-world example of how focusing on the little steps makes the impossible become possible.

The Secret. 2006. www.thesecret.tv. An excellent presentation on the power of positive visions, but unfortunately nothing on the critical steps that you must take to turn positive visions into positive realities.

What the Bleep Do We Know? Science and Spirituality. www.whatthebleep.com. A thought-provoking presentation on "reality" and the role that your mind, mental imagery, and spirit can play in creating new or better realities.

Free Articles

Many articles relevant to performance excellence and quality living are available free at www.zoneofexcellence.com. Click on Free Articles or Journal of Excellence. The following articles are examples of what is available.

"An Analysis of a Children's Relaxation/Stress Control Skills Program in an Alternative Elementary School Setting." Shaunna Taylor and Terry Orlick.

"Coping With Cancer: Lessons From a Pediatric Cancer Patient and His Family." Julie Koudys and Terry Orlick.

"Excellence Through Collaboration." John Partington.

"Excelling in the Olympic Context." Terry Orlick.

"Focusing for Excellence: Lessons From Elite Mountain Bike Racers." Danelle Kabush and Terry Orlick.

"Interview With Chris Hadfield, Canadian Astronaut." Chris Hadfield and Terry Orlick.

"Interview With Curt Tribble, Elite Surgeon." Curt Tribble and Terry Orlick.

"Lessons Learned: In Pursuit of Excellence." Kelly Doell.

"Making the Impossible, Possible, Within a Relationship: An Interview With Lisa and Mike." Terry Orlick.

"Mental Strategies of Elite Mount Everest Climbers." Shaunna Burke and Terry Orlick.

"Mental Strategies Used by Professional Actors to Enhance Quality Performance." Tim Murphy and Terry Orlick.

"Nurturing Positive Living Skills for Children: Feeding the Heart and Soul of Humanity." Terry Orlick.

"Patients as Performers." Curt Tribble, Doug Newburg, and Jeff Rouse.

"'Perspective'—Can Make a Difference!" Cal Botterill and Tom Patrick.

"Success Elements of Elite Performers in High Risk Sport: Big Mountain Free Skiers." John Coleman and Terry Orlick.

"The Essence of Excellence: Mental Skills of Top Classical Musicians." Carole Talbot-Honeck and Terry Orlick.

"The Impact of a Positive Living Skills Training Program on Children With Attention-Deficit Hyperactivity Disorder." Kealey Hester and Terry Orlick.

"The Process of Perspective: The Art of Living Well in the World of Elite Sport." Matt Brown, Kathy Cairns, and Cal Botterill.

"The Quest for Gold: Applied Psychological Skills Training in the 1996 Olympic Games." Colleen Hacker.

"Thinking Sound: Reflections on the Application of Mental Training to Opera." Hans Gertz.

"Excellence in Space." Marc Garneau.

"Teaching Positive Living Skills to a Family With Special Needs." Melissa Klingenberg and Terry Orlick.

"Teaching Skills for Stress Control and Positive Thinking to Elementary School Children." Jenelle Gilbert and Terry Orlick.

INDEX

Note: The italicized *f* and *t* following certain page numbers refer to figures and tables, respectively.

ABOUT THE AUTHOR

Courtesy of the author

Terry Orlick, PhD, is a world-renowned leader in the applied field of sport psychology, mental training, and excellence. A former gymnastics champion and coach, Orlick has served as a high-performance coach for over 35 years to thousands of Olympic and professional athletes in more than 30 sports. He has served as a performance-enhancement consultant and focus coach in numerous Summer and Winter Olympic Games, as well as a consultant for various professional teams and leading business corporations.

Former president of the International Society for Mental Training and Excellence, Orlick has authored more than 20 highly acclaimed books. He has created innovative programs and books for children and youth to develop humanistic perspectives and positive mental skills for living, including *Cooperative Games and Sports* (2006, Human Kinetics) and *Feeling Great: Teaching Children to Excel at Living* (2004, Creative Bound).

Orlick, a graduate of Syracuse University, the College of William & Mary, and the University of Alberta, is a professor in the School of Human Kinetics at the University of Ottawa, Canada, and founder of the innovative *Journal of Excellence.* He holds distinguished service awards from numerous Olympic and education associations, as well as certificates of merit from governments, universities, sport organizations, and schools for distinguished service to the community. He has given lectures on the pursuit of excellence in virtually every corner of the world. Orlick lives with his family at Meech Lake, Quebec.

You'll find other outstanding mental training resources at

www.HumanKinetics.com/mentaltrainingforathletes

In the U.S. call 1-800-747-4457

Australia 08 8372 0999 • Canada 1-800-465-7301
Europe +44 (0) 113 255 5665 • New Zealand 0800 222 062

HUMAN KINETICS
The Premier Publisher for Sports & Fitness
P.O. Box 5076 • Champaign, IL 61825-5076 USA

eBook
available at
HumanKinetics.com